WOMEN of NAUVOO

Lucian Foster captured the Nauvoo Temple on the hill from his studio on the flats of Nauvoo near the corner of Parley and Hyde streets sometime in 1845–46. Building the temple was the focus of the Nauvoo Saints for nearly six years beginning in 1840. The sisters contributed their time, talents, and financial resources to help build the temple and participated in the Spirit-filled events during the winter 1845–46, when five thousand Saints received their temple blessings.

Women of Nauvoo

RICHARD NEITZEL HOLZAPFEL
JENI BROBERG HOLZAPFEL

Bookcraft
Salt Lake City, Utah

Library of Congress Catalog Card Number: 92–72663

ISBN 0–88494–835–8

6th Printing, 1996

Printed in the United States of America

For Zanna and Marin—
spiritual heirs to the blessings
and promises of the
sister Saints in Nauvoo.

CONTENTS

PREFACE

We walked the roads of old Nauvoo, now partly restored, during our first visit there together in 1984. During one evening, we strolled down a dusty road in the moonlight from Heber and Vilate Murray Kimball's home to the Joseph Smith properties on Water Street.

That particular evening, we remembered how Heber stopped at the Murray farmhouse to get a glass of water years before in New York. The owner of the farm asked his sixteen-year-old daughter, Vilate, to bring a glass and serve the thirsty young man. From that first meeting, a long courtship and loving relationship began.

A feeling arose in our hearts as we contemplated a walk Heber and Vilate made in Nauvoo during a particularly trying time when their faith was tested to the utmost (see pages 96–97).

This book is a small effort to rediscover and recall the rich spiritual heritage found in Nauvoo, especially among the great sisterhood that transcends both time and place. The sisters in Nauvoo, while sharing a common connection with the restored gospel, were quite diverse. Sometimes these sister Saints exhibited great faith, and at other times their faith faltered and failed them.

When faced with personal trials or institutional crises, each sister made her own decisions. A classic example is the story of Martha Hall Haven and Sarah Hall Scott, two sisters who arrived in Nauvoo in 1843 with their husbands.

Both women were full of hope and expectations as they gathered with the Saints on the Mississippi River. Each one, however, was an individual—complex and difficult to understand at times. Each reacted to the Nauvoo experience quite differently; finally, Sarah left Nauvoo, disappointed with life there and the direction the Church took in doctrinal matters. On the other hand, Martha rejoiced in the experience and headed west with the main body of Saints in 1846.[1]

The stories contained in this book represent numerous unrecorded stories of women in our history. Unfortunately, many contemporary diaries of both men and women connect these individuals only to their husband's name and refer to them as Brother So-and-so "and spouse." Historians are writing path-breaking studies dealing with nineteenth-century Mormon women, including those who settled Nauvoo some one hundred fifty years ago.[2] Our own work in this book relies heavily on these articles and books written at a time when women's studies, in American history in general and in Mormon history in particular, are blossoming. Specifically, the works of Lavina Fielding Anderson, Maureen Ursenbach Beecher, Jill Mulvay Derr, and Carol Cornwall Madsen are most helpful. A representative example of their insightful efforts is found in Maureen Ursenbach Beecher and Lavina Fielding Anderson, eds., *Sisters in Spirit: Mormon Women in Historical and Cultural Perspective* (Urbana: University of Illinois Press, 1987). While we developed the many ideas and constructs of this work independently, they nevertheless have been clarified and enhanced by these scholars' research and publications. Few published histories of the Nauvoo period have attempted to go beyond the lives of prominent men and Church institutions. A refreshing exception is the recently released study by James B. Allen, Ronald K. Esplin, and David J. Whittaker, *Men with a Mission, 1837–1841: The Quorum of the Twelve Apostles in the British Isles* (Salt Lake City: Deseret Book Co., 1992). While narrating the early apostolic missions to Great Britain, the authors provide in chapter eleven, "Meanwhile, in Nauvoo" (pages 267–91), a delightful review of the women who sustained these men. A prodigious amount of research and writing on the broader history of Nauvoo has also contributed to this work.[3]

Still, much work needs to be done regarding women's history in general. Louise A. Tilly of the New School for Social Research spoke at a seminar sponsored by the University of California, Irvine, a few years ago. There she related a story of a historian who discussed women's participation in the French Revolution. At the end of the presentation, an older, well-known scholar of the French Revolution stood up and asked, "Now that I know that women were participants in the revolution, what difference does it make?"

Tilly then remarked that an "increasingly urgent task for women's history is to produce analytical problem-solving studies as well as descriptive and interpretive ones, and connecting their findings to general questions already on the historical agenda—not only analyzing its implications, but of connecting the problems of women's history to those of other histories."[4]

While our study is definitely descriptive, it also brings together some informative sources that may allow those interested in Nauvoo to readjust their view of the City of the Saints. Other vehicles, intended for the academic community, are being used to explore

women's issues within the context of Mormon history; still there remains the challenge to connect these studies with the broader discussions of history.

When quoting from letters, diaries, and contemporary accounts,
we have modernized spelling, punctuation, and capitalization when
the text would otherwise be confusing or misleading, and we have
spelled out abbreviated words in the interest of readability. Unusual
or archaic words are defined within brackets.

We hope that this small work contributes to the growing litera-
ture, both academic and popular, of an incredible story of sisterhood
established on the banks of the Mississippi River, and that it will help
to establish a meaningful link with a vanishing world. As Nauvoo
resident Eliza R. Snow wrote, "To narrate what transpired within the
seven years, in which we built and occupied Nauvoo, the beautiful,
would fill many volumes. That is a history that never will, and *never
can* 'repeat itself.' "[5]

The story of the women of Nauvoo highlights the sister Saints as
individuals, as women as well as members of the Church, unique and
diverse from each other, yet bound together in the bonds of community often stronger than biological ties.

ACKNOWLEDGMENTS

Many individuals helped and encouraged us during our research and writing. However, we are totally responsible for the material published herewith. We thank Ronald Barney, Maureen Ursenbach Beecher, George Bickerstaff, Marjorie Conder, T. Jeffery Cottle, Jill Mulvay Derr, Randall Dixon, Scott Duvall, Jana Erickson, Garry Garff, Daniel Hogan, Glen M. Leonard, Carol Cornwall Madsen, Cory Maxwell, Edith Menna, Veneese Nelson, Melissa Ostler, Billy Plunkett, Ronald Read, Ronald E. Romig, Dana Roper, R. Q. Shupe, William Slaughter, Ted D. Stoddard, and David Whittaker.

We also thank the Archives Division, Church Historical Department, The Church of Jesus Christ of Latter-day Saints, Salt Lake City, Utah; Pioneer Memorial Museum, National Society Daughters of Utah Pioneers, Salt Lake City, Utah; the Huntington Library, San Marino, California; the Special Collections and Manuscript Department, Harold B. Lee Library, Brigham Young University, Provo, Utah; the Missouri Historical Society, St. Louis, Missouri; the Museum of Church History and Art, The Church of Jesus Christ of Latter-day Saints, Salt Lake City, Utah; the Minnesota Historical Society, St. Paul, Minnesota; and the Library and Archives, Reorganized Church of Jesus Christ of Latter Day Saints, Independence, Missouri, for copies and permission to reproduce the photographs and manuscript quotations contained in this work.

1

AN UNKNOWN STORY

Such is the heroism of the women of "Mormondom"
but words would fail to tell it all and we can only
look for the record of it in the archives above.
                                    —Mary Ann Stearns Winters

*M*ary Ann Weston Maughan was born and raised a Methodist near Gloucester, England. She was baptized a member of the restored Church at the age of twenty-two and married a Latter-day Saint named John Davis in December of the same year. Within four months, however, she was a young widow without means of support. Her husband had been injured internally as the result of a beating by an anti-Mormon mob, and had also suffered a bad fall, all of which left him ill and bedridden for several weeks. His condition gradually worsened, and he died on 6 April 1841. Mary soon made preparations for the long trip to Nauvoo. She "started to walk a little way" with a company of fellow Saints, but soon came to a place where they were about to "lose sight of [her] father's house." She later recalled:

> I sat down and I might have stayed there if some of the company had not come back for me. I was sick and quite overcome with the grief and sorrow I had passed through in the last three months. . . . We were a sorry company that traveled to Gloucester that morning. Myself and others wept all the way. . . . Now I had left all and was traveling alone to a land unknown to me, but I had cast my lot with the people of God and in him I put my trust.[1]

She also wrote:

> The last and hardest trial was to take leave of my father, mother,
> brothers, and sisters. My dear good mother was most broken-
> hearted to see me go, but Father was more calm. . . . My two little
> sisters clung around my neck, saying, "We shall never see you
> again." I had not told them this, for I knew the parting from
> them would be very hard. Little Jane wanted to come with me,
> but this was impossible, for she was only eight years old.[2]

Among the many who left their homes to gather to Nauvoo,
Mary is part of the little-known history of Nauvoo—the history of
the women who settled the swamplands of old Commerce, Illinois,
known by the Saints as Nauvoo and as the City of Joseph. These sister Saints—often alone and without companionship—made significant contributions to this beautiful city, and endured such difficulties
as Joseph Smith's martyrdom and the western exodus. The institu-

*Patty Session's diary began just a few days before she crossed the Mississippi River to begin
her trip west in 1846. The sister Saints sometimes spent their last few cents to purchase
paper and ink before their departure so they could chronicle their exodus.*

tional records of old Nauvoo—the ecclesiastical, economic, and civic records—tell a story; but the Relief Society minutes as well as the letters, diaries, and recollections of the women themselves tell another story of Nauvoo.[3]

Nevertheless, our view of life in Nauvoo from a woman's perspective is rather sparse. While Nauvoo-period letters, diaries, and journals of men are relatively plentiful, most of the information available about women's lives during this time comes from either a small collection of contemporary women's diaries and letters or a larger collection of recollections and autobiographical statements produced many years subsequent to the events in Nauvoo. This sparsity of primary sources from women of the Nauvoo period may be explained by a non-Mormon immigrant who pointed out, "Pioneer women were quite too busy in making history to write it."[4]

Although the diaries of the men in Nauvoo add to our understanding of the Saints' experiences, what they left unrecorded can often suggest something about the lives of their mothers, sisters, wives, and daughters. The sisters' own records show a rich variety of responses to the Nauvoo experience.[5] The sisters noted or recalled the cheerful and lively moments as well as those of suffering and death.

As converts arrived in the City of the Saints, they testified to the new and strong ties formed with fellow Saints, a good beginning for a new life. While each responded differently to the challenges that life in Nauvoo presented—some with faith and others with doubt—each nevertheless left us something worth preserving.

The Saints arrived at the Mississippi River as refugees from state-sanctioned persecution in Missouri during the winter of 1838–39. Within seven years, they left their homes, farms, businesses, and temple in Nauvoo, Illinois, as a community in exile, and crossed the same river to the shores of Iowa. This time the Saints fled west to the Indian lands beyond the Missouri River to establish Winter Quarters. The following year, a vanguard pioneer company left Winter Quarters to blaze a trail to the Great Basin. In the Great Basin, the Saints established another community, Great Salt Lake City. Soon hundreds and thousands of Saints from North America, the British Isles, and Europe followed.

These pioneers brought with them what they could. More important, however, they brought with them the spiritual heritage of Nauvoo—of which the sisters were particular recipients.

During the seven years the Saints resided in eastern Iowa and western Illinois, they established the headquarters of the restored Church at Nauvoo, Illinois. They built several communities in the area before they were forced once again to find refuge in another location.[6]

Before their departure, however, the sister Saints in Nauvoo received choice blessings and promises through the Prophet Joseph Smith, blessings that sprang from important events beginning in 1842.

On a Thursday afternoon, 17 March 1842, twenty women met in the upper room of Joseph Smith's Red Brick Store in Nauvoo, Illinois. Also in attendance at this historic meeting were several Church leaders, including the Prophet Joseph Smith. Joseph organized the "Female Relief Society of Nauvoo" on this day. Emma Smith was selected to be the first president, with Elizabeth Ann Whitney and Sarah M. Cleveland as counselors, Eliza R. Snow as secretary, Phebe M. Wheeler as assistant secretary, and Elvira Annie Cowles as treasurer.

Emma Smith, the Prophet's wife, suggested the name by which the organization came to be known in this first meeting. She said on that occasion, "We are going to do something *extraordinary*. When a boat is struck on the rapids with a multitude of Mormons on board, we shall consider that a loud call for *relief*. We expect extraordinary occasions and pressing calls."[7]

The establishment of the first Relief Society was a remarkable event, because it was an important aspect of the "restoration of all things." Other women's groups were organized in America before, but the scope and vision invested by Joseph Smith in this particular organization made it a truly distinctive feature of the Church and a unique group among the women's benevolent societies of the day. The women themselves saw their "society," as it was commonly and consistently called in the minutes, as more than simply a charitable organization. The organization of the society also provided an official "seal" for the spiritual blessings granted to the sisters in Nauvoo.

By 1844, more than thirteen hundred women had joined the Nauvoo Relief Society. The society's involvement in the affairs in Nauvoo went beyond the responsibilities of taking care of the poor in Nauvoo.

The involvement of the sister Saints in diverse enterprises during the period was quite remarkable for the time. A few days following the organization of the Society, Joseph Smith said that they "should move according to the ancient Priesthood, hence they should be a select . . . choice, virtuous, and holy [Society]."[8]

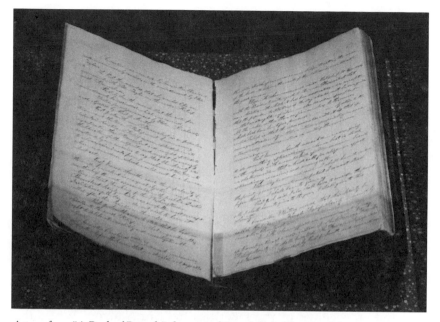

A page from "A Book of Record," the original Female Relief Society of Nauvoo minute book in the handwriting of the first secretary, Eliza R. Snow. An inscription on the title page reads "O, Lord! help our widows, and fatherless children! So mote [may] it be. Amen. With the sword, and the word of truth, defend thou them. So mote [may] it be. Amen."

In Nauvoo, Joseph Smith began to expand the role of women in the Church through the introduction of temple worship and ritual. Women received sacred ordinances and participated along with men—first in Joseph's "Quorum of the Anointed" and later in the completed Nauvoo Temple.[9]

The story of the first Relief Society is an aspect of the broader history of Nauvoo and is a part of the heritage Joseph Smith and the early sister Saints left to the Church today.

Nearly sixty-five years later, Church leader Orson F. Whitney wrote:

> Among the outward evidences of the divine origin of "Mormonism," there is nothing that testifies more clearly or eloquently to the truth of the latter-day work, than the provision made therein for the uplifting and advancement of women; for the salvation and exaltation, in this world and in the world to come, of woman as well as man.[10]

The organization and establishment of the Relief Society in Nauvoo one hundred fifty years ago has left several important legacies to the sisters of the Church and to the membership in general. Among the important and significant treasures preserved from its founding are the minutes of the Relief Society of Nauvoo, an invaluable source. Not only does this record help one understand the historical setting of Joseph Smith's work among the sisters, but through its pages one can begin to see the role women play in the establishment of the kingdom of God.

The first Relief Society minutes, 17 March 1842, were originally recorded into the "Book of the Law of the Lord" by Willard Richards, a secretary of the Prophet. At a later time, these minutes were transcribed into the "Female Relief Society of Nauvoo" minute book. Following her call to act as secretary, Eliza R. Snow kept the minutes of the society's meetings in this important early record.

Eliza Snow, later the society's second general president, fulfilled her stewardship as secretary when she faithfully recorded the activities and proceedings of the meetings held in Nauvoo. When the Saints abandoned Nauvoo in 1846, she included the priceless records among the few items she brought across the plains to the Salt Lake Valley. In Utah, when Brigham Young called her to reorganize the Relief Society among the units of the Church, she carried the records with her from ward to ward to help local priesthood leaders organize units of the Relief Society according to the order set forth by the Prophet Joseph.

In 1905 Bathsheba W. Smith, general president of the Relief Society at the time, spoke to a group of Relief Society sisters in the Pioneer Stake and mentioned this important record book: "I have the book of the Relief Society Sister Eliza kept, and I am very proud of it."[11]

Portions of the Nauvoo Relief Society minutes were incorporated into several published sources, including *History of the Church, Teachings of the Prophet Joseph Smith,* and *The Words of Joseph Smith.*[12] These minutes have been a blessing to the Church and remain one of the invaluable records preserved in the Church archives.

The Nauvoo Relief Society minutes, along with the contemporary diaries, letters, and later reminiscences of the women who participated in the momentous events in the City of the Saints, provide an interesting and illuminating account of the Nauvoo period. This story has largely been forgotten by the Saints, and only recently has it been rediscovered.

2

COMING TO NAUVOO— SISTERS GATHER

> We walked until our shoes were worn out, and our feet became sore and cracked open and bled until you could see the whole print of our feet with blood on the ground.
>
> —Jane Elizabeth Manning

Many of the Saints who fled across the open prairie of the state of Missouri and the Mississippi River bottoms during the harsh winter of 1838–39 to the safety of Iowa and Illinois were courageous women. These sisters were not simply acted upon by forces beyond their control; they were actors in this great drama of Mormon history.[1]

A few years later, these same women, augmented by many more recent converts, left Nauvoo in 1846 to begin their famous trek to Utah. These Latter-day Saint grandmothers, mothers, daughters, and sisters made their way through the wilderness of Iowa to a temporary gathering place, Winter Quarters, before beginning the long journey to the Great Basin.

Thousands of sister Saints and new converts arrived in Nauvoo with excitement and great expectations between the years 1839–46.[2] Every sister, whether young or old, married or single, came to the City of the Saints with a sense of adventure—the very act of accepting the gospel message demanded tremendous courage and sacrifice. For many of these women, leaving family and friends behind to join their sisters in Nauvoo was truly a singular act of faith.

Unlike most of their pioneering non-Mormon contemporaries, Latter-day Saint women gathered to Ohio, Missouri, Illinois, and eventually Utah for non-economic reasons.³ They traveled to these various places with their families or alone for usually one reason, to be with the Saints. The gathering to Nauvoo was no different.

The story of the Saints' gathering to Nauvoo began in January 1839, when plans were established to assist the poorest Saints to move from Missouri. Drusilla Hendricks, whose husband was wounded at the Battle of Crooked River just a few months earlier, recalled this period:

> We were compelled to stay at Far West until after the surren-
> der, when we went home. The mob had robbed the house of bed-
> ding and, in fact, everything but my beds. My husband could not
> yet move hand or foot. Then we had to settle our business mat-
> ters and fix to get out of the state. I went to work and sold what I
> could and gave our land for money to buy two yoke of cattle. Fi-
> nally we had to leave everything, only what we could put into a
> little wagon.
>
> About the middle of January, Father Joseph Smith and Father
> [Isaac] Morley, with five or six others, came and anointed and ad-
> ministered to my husband. They stood him on his feet and he
> stood by them holding to each arm. He began to work his shoul-
> ders. I continued to rub him with strong vinegar and salt and lini-
> ments. The brethren were leaving the state as fast as they could.⁴

The brethren were leaving the state because their lives were in immediate danger. Charles C. Rich left following an attempt on his life at Far West by Missouri militia personnel. His wife, Sarah Rich, was left behind and forced to make her way east to Illinois without his help. When the small group she traveled with reached the Missis-sippi River, the ice was broken up on the west side of the river and was running, so the ferry boat could not cross.

Having traveled so far, and now being only a few hundred yards from their destination yet unable to reach it, Sarah and another woman felt very downhearted. The knowledge that their husbands were on the opposite side in Quincy, Adams County, Illinois, waiting for them worsened the emotional strain of the situation. Because the ferry was not in operation, the only way they could cross was by using a skiff or a canoe to maneuver through the ice to the island and from there to walk on the ice to Quincy on the east side.

While Sarah waited on the riverbank, a male member of the

Portrait of Sarah Pea Rich, painted by William W. Major in Nauvoo before the Saints left their beloved city for the wilderness of Iowa.

group, George D. Grant, told her to cheer up because he would go over and tell Brother Rich she was there. In his attempt to cross, George fell through the ice and was barely saved by two other men. "So when we heard this news we went back to our wagons clearly discouraged," Sarah recalled. "I went into the wagon to cry, while Sister [Louisa Taylor] Stout and my dear father . . . prepared dinner."

Not much time elapsed before Sarah's husband learned that she was there, and he made the crossing himself with another Latter-day Saint brother. "Great was our joy to meet with our dear companions," she enthusiastically remembered, "who were compelled to part with us three months before and flee for their lives from a howling mob." On the following day, both husbands decided to take their wives across the river to better shelter and security, despite the river conditions. Because Sarah was pregnant and near delivery, she agreed to cross over immediately, as she did not know when the baby would be born.

They got into a canoe, and the men rowed them across the river to the point where they could cross the remainder of the way on the ice. Sarah left her aged father on the Missouri shore so he could take

care of the teams and wagons until the ferry boat could cross. She remembered that the old man "stood with tears in his eyes watching us,
not knowing whether we could reach shore or not."[5]

Emma Smith made her departure from Far West, Missouri, with a
group of Saints on 7 February 1839. Her husband still languished in a
"lonesome prison" in Liberty, Missouri. She wrote to him shortly
thereafter:

> No one but God, knows the reflections of my mind and the feel-
> ings of my heart when I left our house and home, and almost all
> of everything that we possessed excepting our little children, and
> took my journey out of the State of Missouri, leaving you shut up
> in that lonesome prison. But the reflection is more than human
> nature ought to bear, and if God does not record our sufferings
> and avenge our wrongs on them that are guilty, I shall be sadly
> mistaken.[6]

Emma finally arrived at the western shore of the frozen Mississippi River. Somewhat fearful of the thin ice, she separated her two
horses and walked apart with two-and-one-half-year-old Frederick
and eight-month-old Alexander in her arms. Julia held securely to
her skirt on one side and positioned young Joseph on the other side
to begin the walk across the river.

Emma also carried Joseph's manuscripts of his Bible translation in
heavy bags, along with her husband's other personal papers fastened
securely to her waist. She then walked across the frozen river to safety
in Illinois.

Mary Fielding Smith, whose husband, Hyrum, was also shut up in
Liberty Jail, told her experiences during the difficult exodus in a letter to family in June 1839. She recounts the tale of her tribulations:

> My husband was taken from me by an armed force, at a time
> when I needed, in a particular manner, the kind [of] care and at-
> tention of such a friend, instead of which, the care of a large fam-
> ily was suddenly and unexpectedly left upon myself, and in a few
> days after, my dear little Joseph F. was added to the number.
> Shortly after his birth I took a severe cold, which brought on
> chills and fever; this, together with the anxiety of mind I had to
> endure, threatened to bring me to the gates of death. I was at
> least four months entirely unable to take any care either of myself

or child; but the Lord was merciful in so ordering things that my dear sister could be with me. Her child was five months old when mine was born; so she had strength given her to nurse them both.

Mary recalled the persecution the Saints encountered following the fall of Far West and their subsequent expulsion: "This happened during my sickness, and I had to be removed more than two hundred miles, chiefly on my bed." The journey was hard on the family. "I suffered much on my journey; but in three or four weeks after we arrived in Illinois, I began to amend, and my health is now as good as ever."[7]

Martha Pane Jones Thomas arrived in Missouri from her home in Kentucky in 1837. She and her family departed the former Mormon capital in Missouri on Valentine's Day, 1839. Martha was eight months pregnant when she began the journey.

We started across the prairie to Tenny's Grove, about twenty miles [from Far West]. The snow was about six inches deep. The children all barefoot, except the oldest boy. To hear them crying at night with their feet cracked and bleeding was a grievous sight for a mother to bear. I would often grease them and put on clean stockings, instead of making them wash them when going to bed.

Hundreds of Saints were on the road heading east at the time. Their escape to Illinois was sometimes accomplished as fast as eight days, and other times it took as long as three weeks. The usual trip took between ten and eleven days. Some of the last Saints out of Far West found camp poles and wood for fires all along the way, provided by the Church's Committee for Removal. One man returning from Illinois to Far West reported over two hundred wagons between the Mississippi River and Far West, all heading for safety in Illinois. For those without sufficient provisions, the way stations provided welcome relief.

Martha Thomas's family "found stations all along the road with provisions." They were "much surprised as this was the first station we ever saw. We acknowledged the hand of God. Drew provisions and went onto the next, until we reached [the Mississippi River]. We could not cross for the ice. Several hundred families were camped on the river bank."

While camped at the river, word came that the militia intended to shoot all the Mormons still remaining in Far West on a certain day. Martha's husband arrived at their campsite from a meeting and said, "Mother, what do you think of our team going back to Far West?" He continued, "The Brethren and Sisters (for there were many widows and children) are all to be shot if they are not out by such a day." Martha responded, "Well, dump the things out by that log." Soon her husband was on his way back to help.

During the evening, the family drove four stakes into the ground and laid some poles, tied up with bed cords so that several quilts could be hung all around, except at one end, "which was left open so the heat of the log fire would shine in and keep [us] warm." Martha thought, "A Queen never enjoyed such a bedroom. It was a comfortable place [and] had one good night's rest in it."

The next day, boats began making one trip across the river per day. "Just imagine," Martha recalled, "I was left on the shore, with no living one with me, but four small children. The sun was down. I could not see across the river. I wrapped the children in the bed clothes. It was very cold and [I] sat down on the bed to watch for the boat. I began to look at my situation, not knowing what moment I might be taken sick [have the baby]. For the first time the tears stole down my face, on my own account. One of the little ones said, 'Mother, are you sick?' 'No,' said I, 'the wind is so cold.' "

Just at the moment of despair, a fellow Saint, Brother Wiswager, rode up. "Seeing I was feeling bad," Martha fondly recalled, he "stayed with me until he heard the boat coming. He had twelve miles to ride after dark." He offered them lodging in Quincy, where he established his own family in a twelve-foot-square house. Brother Wiswager joked, "We have five chidlren, you have five, four grown persons, plenty of standing room!"

In a few days, Martha was "put to bed" and delivered a fine young baby boy, whom she named after Joseph Smith, who was still incarcerated in a prison in Missouri.[8]

Another Missouri Saint, Nancy Tracy, made a "cart out of two wheels of an old wagon" drawn by one horse. The small cart had "a bed sheet for a cover" and little room for any of the family's personal effects. Nancy, her husband, and three small children started their journey from Far West to Illinois sometime in March 1839. "It [was] storming incessantly," Nancy wrote. She continued her narrative:

> We traveled on until we came to the Mississippi bottom. It was three miles across the river bottom. We were five days in crossing

it through mud and water. I had to wade and carry my child six months old and gather brush at night to make my bed upon, for our cart was not large enough to sleep in and when it stormed, which it did nearly all the time, we had to take it as best we could. Well, we crossed the river at Quincy and traveled up the river, stopped one year near Payson, Illinois, and then came to Nauvoo.[9]

The people of Illinois, particularly the citizens of Quincy, reached out to help the refugees from Missouri. Writing to friends in the East, Elizabeth Barlow mentioned the help the Saints received in Illinois: "The people of Quincy had contributed between four and five hundred dollars for the poor Mormons. God had opened their hearts to receive us. May heaven's blessing rest upon them. We are hungry and they feed us, naked and clothed us. The citizens have assisted beyond all calculations."[10]

Following Joseph Smith's escape from his imprisonment in Missouri, he soon took steps to locate the Saints in a new gathering place, Commerce, Illinois, forty-five miles north of Quincy.

The gathering to Commerce, later called Nauvoo, was often a multi-step operation for these Missouri exiles. Leonora and Eliza Snow left their Missouri home and settled briefly in Lima, a community between Commerce and Quincy.

The Snow sisters found much-needed work as seamstresses and lodging for themselves and Leonora's two young children in an upstairs apartment of a home. The sisters, however, did not tell the owners that they were Mormon refugees. Sometime later, Eliza reported hearing the gentleman of the house "proclaiming loudly against the Mormons" in the parlor below their room. His accusations were based on rumors and hearsay. Eliza and Leonora noticed a change in his tone, as he told his visitors about the "two noble women" living in his home, insisting all the time that "no better women ever lived."[11]

Other sisters were able to go directly to the gathering place, so they packed their wagons again and started to rebuild their lives. Julia Ives Pack brought her mother, Lucy Ives, with her to Nauvoo. Lucy was forced from her Missouri home at the "point of a bayonet" in February. Now, eight months later, she died on 20 October 1839 at the home of Stephen and Hannah Hogaboon Markham, "completely worn out by the mobbings and hardships."[12]

On 10 May 1839 Emma and Joseph Smith moved their family into an 1803 two-story log cabin called the Homestead. Joseph Smith III recalled his family's arrival: "[We] left Quincy, May 9, arrived at Commerce the following day, and moved into a log house. . . . Grandfather Joseph and Lucy Smith lived in a small log house [summer kitchen] on the west side of the frame attachment to the block house."[13]

While the exiled Missouri Saints built up Nauvoo on the banks of the Mississippi River as a refuge from the storm of persecution, missionaries in Great Britain were having great success in converting many individuals to the restored Church. Joseph Smith, through the missionaries and other Church leaders, encouraged these new converts to gather with the Saints in western Illinois and eastern Iowa. As Nauvoo had become a safe haven for the driven Missouri Saints, so it now would become a retreat for the politically and economically disadvantaged British Saints.

These ambitious Saints made their way west by whatever means were available. Some sisters, along with family members, arrived by canal boats, wagons, stages, river boats, and horses; and some simply walked the whole way to the new city of the Saints. By 1840, a massive emigration began when British Saints crossed the Atlantic Ocean, commencing their travel from the docks of Liverpool, England, on sailing vessels to New Orleans.[14] Atlantic crossings were slow and tedious. The journey from Liverpool to New Orleans took as many as seventy-one days or as little as thirty-seven days. The average crossing took fifty-four days. From New Orleans the Saints continued their journey by steamboat up the Mississippi River to the boat landing in and around Nauvoo. The difficulty of travel was augmented by the sorrow of leaving family and friends.

The hardships of gathering also came to bear upon loved ones left behind who suffered because family members ventured afar. There is no measuring the last look of anguish on a mother or sister's face as a family member began a long journey, never again to be seen. And there is no reason to doubt that the memory of that look stayed with the convert to the grave.

Jane Robinson, an English girl at the time of her conversion and her migration to America, wrote:

> I believed in the principle of the gathering and felt it my duty to go although it was a severe trial to me, in my feelings to leave my

native land and the pleasing associations that I had formed there; but my heart was fixed. I knew in whom I had trusted and with the fire of Israel's God burning in my bosom, I forsook my home.[15]

The first sister Saints from England left on 6 June 1840 with a group of forty-one excited, newly converted members of the Church. Forty-four days later, after three days in quarantine, these immigrants landed at New York "safe and in good spirits."

Crossing the ocean from England during that period was hazardous and difficult, as was often noted in the Saints' diaries and later reminiscenses. One reporter noted, "The men, women, and children screamed all night in terror."[16] Another diarist recorded:

> The wind blew hard . . . ; many were sick all night. . . . Such sickness, vomiting, groaning and bad smells I never witnessed before, and added to this the closeness of the berths almost suffocated us for want of air. . . . On the Friday night a little girl belonging to a family in the second cabin was frightened by the storm and lost her reason.

Two days later the author wrote, "This night the child which was frightened died."[17]

Sometime later, another immigrant company aboard the ship *Palmyra* ran into a severe storm that lasted eight days. There were no fires and therefore no cooking. The passengers lived on biscuits and cold water when they felt like eating. Young Ann Pitchforth noted:

> The waves dashed down the hold into the interior of the vessel, hatchway then closed, all the utter darkness and terror, not knowing whether the vessel was sinking or not; none could tell— all prayed—and awful silence prevailed—sharks and sins presenting themselves, and doubts and fears; one awful hour after another passing, we found we were not yet drowned; some took courage and lit the lamps.[18]

Mary Field Garner crossed the Atlantic as a young girl with her parents. She recalled:

> After joining the Church my parents were not content to stay in England, but they wanted to be with the main body of Saints at

Nauvoo. As soon as they could save enough money to make the voyage they came to America. . . . The sea was very rough, and there was a bad storm which caused the ship to be driven off its course. Thus it took us seven weeks to make the voyage. We were at sea only a short time when I became seasick.

To Mary's dismay, the "sickness lasted the whole trip," but she rejoiced when they saw land again.[19]

The relief of landing was somewhat tempered by the fact that at New Orleans the Saints had to board a steamboat to continue their journey to Nauvoo. The steamboat trip, especially on the budget most Saints were able to afford, was not a luxurious river cruise. Conditions were very unsanitary—the boats were notoriously dirty and smelled of livestock. The boats themselves were crowded; even those who had cabins often were found sleeping on the floor as they doubled up.

The steam engine was loud with its roaring furnace, and the shrill of the safety valve's whistle constantly reminded the passengers of the danger of explosion. Seasoned travelers slept dressed in case of accident at night when the danger of hitting river snags was highest. The huge wheels splashed noisily as the boat continued its journey. Several letters and diaries mention people falling overboard. Small children were watched continually during the trip up the Mississippi.

Elizabeth Kendall, widow of John Kendall from England and mother of three children, arrived in Nauvoo in February 1843 from her homeland. She arrived at the upper landing in Nauvoo at the conclusion of her riverboat journey from New Orleans. Upon arrival she "hustled about finding a place to leave her children and securing information from those who were there to give it." She started the walk to the city, one mile away:

> She found on the corner of Main and Kimball streets a long, one-story brick building, built with its fronts to the west where a door opened to Main street; parallel with Kimball street it ran back towards the east. Ten comfortable rooms with doors opening into the garden plot, each room with such a door, two windows and a fireplace. This was a tenement owned by a widow, whose tenants were preferably widows. . . . [She] secured the third room from the east end, . . . returned to the landing for her children and her early store of goods; putting them in the room she now called home, she went buoyantly about the town seeking work.[20]

Widow's Row, or Brick Row, was located near the southwest corner of Main and Kimball streets on the flats of Nauvoo. Several women, including Sophia Leyland and Elizabeth Kendall, lived in the single-story building.

Another new English convert, Jane Mellau, wanted to emigrate to America. She and her husband, John, were unable to afford the trip to Nauvoo. John was sent ahead, hoping to find employment to pay for the passage of his young family, which included two children. Four months following his departure, Jane gave birth to their third child, who died within the year.

Jane soon departed England for America and arrived in New Orleans with only four dollars left. This resourceful sister secured passage on a Mississippi steamboat for her family, having worked for a riverboat captain in New Orleans. Upon her arrival in Nauvoo, she was informed of her husband's death.

Taken in by Emma Smith, Jane was determined to continue her life as productively as possible. Early one morning a short time later, Jane made her way down a street to do the family wash when she met her husband face to face—his death had been only a rumor. Soon the reunited couple moved into a rented house and began their new life in Nauvoo together after a long period of separation.

Several newspapers and non-Mormon visitors made comments about the sister Saints newly arrived from England. In 1841 the *Quincy Whig* noted that a group of Saints from England seemed to have "an honest and healthy look." The group included "many comely women, . . . handsome and delicate," as well as ninety children under the age of fourteen.[21] The *Fort Madison Courier* said that the English Saints "appear to be quite [an] inoffensive people and possessed of some means."[22]

A Scottish minister, traveling on the Mississippi in the summer of 1844, was especially interested in the Mormon immigrants he observed, since the British churches were much shaken by the impact of the Church's missionary effort overseas. He met a British sister Saint whom he described as "intelligent on all other points but the Mormonite delusion, on which she seemed crazed."[23]

A Canadian, Eliza Dana, and her sisters were baptized "with aching hearts," because their parents disapproved of their involvement with the Saints. Following their baptisms, however, their mother joined the Church before the family moved to Lockport, New York. Eliza remained at Lockport for eighteen months until the spring of 1844, when she "was united in matrimony" on 18 April to William Gibbs. Soon the newlyweds started toward Nauvoo. She recalled:

> When we got within one hundred and eighty miles of Nauvoo, the roads were so fearfully bad we stopped four weeks for them to improve. While there we received news of the death of the prophet Joseph. Notwithstanding we had none of us ever seen him, it cast such a gloom over our minds that it seemed to blight all our future prospects. In a few days, however, we journeyed on, but when we arrived at Nauvoo it was not the Nauvoo we had anticipated. All was gloom and madness, and as time passed, sorrow and distress seemed to mark us for their particular victims.[24]

Catherine Spencer and her husband, Orson, a Baptist minister, were converted to the Church in Middlefield, Massachusetts, by Catherine's brother-in-law, Daniel Spencer. Daniel had accepted baptism into the new Mormon faith earlier and had come to Massachusetts with the express intention of converting his minister brother and his sister-in-law. After several days of conversation and lively discussions, Catherine said to her husband, "Orson, you know this is true!"[25] Orson did know, and, as a result, the couple were baptized shortly thereafter. For Catherine, baptism meant family conflict. Her share of her father's estate was immediately revoked.

Friends offered help to Catherine Spencer, but only if she would renounce her newfound faith. Her reply was, "No, if they will withhold from me the supplies they readily granted to my sisters and brother because I adhere to the Saints, let them. I would rather abide with the Church in poverty, even in the wilderness, without their aid, than go to my unbelieving father's house and have all that he possesses."[26]

After giving up a paid Baptist ministry and a salary that kept them quite comfortable in Massachusetts, Catherine and Orson joined the Saints in Nauvoo, Illinois. At the age of thirty-five, a short four years later, Catherine Spencer died in the severe winter weather as the Saints were driven from their Illinois home into the wilderness of Iowa in 1846.

Jane Elizabeth Manning, a free black born at Wilton, Fairfield County, Connecticut, on 11 May 1821, was an early convert to the Church. While a young girl, she lived as a servant, not a slave, in the home of a prosperous white family. Jane was a Presbyterian when Charles Wandell, a Mormon missionary, arrived in the area with his companion to preach the restored gospel. Eventually, Jane was converted by the message and introduced her own family to the Church. Soon thereafter, Jane and eight family members immigrated to the Church headquarters in Illinois, where she met Joseph Smith.

Jane, along with her mother, Eliza; her sisters, Angeline and Sarah; her brothers, Isaac and Peter; her sister-in-law, Lucinda Manning; her brother-in-law, Anthony Stebbings; and her small son, Sylvester, left Wilton, Connecticut, in October 1843. They traveled with a larger group of Saints from the area as far as Buffalo, New York. Separated from the main body of travelers when boat authorities refused to allow them on the steamer, Jane led the little family of Saints eight hundred miles to Nauvoo.

Jane remembered, "We walked until our shoes were worn out, and our feet became sore and cracked open and bled until you could see the whole print of our feet with blood on the ground. We stopped and united in prayer to the Lord, we asked God the Eternal Father to heal our feet and our prayers were answered and our feet were healed forthwith."

They were stopped in Peoria, Illinois, and threatened with imprisonment when they were unable to show their "free papers." The group of Saints finally convinced the authorities they were never slaves and were not therefore required to have "free papers." Jane and her family were allowed to continue their journey to Nauvoo.

"We went on our way," Jane recalled, "rejoicing, singing hymns,

and thanking God for his infinite goodness and mercy to us, in blessing us . . . , protecting us . . . , and healing our feet."[27]

Soon they arrived in Nauvoo, and with the assistance of Orson
Spencer they were directed to the home of Joseph and Emma Smith,
where Jane met the Prophet for the first time. She later recalled: "I
was certain he was a prophet because I knew it. I was willing to come
and gather, and when he came in with Dr. Bernhisel I knew him. Did
not have to tell me because I knew him. I knew him when I saw him
in Old Connecticut in a vision, saw him plain and knew he was a
prophet."[28]

The band of converts was greeted warmly by the household, including Emma, who bid them all welcome. They were seated in one
of the rooms of the newly completed Mansion House. Joseph took a
chair near Jane and asked, "You have been the head of this little
band, haven't you?" "Yes, sir," answered the small black woman.[29]

Jane related their travels to the City of the Saints. The entire
family was invited to stay at the Mansion House until they found
work and other accommodations. Jane, however, remained at the
Prophet's home, working with Emma to care for guests who stayed
with the family.

Another woman arrived in Nauvoo during this same time. Eliza
Monroe was the only child of a native East Indian woman and a
young British army officer. Like her mother, her hair and skin were
dark. Eliza traveled to England following her mother's death. Life was
much different there, but Eliza heard the "good news" of the Restoration and soon made arrangements to travel with a group of Saints to
Illinois. Helen Mar Kimball Whitney fondly remembered her as
being "slender and full of grace and refinement, with none of the
proud and haughty airs of an aristocrat."[30]

One aged convert sent her son, Isaac C. Haight, ahead to make
preparations for her trip to the Church's new gathering place. He
started on 7 June 1842 and arrived at Nauvoo on 5 July. During the
next summer, Isaac returned east to help his mother and father, Katu-
rah Horton and Caleb Haight, gather with the Saints. The company
left their home in New York on 13 September 1843. Isaac's journal
reviews the difficult trip west:

> 13 September 1843. Left Movania in company with father,
> mother, the Bateman family, and Wilson Arden and family for
> Nauvoo. All in good health, but mother. She was very feeble, but

anxious to go to Nauvoo she thought she would try the journey.
She stood the journey very well the first week.

23rd [September]. She then began to fail. . . . We had to stop
that [day] and the next. 25th [September]. Started again. Mother
had to lay on a bed. We arrived in Kirtland [Ohio] on 27th.

28th [September]. Put mother on the canal boat.

Isaac accompanied his mother on the trip to Cincinnati and sent
his father and other family members ahead.

6th [October] Mother's health is so delicate that I fear she
will not live to get to Nauvoo. 16th [October]. Arrived at Nauvoo; found my family all well. Mother is quite feeble. . . . Father
and company arrived by land.

18th November. [Mother] died without a struggle or a groan
and has gone to rest in the Paradise of God with the Saints that
have gone before, there to remain until the morning of the resurrection of the just when we shall again behold her clothed with
bright immortality and eternal life.[31]

Mary Ann Stearns, not yet ten years of age, was in England while
her stepfather, Parley P. Pratt, served a Church mission. She traveled
to America and, following the landing, boarded another ship on 1
January 1843 to travel "from the mouth of the Mississippi up to New
Orleans." Mary wrote:

The weather was delightful. Oranges were on the trees, and cotton was still in the fields. The captain of the pilot boat invited
[us] to take New Year's dinner with [him]. . . . We had a fine dinner, a great treat to us after being on the ship ten weeks. . . . They
treated us very cordially, sent nice fruits to mother and children.

Mary's mother stayed with her children while Parley P. Pratt and her
daughter went to dinner. The children had "not quite recovered from the
measles." Eventually, the company of Saints arrived at New Orleans and
disembarked. All two hundred and fifty went on board the *Goddess of
Liberty* for the trip to St. Louis. From there, the company traveled toward Nauvoo, except Mary and her family, who stayed the winter at
Chester, Illinois, because Parley was unwilling to venture into Missouri
after the abuse he had experienced when the Saints were expelled.

Months later, the family made the trip from Chester to Nauvoo. The trip was an eventful one as the riverboat *Maid of Iowa* made its way up the icy waters of the Mississippi toward its destination. Another steamboat loaded with Saints, *Amaranth*, moved along with Mary's group. She recalled:

A little boy of [the] company about eight years old fell overboard and was drowned. I attended the funeral and was much impressed by the accident. By the last of March, the ice breaking up, the two steamers started up the river. Sometimes one would be ahead and then the other, our little boat being much hindered by the large cakes of ice. We were two weeks making the journey, and on the 5th of April, I had a little sister born who was named Susan for our Grandma Frost. The 6th being my own birthday, I regretted it very much that they could not have come together. Brother Snow, with his company, landed at Nauvoo in the forenoon of April 12, and our company in the afternoon of the same day.

Joseph Smith arrived at the landing to greet the Saints, and following "a general handshaking," he came to Mary's cabin. Mary noted:

After cordial greetings, he took a seat and taking the little boys, Parley and Nathan, upon his knees, seemed much affected, . . . tears streaming down his face. Brother Pratt, seeing the general emotion this caused, said, in a tender, jesting fashion, "Why, Brother Smith, if you feel so bad about our coming home, I guess we will have to go back again," tears of joy filling his own eyes. This broke the spell, smiles returned, and joy unbounded filled every heart.

Soon the family was taken to Joseph and Emma's home to be nursed and cared for, following their long journey.[32]

Not all those who arrived in Nauvoo during this period were converts. Many people came to investigate the new faith and to meet the Prophet—among them was Mary Ann Hoopes Yearsley.

Mary Ann Hoopes married David D. Yearsley on 4 September 1830, the year the Church was organized. Eleven years later, Mary Ann and David arrived in Nauvoo to meet the Mormon prophet and to see for themselves what Mormonism was all about. Following their introduction, Mary Ann, satisfied that Joseph was a prophet, asked him to baptize her. The baptismal service began at the edge of the Mississippi River, where Joseph took her by the hand and went with her into the river to perform the ordinance. Mary recalled, "After the ordinance was performed, the Prophet swam out into the river a short distance, which greatly surprised [us] as [we] thought it a very strange thing for a Prophet to do."[33]

Another nonmember, Charlotte Haven of Portsmouth, New Hampshire, arrived in Nauvoo sometime in December 1842. She left Quincy on a stagecoach. Writing to her family in New Hampshire on 3 January 1843, Charlotte noted:

> Our stage much resembled an Eastern butcher's wagon, and we soon ascertained that the curtains on the sides were destitute of fastenings, for they flapped up and down, to and fro, admitting a bracing circulation of air at every gust, which seemed to come direct from Arctic regions. The driver, who occupied the seat before us, told us we must on no account stop talking, "for," says he, "people freeze to death on these prairies before they know it."

She continued telling family members of a young Mormon girl they picked up along the way. The girl was dressed only in "a calico dress, thin cotton shawl, sun bonnet, and india-rubber shoes." The occupants of the stage offered to share with her their heavy buffalo robe. Charlotte wrote:

> At eleven o'clock we came in full sight of the City of the Saints, and were charmed with the view. We were five miles from it, and from our point of vision it seemed to be situated on a high hill, and to have a dense population; but on our approach and while passing slowly through the principal streets, we thought that our vision had been magnified, or distance lent enchantment, for such a collection of miserable houses and hovels I could not have believed existed in one place. Oh, I thought, how much real poverty must dwell here!

Charlotte was obviously a vivacious and attractive young girl. When she took her first walk around the city, passing by the temple, she said, "I verily believe every man at work cutting stone laid down

Nauvoo Main Street scene. Joseph and Emma Smith's Mansion House is located at the right; Sidney and Phebe Rigdon's one-story frame home (the city post office) is located just north; and the old hotel is located across the street.

his tools and gazed at me as I passed." Charlotte never joined the Church, but she participated widely in the many balls and socials in the community. As a member of the "Gentile" minority, a group she called "our little society," she was part of a larger aspect of the city. [34]

The "little society" attitude probably did not reflect the larger non-Mormon population, which may have reached nearly two thousand people. A city ordinance allowed for the exercise of religious belief for all citizens. A visiting Methodist minister, like many other clergy, was invited to speak to the Saints. He did so and was surprised "a little, as I did not expect to find any such thing as a religious toleration among them." [35]

Sister Saints continued to arrive in Nauvoo during the entire time Joseph gathered the members of the Church to build a community of the faithful. Following his death, the Saints continued to pour into the city.

Irene Hascall, a bride of only a few months, arrived in the city with her husband, Francis M. Pomeroy, from North New Salem, Massachusetts, sometime in May 1845. The new family traveled by way of Hartford, Connecticut, to New York and on to Philadelphia. By means of rail and of canal boats, they arrived at Pittsburgh and then traveled on the Ohio River to St. Louis and finally up the Mississippi River. This migration of sister Saints to the City of Joseph continued even after the first wagons crossed the Mississippi River in February 1846 to begin the trek west.

Irene Hascall Pomeroy's mother, Ursulia, and brother, Thales, left their home in Boston and boarded a ship headed for New Orleans. Ursulia's husband, Ashbel Green Hascall, went to California with Samuel Brannan on the ship *Brooklyn* several months earlier with plans to meet the family in Utah—the Saints' destination in the west. The family never saw him again, however, as he died before reaching Salt Lake City.

After arriving in New Orleans, Ursulia Hascall and her son, Thales, traveled up the Mississippi River to St. Louis and transferred to another steamboat bound for Nauvoo, arriving in May 1846. The aged matriarch was greeted by her daughter, son-in-law, and new granddaughter. A few weeks later, four generations of the Hascall-Pomeroy family left the City of the Saints and traveled west for a new home in the Rocky Mountains.

3

DAILY LIFE—WOMEN ON THE ILLINOIS FRONTIER

In Nauvoo City we reside,
Where we in peace can now abide,
Our dwelling measures "Thirteen Feet,"
With walls rough-hewn and white-washed neat.
—Abigail Pitkin

*W*estern historian Emerson Hough said that the chief figure of the American frontier was the "sad-faced woman, sitting on the front seat of the wagon, following her lord where he might lead."[1] Men are given most of the credit for settling and subduing the frontier; their qualities are those that historians write about as characterizing that period of our history.

Women are often given only secondary credit for carrying out the "duties of a wife" and are called "brave," "mother of the frontier," and "worthy companion and counsellor of those noble and fearless men."[2] However, the truth may be, as one writer notes, that the "sacrifices in moving west have been made largely by women."[3]

The Illinois frontier changed rapidly during the early part of the 1800s.[4] Most of the shores along the waterways, especially the Mississippi River, were settled by 1830. Chicago had only Fort Dearborn and a dozen or so houses at the same time. On the central prairies farther from the waterway, the frontier existed in some places as late as 1850.

The area of Nauvoo was settled by Indians as early as 1805 when the Sac and Fox Indians united and maintained a small village in the area. Eventually, the Indians were forced from their Illinois villages in the 1820s. Between 1800 and 1810, the population of Illinois grew to nearly thirteen thousand; in 1820, the federal census taker counted over fifty-five thousand inhabitants. Illinois became the twenty-first state in December 1818.

Eleven years later, Hancock County was organized, and a post office, called Venus, was established near one of the early homes. This post office served two dozen families in the area by 1830. In 1834, Joseph B. Teas and Alexander White surveyed the land near Venus and renamed the town Commerce. The small community served about a hundred farmers, merchants, and traders in the area. Several stores were established before the Saints began to arrive in the area in 1839.

When Emma Smith arrived with her family, they moved into a small cabin overlooking the river. There were several homes and businesses scattered along the east banks of the Mississippi for about one and a half miles, but only a few were vacant for the large group of Saints. Many sister Saints found protection from the elements in dirt dugouts, tents, or their wagons until log homes could be built.

Frances Turley's family, consisting of six children and her husband, Theodore, lived in a tent "for the space of thirteen weeks" before they finished the first Mormon home built in Commerce. On 21 September 1839, with the log home just completed, Theodore left Commerce to begin serving a mission for the Church in England.[5]

Another convert family from the East was making its way to the Mormon Zion in Missouri when they heard that the Saints were gathering to Commerce. When they arrived, "every house was full." It was too late in the year to begin their own home, so they found a "blacksmith shop" abandoned earlier by two families. This "was the best Father could do," his daughter recalled. The shop "had no floor, nor door, nor chimney. Father made a sod chimney (there were not rocks), a clapboard door, and we lived in that all winter."[6]

The problem of finding adequate housing continued through most of the settlement period. In England, where missionary work continued and emigration efforts were steady, Church leaders warned the Saints that upon arriving in Nauvoo they could not "expect to rent houses and enter at once on a comfortable living—but must pitch tents and build temporary cottages. Thirty to forty yards of calico will make a good tent and four to six weeks work with little expense will erect a small cottage."[7]

The Nauvoo of the Mormon period was a section of wilderness area made up of thickets and forest. Inland about a quarter of a mile was some rich farmland, originally part of the earlier Indian agricultural settlement before the first white settler arrived. Access to the town of Commerce was virtually impossible from these farmlands through the thickets, but farmers could have driven their wagons north to the Carthage Road and then westward to Commerce, which was located on the banks of the river.

When the Mormon women arrived in Commerce, their work was seemingly never done; even social gatherings often had a work purpose. These sisters labored to the limit of their strength, in almost every waking hour. They were often perpetually tired, and the fatigue was not lessened by giving birth to a succession of children, born usually without the benefit of a doctor.

Although Joseph was a man of his times, he nevertheless could be found at home doing things that surprised other men—no doubt Emma appreciated these efforts, especially in light of the number of visitors who came to the home for dinner or overnight accommodations, sometimes lasting days and weeks.

One annoyed man reported that Joseph built kitchen fires, carried out ashes from the fireplace, carried in wood and water for home use, and assisted in taking care of the children—duties often relegated to women. "Some of the home habits of the Prophet . . . were not in accord with my idea of a great man's self-respect," Jesse W. Crosby noted.

Finally, Crosby, full of self-assurance, confronted Joseph, hoping to give him some advice on how to manage his home. "Brother Joseph, my wife does much more hard work than does your wife." The Prophet mildly reproved him by saying that a man who did not love and cherish his wife "and do his duty by her, in properly taking care of her," in this life would not be with her in the next. Thereafter, Crosby noted, "I tried to do better by the good wife I had and tried to lighten her labors."[8]

In fact, the endless work, the heat of summer, the cold of winter, and continual persecution tended in combination to make these women look older than their years, and this is reflected in the few photographs that exist from the early Mormon pioneer period.

Many of these women left comfortable homes with water pumped in and separate rooms for privacy. Most furniture, utensils, dishes, and cupboards were left behind, destroyed, or lost during the persecution in Ohio and Missouri. Still, Abigail Pitkin, an unmarried sister in Nauvoo, was able to look upon her situation with remarkable cheer-

fulness and amusement, as is demonstrated in a letter she wrote her
sister:

> I often thought I'd like to give
> You an account of where we live.
> What's our employ, what we possess,
> How we appear, and how we dress.
> In Nauvoo City we reside,
> Where we in peace can now abide,
> Our dwelling measures "Thirteen Feet,"
> With walls rough-hewn and white-washed neat.
>
> Our bed springs up against the wall
> Because our room is rather small;
> For we in building count the cost
> Lest too much money should be lost,
> For mobs you know have saucy grown
> And will not let us have our own.
> Our table measures just "Three feet,"
> With falling leaves and varnished neat.
>
> With chairs we're blessed with only two
> Missouri claims the remaining few;
> Our glass above the table stands,
> Cracked through the center by your hands,
> Which oft reminds us of the scene
> When it was decked with evergreen.
> On shelves our dishes are ranged neat
> By pegs supported, quite complete.
>
> For old Missouri's wicked clan
> Our cupboard kept, and warming pan.
> We have a heifer very small
> At present gives no milk at all;
> And fowls which throng our door
> But lack of corn will keep them poor,
> Poor things, they'll have to make us meat
> When we have nothing else to eat.
>
> We have a bag to hold our flour,
> Now nearly full stands near the door,
> And many old trunks scattered round,

In which our cabin doth abound.
Our old red boxes join the ring,
Of them awhile I fain would sing.
Like trusty friends they've by us stood,
And from them we've derived much good.

We've many useful things around
That scarce will get a passing sound.
I'd not forget to name the sink
For that is useful, oft, I think.
On subjects long I must not dwell,
But shortly now the tale must tell
How we, like "Dorcas," garments make
For which we goods or money take.

In building often we engage,
But that our foes doth much enrage.
Our homes to them seem very fair,
Which leads them on to act more rare.
In dress and manners we appear
Much as we did when you were here.
Our names we keep but rather would
Exchange for better if we could.

We've many friends and many foes,
Many wants and many woes,
But still I am content to be
A "Mormon," not a "Pharisee."
I still remain your friend, A. P.
And wish in faith we could agree.
May health and peace your steps attend
And wisdom guide you to the end.[9]

Although many of the Saints started from scratch as they tried to reestablish their homes on the banks of the Mississippi River, merchants quickly supplied a vast array of items to those who could afford them. At first, however, very few could.

A typical kitchen in Nauvoo was probably similar to the other Illinois frontier women's situations. Cook stoves were available, but few Saints could afford the price, especially during the early period of Nauvoo's history when money was scarce.

Sutcliffe Maudsley's portrait of Mary Fielding Smith, painted sometime between 1842 and 1844. Around this same time, Maudsley painted similar portraits (same size and pose) of Hyrum, Joseph, and Emma Smith.

Charlotte Haven noted the cooking situation in a letter to family shortly after her arrival in Nauvoo: "A Herculean task it seemed to me, with the fire-place and such cooking utensils; but we had a nice dinner—venison, hot biscuits, potatoes roasted in the ashes, etc.—for we were awfully hungry."

Among the items used to cook their dinner was an object called a "spider." Charlotte explained, "This last our grandmothers might have called a bake-kettle; it has three legs and an iron cover, which is covered with hot coals when anything is baking."[10]

Writing to her sister on 22 January 1843, Charlotte mentioned the venison prepared on Christmas Day. It was "roasted by being held on a long pointed stick over a bed of coals. We also had baked beans, biscuits, and vegetables cooked alternately in the spider and tin dipper, except the potatoes which were roasted in the ashes." On a later occasion the family invited two gentlemen to dinner. The turkey "was cooked by being suspended by a string from the mantel-piece, with the 'spider' beneath to catch the gravy." Shortly thereafter, the "'spider' [was] cast into the shade by a Yankee Notion cooking stove," and "flat-bottomed tin candle-sticks" were supplanted by several "glass lamps and spirit gas."[11]

Kitchen items were simple homemade wooden utensils, including cutting boards, rolling pins, spoons, and doughboxes. Eventually, an increasingly available selection of manufactured items could be found in the stores of Nauvoo.

Local newspapers and contemporary letters and diaries listed several types and varieties of crops available to the Saints throughout the year. The major crops included apples, cotton, cucumbers, flax, hemp, Indian corn, gooseberries, grapes, melons, oats, peaches, potatoes, pumpkins, rice, squash, tomatoes, and wheat.

Flax was an important item, and almost every garden had a patch of flax. Gathered in the fall, the family worked together in the winter months to prepare it for spinning and weaving. Women, who were generally responsible for making clothing, spent much of the winter time repairing and making clothes for their family.

From mid-February to April, depending upon the weather, the sisters gathered sap and made syrup and sugar. Following a good thaw, sap from maple trees in the area was gathered when a tree was tapped. Some twenty gallons of sap were needed to make just one half-gallon of syrup. Once sufficient sap was collected, it was boiled down for sugar or syrup.

During the spring a kitchen garden was prepared; and in the summer, fresh vegetables from the garden were enjoyed. Writing to her husband, Bathsheba Smith said:

> We have had the garden plowed. It looks very well, but would [do] better if it did not rain so much. The worms trouble all the neighbors' gardens, and have not mine but little. A great many people have had more or less out of our garden such as lettuce, onions, radishes, and greens. . . . Our early potatoes are getting quite large. The corn is in tassel. Cabbage looks well. Vines rather poor. Tomatoes in bloom. Beets quite large. [We] will soon have peas.

Much of the fruit was eaten fresh, "stewed for pies," or dried for winter use. Cucumbers were made into pickles. The sisters made sure that their gardens produced everything the families could use, but the final touch always included flowers. "A good many of our flowers are in blossom," Bathsheba added to her list of garden produce.[12]

Writing to family in the British Isles, Ann H. Pitchforth gave them some vivid details of daily life in her new home on the frontier in Illinois:

> Meat is cheap, two pence (four cents) a pound of choice pieces, one pence a pound the other fowls, one shilling (twenty-five cents) eggs two pence (four cents) a dozen. Meat is cheap, but vegetables are high. We hope by next year to grow our own. Cabbages are five cents a piece, turnips are high. Potatoes are high.[13]

Many families had a cow on hand to provide necessary fresh milk and other dairy products. In most cases, the mother had the responsibility to care for the animal, unless a child was old enough to perform the daily task. Through the local paper, the *Nauvoo Neighbor*, the Saints were informed on the correct way of milking a cow: "If you would obtain all the milk from the cow you must treat her with the utmost gentleness; she must not stand trembling under your blows nor under your threats. She may at times need a little chastisement, but at such times you need not expect all her milk."[14]

The milk from a cow was often made into butter or cheese, which drained from cloth bags or perforated buckets hung from rafters in an out building. Bathsheba Smith told her husband that she had "sold six pounds of butter since" he left for his mission.[15] Home production not only provided for families' needs but also provided extra items to trade for those things families could not produce themselves. Bad weather, economic conditions, and other factors induced certain types of food shortages in Nauvoo.

Shortages included the basic commodities of butter, eggs, milk, and flour. Flour was a scarce commodity in any frontier community, and Nauvoo was not any different. Bathsheba noted in one letter to her husband, "I am about out of flour." She did have plentiful supply of another item she identified as meal—the ubiquitous cornmeal.[16] It appeared in every kitchen and in most daily fares.

The sisters made "ash cakes" from cornmeal in their fireplaces. Usually this meant they first cleaned the hearth and then placed the cornmeal cakes (a mixture of salt and boiled cornmeal) on the hottest part of the hearth and covered it with hot wood ashes. After it had finished baking, the ash cake was removed from the ashes, then washed and dried and served as part of a meal, or as was the case in many homes, the main part of a meal.

Cornmeal could be cooked in several ways, including johnnycake and a variety of other types of breads with ingredients ranging from molasses to buttermilk. Cornmeal was used to make hasty pudding; and, when sweetened with maple sugar or honey, it was dessert.

The sisters tried to make variations on this basic commodity, but family members still found the daily fare monotonous. On one occasion, Mary Fielding Smith's son John went with his cousin to have dinner with his Aunt Emma and Uncle Joseph. With a boy standing on each side of him, Joseph prayed, "Lord, we thank thee for this johnnycake, and ask thee to send us something better. Amen." Following the prayer, the bread was cut and served to the family, but before they could finish it, a man knocked at the door and asked for the Prophet. "I have brought you some flour and a ham," he said. Joseph took the gifts gladly, blessed the good brother for offering them, and then turned to the family. "I knew the Lord would answer my prayer."[17]

For others, their prayers were not answered in the same way. Mary Field's father and two sisters died shortly after their arrival in the City of the Saints from their homeland in England. She remembered the situation:

While at Nauvoo my father, William Field, and my two sisters, Eliza and Rachel, died leaving mother with six children to provide for. We were very poor and had very little to eat—cornmeal being our main food. When the other food became exhausted we were put on rations of one pint of [corn]meal a day for the seven of us. We could cook it as we wished. Oh how hungry we were for something else to eat! The children cried for a piece of white bread, and mother ofttimes would cry with us.[18]

The *Nauvoo Neighbor* not only gave practical advice but also often ran recipes for such favorites as Admiral Peacock's Pickle for Meat. "The beef, after lying in the pickle for ten weeks," the paper reported, "has been found as good as if it had been salted three days and as tender as a chicken." On other occasions, recipes for potato pancakes, applesauce cake, ginger cookies, and rusk, a cornbread cereal, were published. Other useful cooking tips included information on how to salvage frozen potatoes, the best method for fattening turkeys, and numerous ways to preserve meats, fruits, and vegetables.[19]

While women of Nauvoo had access to newspaper recipes, they probably relied on the cooking traditions they brought with them or those recipes shared among neighborhood friends.

Another important domestic duty of the sister Saints included preparing for the harsh Illinois winters. The sisters cured meat and dried a variety of fruits and vegetables. Some of the fresh berries and currants were made into jellies and preserves. Apples were also made into cider. This lifesaving task usually involved the children of the home as well.

As the Saints attempted to build a community with precious few resources, many were unable to supply sufficient provisions for their families.

Drusilla Hendricks had most of the responsibility for taking care of the family, including her husband, who was left an invalid after being wounded in the Battle at Crooked River. "I had to lift [my husband] at least fifty times a day, and in doing so I had to strain every nerve," she recalled. With five children under the age of ten, this young mother tried to survive in Nauvoo by taking in boarders, tending a garden, milking cows, feeding livestock, maintaining her home, and preparing the family's daily need for food and clothing.

Her skill at maximizing her resources is demonstrated in an excerpt from her reminiscences:

I paid fifty-six dollars for house rent and got me two bedsteads, four chairs, five falling leaf tables. Kept one of the tables myself and let Brother Lewis have one for moving us to Nauvoo, sold two to Sister Emma Smith for provisions. The brethren gave us a lot and [put] up a log house, and I hired a man to cover it and build a chimney. I and Sister Melinda Lewis chinked and plastered it. We raised a good garden. I began to make beer and gingerbread and go out on public days, this showing that necessity is the mother of invention. I paid a good deal of tithing by making gloves and mittens. I had about thirty pair on hand. I still [did] washing for bread or molasses for my children.

Drusilla recalled an incident that sustained her faith in knowing God was concerned for her family's welfare:

Flour was hard to get. The winter set in early November [1842] and was very hard. I had to buy wood. I only [had] cornmeal for bread. . . . My husband asked me to lay aside my work and pray [for help]. . . . When I was through I felt like I had poured out my whole soul to [the Lord] and I knew that we should have something [to eat]. I had no doubts.

Soon after this experience, a gentleman sold the Hendricks family some fresh pork on credit, which was not due and payable for twelve months. "Who could not see the hand of the Lord in this miracle worked on [a] natural principle?"[20]

Not only did women in Nauvoo often lack food items and equipment needed in their daily work, but the kinds of food they cooked and the clothes they wore were in many instances much different from what they were used to having. This situation was especially true of the recent converts from England. Many sisters even took on chores that were not considered women's work in the East.

In the frontier community of Nauvoo, women made soap and candles, both long and tiring chores. They spun thread and weaved cloth to make clothing and even worked at shoe making. A wringer and a washboard always stood nearby. For clothing to be very clean, the white things were boiled with homemade soap, making wash day a day-long affair. Care of animals often fell to women; they built fences, took care of the "kitchen garden," and helped in the fields— all this while pregnant about thirty percent of the time. Women's daily activities and responsibilities changed, increased, and became far more difficult. For the English Saints, the change could be even more drastic and dramatic.

Home production, while becoming less important in the major urban centers in the East, still was a significant part of the Nauvoo economy. Irene Hascall Pomeroy made a "double brim [straw hat] for a shoe maker" and received a "beautiful pair of kids' shoes" in return.[21] The barter system was the mainstay of individual commerce in the city.

Some eight or nine thousand Saints were in Nauvoo and its vicinity by the summer of 1841. Within a year, Nauvoo eclipsed every other Illinois city in size, with the exception of Chicago. Almost single-handedly the Saints made Hancock County the most populous county in Illinois by the 1845 census.

Nauvoo was a city of log, frame, brick, and limestone homes and

Interior view of Joseph and Emma Smith's first Nauvoo home (the Homestead). The earliest Latter-day Saints' homes were often small wood frame or log buildings. These structures were primitive in nature, but were better than the tent and wagon shelters many lived in upon their arrival in Nauvoo before a log cabin could be built.

buildings by 1843. A non-Mormon resident of Hancock County estimated that at its peak Nauvoo had some "twelve hundred hand-hewn
log cabins, most of them whitewashed inside, two to three hundred
good substantial brick houses, and three to five hundred frame
houses.[22] We must remember, however, that during the entire Mormon period, houses, even next door to each other, were different
styles, some more substantial than others.[23]

Like all frontier communities, Nauvoo replaced its first primitive
log homes with more substantial structures, maybe somewhat faster in
Nauvoo's case, however. On any given block in the city one might
find families functioning in two traditional ways. One family would
be living in the traditional "first house" or log cabin, where one room
encompassed all the family indoor activities, including cooking, eating, socializing, and sleeping. The home next door might be a second
home, traditionally called the "big house." The big house was usually
a two-story brick home, with a kitchen-eating area separated from
sleeping areas, and, if circumstances permitted, a parlor apart from
all.

Charlotte Haven described her circumstances upon arriving in
Nauvoo at their "little white cottage with green blinds." She wrote to
family:

> The stage left us at the kitchen door. The introduction to this
> room was discouraging enough—full of smoke from a fire just
> kindled in the fire-place, no furniture except a red chest and a
> box of crockery, upon which was extended a half venison, flanked
> by a basket of vegetables, and sundry parcels of groceries.

As she briefly toured the other rooms, she saw "a large box stove
in what is a parlor and dining room, a bedstead without bedding in
the bed room—that was all!"

Soon Charlotte's brother and a boarder provided "a table, three
chairs, a coffee-pot and mill, two large tin dippers, and a *spider*." Two
feather beds upon mattresses of husks were used for sleeping.

Charlotte purchased a rug on the following day from a woman
living near the temple. Unlike the rugs she was used to, this one was
"a coarse, ugly thing, which she called 'hit and miss,'—not a pretty
stripe—that was the 'miss'—and the 'hit' was a few inches of red flan-
nel and blue calico at irregular intervals a long way apart, while the
rest was in very shade of *fade.*" Fifteen yards was purchased reluc-

tantly, but the added comfort during the winter was needed no matter how it looked.[24]

In another letter home, Charlotte described the homes built on the prairie near town. "The houses are still of the rudest construction." They were "mere shelters, many built of logs placed cob fashion, some of only one thickness of boards, and others of sod or mud, with seldom any plastering or floors, and minus chimneys, doors, and windows." In place of chimneys, doors, and windows, the poor Saints substituted a funnel about the roof or through a side wall. A quilt was suspended in the doorway or over a window opening.

"You would think it impossible that human beings could inhabit such hovels," Charlotte commented. She was constantly reminded that they were inhabited by "sundry white-headed, dirty-faced, bare-footed children peeping or thrusting themselves between crevices and cracks." To her surprise, however, "in spite of their scanty clothing and the midwinter prairie breezes that play so freely through their dwellings, these [children] look healthy and happy."

In a sympathetic way Charlotte reminded her family:

When we consider the short time since the Mormons came here, and their destitution after having had every vestige of property taken from them, and after having undergone great suffering and persecution, their husbands and sons in some instances murdered; when we remember that, driven from their homes in Missouri, with famine before them, five thousand men, women, and children crossed the Mississippi to this State in the winter of 1841 [1838–39], we cannot wonder that they have no fitter dwelling place and so few of the comforts of life.

She did recognize the advances being made: "Better and more substantial buildings are fast being erected in city and country, and in a few years things will present a very different appearance."[25]

Most homes, especially the first log structures, were generally very simple; they remained unpainted or whitewashed at most, with no wallpaper. Most windows were uncurtained, unless they were paneless, and then a blanket or sheet was placed over the opening. The furniture was almost always undecorated and plain but very practical. A few special pieces or maybe a few family treasures were brought from their previous homes in the East.

Sally Randall reported that her husband obtained "a lot with a log cabin on it, and it [is] paid for. The house is very small, but I think we can get along with it for the present. He had a table and three chairs. We have no bedsteads yet, but shall have soon."[26]

Ann Pitchforth's reactions to the housing cost in the new frontier community of Nauvoo are outlined in a letter to friends and family:

> Rents are very high owing to the increasing value of the land in the city. I intend to save money to buy a house and lot as most people here do; then I shall have no rent to pay. We have a very small house with two rooms and a shed, no upstairs, and the rent is nine pounds and ten shilling [$47.50] a year. By paying twenty pounds [$100] down, I can secure a house and one acre of land and leave the remainder to be paid by ten pounds [$50] a year till paid off. Forty pounds [$200] will buy a house and lot and all in the city. Of course, there are many houses five times as much, but we could improve ours little by little as we could afford.

Sometimes, the euphoria manifested by recent converts was demonstrated in their letters home following their arrival. Ann Pitchforth continued her description of the City of the Saints with an overly simplistic view of this frontier community and increasingly important river city: "There is universal love among them. They are all kind to one another, and very few houses, indeed, have either locks or bolts. All leave everything outside their houses with the greatest of safety."

She did acknowledge, however, "Some bad people get here now and then, but the extremely plain, honest dealing of the people does not suit their chicanery, and they soon get found out and often leave the place."[27] Another sister wrote family members in Massachusetts: "I will not pretend to say that there is nothing improper done or said in this place, for I know there is and there must be where the people of God reside. But there is nothing going on here, that I consider to be wrong, that is upheld by the Church."[28] Sometimes the municipal officers, assisted by the police, helped the "bad people" to leave.

Although Nauvoo was the City of the Saints, it was also an economically important river town.[29] It was founded as the Mississippi River steamboat industry was at the threshold of its golden era. As many as ten steamers passed by Nauvoo weekly, carrying Indians, soldiers, and various types of goods during the town's early years, and by 1843 some four or five steamboats stopped each day. Not only steamboats but also a wide variety of other watercraft plied the currents along Nauvoo's shoreline, including barges, canoes, dugouts, flat-boats, keelboats, and log skiffs. These brought a variety of people in contact with the Saints of Nauvoo.

As a result, trappers, gamblers, Indians, riverboat men, bar-tenders, magicians, musicians, roustabouts, slaves, and prostitutes ar-rived at the wharfs of Nauvoo. The city council acknowledged the existence of "houses of infamy . . . and disorderly characters in this place, who were disposed to corrupt the morals and chastity of our citizens."[30] They passed an ordinance "concerning brothels and disor-derly characters" that prohibited such things within the city limits. Nonetheless, Nauvoo's women included more than sister Saints com-ing together to build the kingdom of God.

John C. Bennett, along with several other "businessmen," built a house of prostitution near the Sunday gathering place of the Saints—the grove. Bennett and his partners then painted a large sign on the front to announce its purpose in an effort to attract a clientele. One contemporary source noted, "We could not get [to the grove] without passing this house and looking right at it, and one or two thousand people would go . . . [past it] on a Sabbath, and they didn't feel very good seeing that house there with great big letters facing them."[31] Eventually the house was "condemned" and destroyed by putting it on rollers and pushing it into a ravine.

The average life span for women in America during the nine-teenth century was but forty years; for men, thirty-eight. In frontier communities like Nauvoo, it was shorter still. Women, however, were subjected to illness more frequently than men. The major causes of poor health on the frontier were the lack of sanitation and the rigors of life. The sisters in Nauvoo, like other communities in Illinois, worked in the kitchens in the hottest weather, breathed in smoke and soot, and were constantly subjected to either too much or too little heat. The lack of dentists was particularly hard on pregnant women.

Nursing and even doctoring was predominantly the woman's work, though several doctors resided in Nauvoo by 1842. Neverthe-less, in the midst of erecting homes and barns, plowing, and planting, in the summer of 1839 many of the Missouri exiles fell ill with the "meanest of all diseases." Called the "ague" by the Saints, it was prob-ably malaria carried by the anopheles mosquito, which thrived in the swampy flats of Commerce. The sickness was common in spring and fall, and newcomers were especially vulnerable.

Already physically weakened by the forced exodus from Missouri during the previous winter and spring, many experienced the chills and fevers of the disease. Those in good health fell ill, and the condition of those in bad health worsened. Many died during the first two years in Nauvoo. The disease was more relentless and deadly than even the mobs they faced in Missouri.

Elizabeth Ann Whitney described her family as "all sick with ague, chills, and fever, and [we] were only just barely able to crawl around and wait upon each other." During this very time, Elizabeth Whitney delivered her ninth child, a boy. Soon Joseph Smith visited their home and invited them to come live at the Homestead. Elizabeth wrote, "[We] went to live in the Prophet Joseph's yard in a small cottage."[32] Soon, the sick among the Saints took every available bed in the Smith household, and many more of them were made as comfortable as possible in makeshift bedrolls in the yard.

Emma and Joseph moved into a tent erected in the yard of the Homestead. Emma found little time for anything but nursing those who came to receive help under her hands. Soon she found herself attending both her husband and her young son Joseph III, who had both caught the disease while helping others.

Emma brought many other families into her home, including the Zina and William Huntington family. Both parents and all three children were sick. Zina had contracted cholera and was near death when she arrived at Emma's house. Even with the extra care given her, Zina Huntington died; however, before she died, she spoke words of comfort to her family. Her eighteen-year-old daughter recalled that her mother called her to the bedside and said:

> Zina [Diantha], my time has come to die. You will live many years; but, O, how lonesome father will be. I am not afraid to die. All I dread is the mortal suffering. I shall come forth triumphant when the Savior comes with the just to meet the Saints on the earth.[33]

Zina Diantha was deeply stricken by her mother's death on 8 July 1839. Months later, her mother's words came into her mind and spoke comfort to her: "Zina, any sailor can steer on a smooth sea. When rocks appear, sail around them." Zina Diantha took comfort in these words and prayed, "O Father in Heaven, help me to be a good sailor, that my heart shall not break on the rocks of grief."[34]

By 20 October, the Nauvoo high council announced to the community an appeal to please resist going to Emma's home for help. She was "exempt from receiving future crowds of visitors as have formerly thronged [the] house."[35] During this terrible season of sickness, Church leaders sought redress from the federal government for losses in Missouri, hoping that financial compensation from them or the state would ameliorate the worsening situation in Nauvoo by providing necessary provisions and shelter for the Saints.

After repeated efforts to obtain some redress at local and state levels for their losses, including land and personal property, Church leaders finally decided to approach the federal government in Washington. Joseph left Emma for the nation's capital on 29 October, with Sidney Rigdon, Elias Higbee, and Orrin Porter Rockwell.

Writing to Emma, Joseph was obviously painfully aware of her situation in Nauvoo:

> I shall be filled with constant anxiety about you and the children until I hear from you and, in a particular manner, little Frederick. It was so painful to leave him sick. . . . [Try to] get all the rest you can. It will be a long and lonesome time during my absence from you, and nothing but a sense of humanity could have urged me on to so great a sacrifice, but shall I see some perish and [not] see redress? No, I will try this once in the [name] of the Lord; therefore, be patient until I come, and do your best. . . . Believe me, [my] feelings are the best kind toward you all. My hand cramps so I must close.[36]

Joseph's concerns for his wife were well founded. Emma was pregnant again, and her two sons, Frederick and young Joseph, were both sick. Frederick's fever finally broke shortly after his father left, but young Joseph still had the "chill fever." He lost a great deal of blood from a nosebleed and rebounded only to be struck with a second bout of the disease, which greatly worried Emma.

The day following Joseph's departure for Washington, someone brought Orson and Nancy Hyde to Emma's home with the "ravaging disease." On the following day, Sarah Mulholland brought her husband, James, the Prophet's secretary, to Emma for help. Emma nursed Brother Mulholland for five weeks and then wrote her husband in Washington, "His spirit left its suffering tenement for a better mansion than he had here."[37]

Another sister, Mary Noble, nursed her two children and a husband. The children died, and her husband "was nigh unto death" through the month of July. At one point, with tears she asked if he "was dying too."[38] He survived, however, but not before his wife went through tremendous stress and grief as mother, wife, and nurse.

During one year, the ague accounted for more than 25 percent of the deaths in Nauvoo. The worst months were August, September, and October, which were also the heaviest periods of fever-related death.

Zina Diantha Huntington Jacobs's diary entries for April 1845 (from which excerpts follow) reflect the process and intensity of the sickness:

April 10 [1845] Quite unwell with the ague in my face. . . .

12th I am no better; see painful nights. Sarah Ann Woode came to assist me. . . .

14th Mother and the neighbors came in to see me. They are very kind, for which I feel truly thankful.

15th . . . I was no better. Sister Eliza Free came to assist me. I trust that she and her sister Emmeline may ever be blessed and ever find friends to assist them and their children in time of need for their kindness to me in my sickness. Also Mother Lyman, Mother Huntington, and Lee girls, Fanny, Julia, Sister Brewer, Sanders, Merrick, and others. Also Amasa Lyman's wife. I feel grateful to God and my friends.

16th My face still worse. . . .

17–18th Sleepless nights almost.

19th The sun [is] about three quarters of an hour high. My face broke about halfway between my chin and ear, rather nearer the chin. Discharged wonderfully. O living mortality, how soon thou canst decay. . . . Eliza and Emily Partridge came over and made my bed and prepared me some supper. All these kindnesses I never shall forget, and the oft times Mother has sent me milk and things for my comfort. (Fanny Merrick came to help me.) . . .

20th I am still getting better. Father comes every day to see me.

21st . . . Brother Lee's wife, Eliza, and Emmeline Free, and Clarissa Decker called.[39]

Along with the ague, Mormon women dealt with consumption

Interior view of Joseph and Emma Smith's second Nauvoo home (the Mansion House).
Eventually, as their economic situations improved, many Latter-day Saints moved from
their first homes into "big houses." These second homes were bigger frame or brick structures that stood in stark contrast to the primitive log homes in the city.

(tuberculosis), chronic diarrhea, assorted childhood maladies, and
other forms of illness. Women also served as midwives. Ann Green
Duston Carling (an English convert from Herefordshire), like several
other sisters in Nauvoo, was set apart for her midwifery duties by
Joseph Smith.

Midwives often carried their precious medical equipment in small
black "baby satchels." Included among the instruments were
"scalpels, needles, scissors, tweezers, saw blades, a small hammer, a
spool of heavy thread, a few obstetrical instruments, plus a package of
scorched cloths which had been ovensterilized."[40]

A unique bonding between doctors and their patients is expected, but bonding between a midwife and an expectant fellow sister
Saint increased when the midwife had experienced childbirth herself.
A sisterhood was created in a special way between them as they
helped each other in suffering and sometimes death. The bonding
created a tie that was often stronger than family relationships, a

bonding characterized by a common desire to build the kingdom of God.

Commonly shared remedies included a variety of cough syrups. Pine tar cough syrup was made by mixing a small amount of pine tar and honey together. Another, red clover cough medicine, was made from red clover, which grew almost everywhere. A good cup of red clover blossoms was put in an earthenware crock with some boiling water. The pot was covered and the contents allowed to cool before straining.

Another important aspect of women's work and activity on the frontier was entertainment, both formal and informal. Entertaining was a diversion often more taxing on the women than the men of Nauvoo. Evening social gatherings generally served an industrial function. For example, the men might be raising a barn or clearing land, in which case they would bring their sharpened tools and probably engage in competitions as they worked.

The women's work was also cooperative, as in quilting. But the sisters often worked for days beforehand getting food ready and afterwards took unfinished handwork home to finish. They also cleaned up after the meal, including washing the dishes with water they brought into the house and heated themselves.

The frontier reputation for hospitality is well known, and Nauvoo was no exception. The main responsibility, however, rested upon the sisters to entertain the guests by providing food and shelter. On one occasion while entertaining guests, Joseph remarked to W. W. Phelps, "What a kind, provident wife I have!" His history continues:

> At this moment Emma came in, while Phelps, in continuation of the conversation said, "You must do as Bonaparte did—have a little table, just large enough for the victuals you want yourself." Mrs. Smith replied, "Mr. Smith is a bigger man than Bonaparte: he can never eat without his friends."[41]

The diaries of the men of Nauvoo reveal the nature and extent of such activities; few, however, mentioned the effort involved, particularly on the part of the women—it was simply expected.

4

NAUVOO—
A CITY OF WOMEN

We were . . . glad of a resting place out of the reach
of those who had sought our lives. . . . We were truly
a thankful and humble people.

—Sarah Rich

*W*hile the sister Saints by and large remained in Nauvoo fixing
their homes, planting their gardens, raising their children,
burying their deceased family members and friends, and meeting together formally and informally, business, political, or Church-related
activities often took the men away from the city, some for short dura-
tions and others for much longer.

Even when the men were in the city, their days and nights were
often filled with work and Church-related activities. This left the
women an opportunity to build important new personal networks,
some of them informal, others highly structured and formal.[1]

Beginning in Nauvoo, a network of sisters began to establish a
strong female bonding, a sisterhood that survived not only the
troubles and turmoil of the Nauvoo experience but also the difficult
pioneer crossing of Iowa in 1846. Annie Wells Cannon stated:

In the forced exodus from Nauvoo, the [sisters], though separated
in different companies coming west, carried the spirit [of sister-
hood] through the journey, over prairie, plain, and mountain, and
ministered in the camps of Israel at Sugar Creek, Garden Grove,
Mt. Pisgah, and Winter Quarters. In the rude temporary homes at

Winter Quarters, meetings were held to comfort, encourage, and keep up the morale of the women.[2]

Rekindled in Winter Quarters during the winter of 1846-47, this sisterhood was brought to the valley of Salt Lake, where it blossomed in every Mormon community throughout the Intermountain West. One woman historian suggested that "nineteenth-century women routinely formed emotional ties with other women." Further, she argued, "a specifically female world did indeed develop" in the nineteenth century. Female bonding created a supportive network of women that was "institutionalized in social conventions or rituals which accompanied virtually every important event in a woman's life, from birth and death."[3]

The sister Saints in Nauvoo experienced many of the same deprivations and joys that other frontier women chronicled; as a result, they too formed a network. However, the female bonding that had its impetus in a larger degree in Nauvoo than ever before in Church history eventually took on new meanings and directions as a result of the doctrinal tidal wave that swept the social, economic, political, and religious landscape of Nauvoo. The social order developed in Nauvoo contrasted with other Illinois frontier communities of the period.[4] One of the bases for an intensified bonding among Mormon women was the periodic absences of husbands, fathers, and brothers from Nauvoo.

Women communicated with absent husbands or family members and friends back home mainly through letters. Writing to her mother in New England, a young woman emphasized this:

> It is with mingled feelings of pain and pleasure that I attempt to address a few lines to you. Yea, it is a great grief to me when I think how far I am separated from you; but the reflection that although far distant, there is a way we can communicate our thoughts to each other.[5]

Vilate Kimball reveals a similar feeling in a letter to her husband. She began, "My bosom friend, the love of my youth, gladly do I retire from the busy cares of life to spend a few moments in silent conversation to you." She longed for the opportunity to be with him, "O that I could take the wings of the morning and fly to your embraces, how

Vilate Kimball's letter to her husband is representative of the numerous correspondences written by women in Nauvoo to family and friends back home, or to husbands, sons, and brothers who were absent on personal or Church business.

much easier I could unbosom my feelings, but yet I am thankful that we even have this privilege of conveying our thoughts to each other."

Vilate noted that she had received a "sweet parcel" that Heber had sent by means of a fellow missionary. Along with the package was a "precious letter." Such letters were read over and over again and passed on to other friends and family members. Vilate wrote, "I have read it over and over with tears in my eyes; the feelings expressed therein [are] worth more to me than words could be without them." Vilate closed with this tender note, "Now, my dear, this page is all devoted to love from me and the children. My daily prayer is that you may finish your mission with honor and be returned in safety to our embraces."[6]

Letters were delivered by chance travelers, by Church missionaries and leaders who left Nauvoo on Church business, and by the postal system. Mail delivery from such frontier communities was often irregular and slow—and always undependable. There is also some evidence that during the latter part of Nauvoo's Mormon history, mail was purposely interrupted by anti-Mormon activists in Hancock County.

The fact that many letters were started on one day and finished several days, sometimes weeks, later indicates the infrequence of mail service. Many letters have postmarks other than Nauvoo, which indicates that some of the letters were paid for by the receiver or that a letter was given to a missionary who put it in the postal system at his final destination, in many cases several hundred miles closer to the intended recipient.[7]

Nauvoo letters not only reveal the daily life of the women of Nauvoo but also preserve their feelings, hopes, and desires. Several sister Saints left precious letters full of insights to their lives.

In 1844 Vilate Kimball wrote her husband a tender letter; she began:

> My dear Companion, It is one week yesterday since I closed a letter to you; although I have not spoken to you for a week, yet you have not been out of my mind many moments at a time when I was awake; and when I am asleep, I often dream about you.[8]

Bathsheba Smith moved into five homes during one year. Following their wedding, the young couple lived with the Smith family for four weeks before moving into their first home, a rented log cabin with a leaky roof and a chimney that smoked. With stout hearts, the newlyweds knelt at their bedside on the first night and thanked God for his blessings in bringing them together.

Soon thereafter, Bathsheba and George A. Smith moved across the river to Nauvoo and found an unfinished log home to rent. It had no glass in the windows, so Bathsheba hung blankets up to keep the cold out and to provide some privacy. They moved another time. This particular home was "the worst-looking house we had yet lived in," she recalled, but it had "the desirable qualities of neither smoking nor leaking."[9]

They soon purchased and began building a two-story frame home. Anxious to have a permanent home, especially since Bathsheba was nearly nine months pregnant, they moved into the unfinished structure. Twelve days later, on 7 July 1842, George A. Smith, Jr., was born. Bathsheba not only began to care for her new son but also became responsible for completing the work on the home when her husband was called on a Church mission two months later.[10] Bathsheba's letters chronicled the private and public news of Nauvoo. She anxiously awaited letters in return—shared them and saved them as precious items to be treasured. She wrote George A.: "When I get a letter first, all the rest come to hear it. The brethren's wives have all been to see me this week."[11]

Her letters kept George A. informed, including her preparation for the long winter. "I have got my corn and fodder secured; broom corn, sunflower seed, and beans likewise. Melissa and me did it."

In closing one letter, Bathsheba noted, "I have had so many melons and my dear was not here to help eat them. Oh, I am so lonesome, all alone [except] baby." She then took the pen and, placing it into the hand of the child while guiding it, wrote, "I is a good boy. I write to you. G. A. Smith, Jr." Bathsheba concluded, "I do not know whether you can read baby's writing. Write every chance. You do not know how I want to see you."[12]

Missionary work included short-term missions to nearby communities and long-term assignments throughout North America and across the ocean to Great Britain. The success in the British Isles was phenomenal. Hundreds, then thousands, listened and believed the husbands, fathers, brothers, and sons sent from Nauvoo to gather the faithful. Mormon women kept the faith at home, providing for their families and fighting the loneliness of separation lasting anywhere from several months to several years.

Almost every household in the Nauvoo area was stricken with

malaria during its first outbreak in the summer of 1839. Among the Church leaders who fell ill were many members of the Twelve Apostles.

The Twelve Apostles were called to leave the United States for a mission in the British Isles, but their departure was delayed by malaria. On 14 September, Brigham Young left his sick wife and ten-day-old daughter and crossed the river to Nauvoo from his temporary home in the abandoned Fort Des Moines to leave on his mission. At Vilate and Heber Kimball's home, however, Brigham collapsed from exhaustion and remained sick for four days. Now Heber had not only his own sick wife, who was about eight months pregnant, and children to take care of but also his fellow Apostle.

Mary Ann Young soon heard of Brigham's situation. She "got a boy to carry her up in his wagon to my house that she might nurse and comfort Brother Brigham to the hour of starting," Heber wrote. Four adults and several children were all sick in a small fourteen-by-sixteen-foot log cabin.

On 18 September, Heber bid his wife good-bye, "who was then shaking with a chill, having two children lying sick by her side." He "embraced her and [his] children and bade them farewell" as he and Brigham made it to a wagon. Both wives were unable to come to the door to see them off. Heber helped Brigham into a wagon and began their journey. Heber recorded, "My inmost parts would melt within me at leaving my family in such a condition, as it was, almost in the arms of death. I felt I could not endure it. I asked the teamster to stop."

Heber asked Brigham to gather all the strength he could to sit up and bid their wives good-bye. "This is pretty tough," Heber said, "but let's rise up, and give them a cheer." He and Brigham did so as they waved their hats three times over their heads and shouted, "Hurrah, hurrah, hurrah for Israel!" Vilate and Mary Ann, upon hearing the shout of farewell, managed to get to the door of the cabin with smiles on their faces, and, while leaning on the doorframe, they waved and called out, "Good-bye; God bless you!" [13]

Both Brigham and Heber returned the good wishes and then told the driver to go ahead. This brief salutation both relieved and sustained the two men as they left their wives for a period of almost two years.

Brigham left some money for his wife, but debts had to be paid. His first letter to Mary Ann, written only hours after parting, explained the various obligations owed. She had only $2.72 left following the disbursement of the funds. "This is almost robbing you I know, but I do not know what else to do. Brother Joseph has pledged himself that the wives of the Twelve should have what they wanted. . . . I do feel as though the Lord would provide for you and me."[14] Brigham himself had neither passage fare nor clothing for his journey. He relied upon the Lord to sustain his family and himself as he began the long journey to the British Isles.

Louisa Barnes Pratt's husband was called to leave Nauvoo as a missionary assigned to the Pacific Isles in 1843, leaving her with four children. Addison, her husband, did not return to Nauvoo, but to Salt Lake City in 1848, where his family had moved during his long absence. Louisa wrote:

> When it was first announced to me his mission was to the South Pacific ocean, and for an absence of three years, a weeping spirit came upon me which lasted for three days. I then became calm, and set about preparing his wardrobe for the event. He was often in a thoughtful serious mood.

She continued, "The parting scene came. . . . The two eldest daughters wept very sorely." The family walked with Addison to the steamboat landing while Addison carried the youngest child in his arms. "It was unfortunate," Louisa noted,

> at the last as he stepped on to the steamboat the children saw him take his handkerchief from his eyes; they knew he was wiping away his tears; it was too much for them. They commenced weeping; the second daughter was inconsolable—the more we tried to soothe her, the more piteous were her complaints. She was sure her father would never return.[15]

The young family returned to their small log cabin, and Louisa "immediately set about building a framed house, buying the lumber on credit." When completed, she won "the reputation of being a punctual business woman." She relied upon her own abilities to pay for the house and support her family by barter and trade. She employed her abilities as a seamstress and set up a school in her new home to pay the bills.

Another young bride, nineteen-year-old Bathsheba Smith, writing her husband, George Albert Smith, on 16 July 1843 noted:

I wish I could have been with you and stayed until you started, for it seemed such a long time until the boat came. I thought perhaps you would come home again in a few minutes, but I was disappointed. I wanted to see you very much. I would have gone to you if I could. O my dear, it is nothing to cry when one feels as I did when I saw the boat going down [the river]. I was pleased to think you would not have to wait any longer, but then how could I bear to have it carry you off so rapidly from me. I watched it until I could not see it any longer; then I held my head for it ached. Soon your father and mother came in. George A. cries, "Pa." He feels bad [and] wants to see you. He often goes to the door to see you. When we say, "Where is Father?" he will say, "a da pa."[16]

The bitterness of such departures made reunion sweet, however. Eliza R. Snow wrote of her brother's return from a mission to the British Isles:

This day I have the inexpressible happiness of once again embracing a brother who had been absent nearly three years. I cannot describe the feelings which filled my bosom when I saw the steamboat Amaranth moving majestically up the Mississippi, and thought perhaps Lorenzo was on board; my heart overflowed with gratitude when, after the landing of the boat, I heard Pres. Hyrum Smith say to me, "Your brother has actually arrived." It is a time of mutual rejoicing which I never shall forget.[17]

Men were not the only ones to leave and return to the City of the Saints on the Mississippi River during the gathering period.

In 1839, Laura Clark Phelps left her small children in the care of "an old lady by the name of Stevenson" while she returned to Missouri. She wanted to free her husband, who had been incarcerated there during the Missouri persecutions. At Columbia, some one hundred fifty miles away from her children in Illinois, Sister Phelps assisted in the escape of her husband and Parley P. Pratt; another prisoner, King Follett, also escaped but was recaptured.

Upon her return to Nauvoo life, Laura Phelps settled down for a few months until August 1840, when she left her older children in Nauvoo while she, her husband, and baby started for Ohio to visit her in-laws for the first time. Eleven-year-old Mary was sent to the Murdock home with her sister. Mary recalled:

Oh! What a strange place it was. Brother Murdock had just married an old maid. She was very particular and everything had to be done just so. At just such a time—we had to have just such an hour to eat, go to bed, and get up. It seemed like we were in prison. We never were allowed a light to go upstairs to bed, but we would go up, get into bed, hug each other, and go to sleep the best we could. They were very particular, however, about making us go to meeting every Sunday.

Mary enjoyed one aspect of the stay, however. "Mrs. Murdock was a fine seamstress and she taught me to sew." Later, she fondly thanked Sister Murdock for the learning experiences gained during the stay.[18] The "imprisonment" must have seemed forever for the young girls. Finally, after ten long months, their mother and father returned to Nauvoo.

Sometimes women accompanied their husbands on missions. The first to cross the ocean to the new mission field in Great Britain was Mary Ann Frost Pratt. Mary Ann's sister, Olive Grey Frost, also went with the family in the fall of 1840.[19] During the next few years several women—including Charlotte Curtis, Artemesia Beaman Snow, Jennetta Richards, Asenath Melvina Banker, Francis Smith Robbins, and Mary Minerva Snow Gates—went with their husbands on Church missions. By and large, these trips were a respite from the sickness and primitive conditions of frontier life in Nauvoo.

Nancy Tracy's husband, Moses Tracy, was called on a political mission to "the state of New York," where he was to distribute Joseph Smith's *Views on Powers and Policy of the Government of the United States.* Joseph Smith offered himself as a candidate for president on his personal merits as an interested and involved citizen, not as a religious leader with peculiar insights into national policies.

Nancy recalled, "I wanted to go with him to see my mother and relatives. Consequently, he was advised to take me with him by Hyrum Smith, the patriarch," just before the martyrdom. When they returned to Nauvoo several weeks later, "it was in mourning for these two great and good men."[20]

Wilford Woodruff was called to leave Nauvoo to take charge of the British Mission in 1844. His wife, Phebe, was also called to accompany him, not to visit relatives but to assist in the ministry. She was given a special blessing by Church leaders on 28 August 1844, just before her departure:

Beloved Sister, in the name of the Lord we bless you as you are about to make your departure over the sea in company with your husband where he is going to preach the gospel of Jesus Christ. You shall be blessed on your mission in common with your husband, and thou shalt be the means of doing much good for you shall have the desires of your heart in all things. Your life and health shall be precious in the eyes of the Lord, and in the hour of distress and trouble thou shalt be preserved by the power of God. Thou shalt be satisfied with your mission. Thy life shall be prolonged, and thou shalt be a comfort to thy husband. Thou must hold him by faith that he may be useful through his life. If thou wilt go in all humility, thou shalt be preserved to return and meet with the Saints in the temple of the Lord and shalt rejoice therein, and thy children shall be preserved until thou shalt return and meet with them again. Thou art sealed up unto eternal life, and we seal all these blessings upon thy head and all others which thou shalt desire in righteousness; even so, Amen.[21]

Thomas Ward's 1845 painting of Phebe Carter Woodruff and her son Joseph Woodruff. Ward was among several English immigrant artists in Nauvoo at the time. Phebe accompanied her husband on several missions, including the mission to England, during the Nauvoo period.

Upon the Woodruffs' arrival in England, the Church's *Millennial Star* announced, "We have detained the press this month in order to announce the arrival of Elder Wilford Woodruff, one of the Quorum of the Twelve Apostles, accompanied by Sister Woodruff and child; also Elder Hiram Clark, and Sister Clark; Elder D. Jones, and Sister Jones."[22]

While these three women—sisters Woodruff, Clark, and Jones—journeyed to England, other sisters left Nauvoo to visit family and friends. Louisa Tanner Follett left the city to visit in the East following her husband's death in 1844. On her way home, she wrote in her diary the feelings that arose in her heart as she prepared to return to Nauvoo:

> September 5, 1845—Oh, how I long to gaze one more [time] on the beloved City of the Saints and meet the warm embrace of my children and friends. I have left Babylon for the last time, and thanks be to God for his preserving care during my long and protracted journey.[23]

Following a trip up the Mississippi River, she continued her account of the journey:

> Sunday, September 7, 1845. At length we got safe over [the Keokuk Rapids], which brought [us] in sight of the beloved city. . . . At ten o'clock we safely landed at the Stone House, where we met with the most cordial welcome from our friends and relatives in Nauvoo. . . . Although my health is much impaired, yet when I take a retrospective view of the past, I feel that I have abundant reason to bless God that amidst the danger to which I have been exposed that I have been mercifully preserved and brought to join my afflicted family and brethren in Nauvoo.[24]

Ten-year-old Margaret Gay Judd and her family left their home in upper Canada to gather with the Saints, but lived temporarily in Walnut Grove and La Harp, New York, before finally arriving in Nauvoo in 1841. Margaret recalled, "How happy Mother was! She was a devoted Latter-day Saint, and her one thought from the day she was baptized was to gather with the Church."

When the Judd family arrived in Nauvoo, housing was difficult to locate. A friend, Brother Noble, invited them to stay with his family until they could find something appropriate. Margaret recalled:

Mother had her misgivings, for she knew Mrs. Noble too well to believe they could live in peace, but necessity knows no law so my parents accepted his kind offer, and things went along pleasantly for a little while, but the lady of the house soon began to show the cloven foot. She did not belong to the Church and was as bitter as gall and very quarrelsome. [She] never let an opportunity pass without saying something disagreeable about the Church, especially about the Prophet. All the apostate lies she could hear she took great pleasure in making Mother listen to, but Mother had made up her mind that she would not quarrel with her. It was pretty hard to have to hear her sneers, insinuations, and abuse continually. I remember once Mother had me sit down and read the Book of Mormon—that was too much! She took a cup of water and dashed it over me and the book. Well, things went from bad to worse until Mother could not stand it any longer.

Eventually, Margaret's father bought a lot and obtained some lumber to build a "shanty." The family moved, and "Mother was delighted to get out of a comfortable home into all the discomforts of a shanty where, when the sun shone it was hot, and when it rained it was wet," Margaret recalled. She never "uttered a word of complaint," since nothing "could keep her from enjoying her religion."[25]

Women were engaged in many other pursuits besides domestic responsibilities. The *Nauvoo Neighbor* noted that the "Female Association for Manufacturing of Straw Bonnets, Hats, and Straw Trimming" would meet at the concert hall. The notice was signed by "Nancy Rockwood, President."[26] Another area where women contributed significantly to community life was in the many schools organized in Nauvoo. Often these schools were held in whatever room could be found—in homes, back rooms of businesses, and the assembly room over Joseph Smith's Red Brick Store.

Hannah Holbrook moved into her new home in January 1843 with her husband, Joseph. By the end of February she was teaching school to several "scholars" at $1.50 per student per quarter in one of the rooms of her newly completed home. Her husband noted that her earnings "became much assistance to me."[27]

Martha Cory taught school with her husband, and together they had as many as one hundred and fifty students. They began their efforts in a leased room designed for a school room, but as they attracted new students they moved to a newly completed music hall, which accommodated the large number of students. As much as 50 percent of the teachers in Nauvoo were women. Domestic duties, however, remained the emphasis for the women in Nauvoo.

The religious life of the sister Saints revolved around many formal and informal meetings. In the standard winter settings, protracted evening meetings were held in homes and larger public buildings in the city and in nearby Mormon communities. As the sister Saints emerged from nature's long winter "darkness" into God's "marvelous light," they rejoiced in the gifts and blessings of the gospel.[28]

Eliza R. Snow attended one of the many "blessing" meetings held in the homes of the Saints. She recorded on 19 December 1843: "Tuesday evening [Lorenzo] having returned, we had the pleasure of the company of Father [Isaac] and Mother [Lucy] Morley: it was an interesting season, in the order of a blessing meeting, Father Morley officiating."

Eliza recorded the blessing in her diary, part of which included these statements:

> Sister Eliza, In the name of Jesus Christ I lay my hands upon thy head, and I confirm all thy former blessings together with the blessings of a patriarch upon thee. . . . The Lord thy Savior loves thee and has been bountiful in pouring his blessings upon thee, and thou shalt have the blessing to be admired and honored by all good men. Thou hast the blessing to speak in wisdom and to counsel in prudence, and thou shalt have the blessing to be honored. . . . Thy influence shall be great; . . . thy name shall be handed down to posterity from generation to generation; and many songs shall be heard that were dictated by thy pen and from the principles of thy mind, even until the choirs from on high and the earth below, shall join in one universal song of praise to God and the Lamb.[29]

Prayer meetings were a weekly experience held in the Nauvoo Saints' homes. Usually a local elder invited his neighbors to his home for such gatherings. The sister Saints in Charlotte Haven's neighborhood invited her to attend their meetings. On one occasion Charlotte went to Sarah Kimball's home for a prayer meeting. She wrote to her brother and sister, "You must know the Saints take an interest in our spiritual welfare, by sending us to read the Book of Mormon,

The Voice of Warning, and the Book of Covenants, and invite us to attend prayer meetings."[30]

A few weeks later Charlotte Haven wrote her family again and mentioned another prayer meeting:

> Sunday evening prayer meetings are held at the private houses in different parts of the city. Elder C., who lives in this neighborhood, has kindly invited us to attend those held at his house, so I with the Judge have been there three Sunday evenings during the winter. The room is well filled, and the meetings are presided over by the elder, are orderly, and are conducted similarly to the Methodist ones I have attended in country in New England. All are at liberty to speak, and sometimes a subject is discussed. One evening it was baptism for the dead. There were only two or three speakers on that subject.

Near the end of this particular meeting, a sister Saint arose to bear her testimony and relate some of her own personal experiences and tragedies. "She told of the joy she had felt when the new faith was revealed to her in her own English land" and of the trials of her faith as she gathered with the Saints.

The sister's story of personal suffering "hushed the assembly into a profound stillness, the words of the heart found a response in every bosom, and upon every countenance tears of sympathy were visible, as they listened to the mournful tones." She lost her husband and four children during the Missouri persecution, and now her "only surviving son lay prostrate with a fever." Charlotte concluded the story:

> In a mother's agony she besought the Lord to withhold his chastening rod, and spare her the only remaining prop of her old age; but if he saw fit to take that also, she fervently prayed that she might bow submissively to his will. It was beautiful to see in the prayer of this sorrowing mother.[31]

Prayers of faith and blessings did not always bring about the desired response, but many sister saints took courage and believed that the will of the Lord was being accomplished.

Jennetta Richards, having arrived from Massachusetts, wrote to her husband's family to thank them for the hospitality she enjoyed there. She wrote, "I arrived at Nauvoo, [but] I felt my strength completely exhausted." Over the next several weeks her health worsened to the point of her being incapacitated; only then did she begin to feel somewhat better. In a tone of accepting the Lord's blessings, she wrote, "If faith does not heal in every instance, it keeps me alive."[32] Friends, family, and Church meetings helped sustain these women in the most difficult times.

For many, Nauvoo was a happy place where nature could be appreciated, especially the sunsets over the Mississippi River. As a young girl, Mary Ann Stearns enjoyed the view from her family home, situated one block north of the temple site. "The view from that point," she recalled, "was a grand one."

> We could see over into Iowa, and for miles up and down the river, as well as the lower part of the city that was built on the flats that extended down to its banks. Many a time, with companions, I have stood on the brow of the hill and watched the sun sink down behind the Iowa hills, in the far distant west.[33]

Contemporary sources confirm this childhood memory as not simply an idealized recollection of the good old days, but as a reality that many Saints vividly recalled years later. Charlotte Haven wrote to her family in the East on 5 March 1843:

> We are having beautiful sunsets these days, and from our parlor window we have an extensive western view, and later on in the night the heavens are all aglow with light from the prairie fires. Between the river and the Iowa bluff eight or ten miles west, ten to twenty fires are started, burning the refuse grass and straw preparatory to putting in spring crops. Often I sit up a long time after going to my room, watching these long lines of fire as they seem to meet all along the horizon. The sun is down and darkness is fast gathering, so I must close, with much love from your sister, Charlotte.[34]

Martha Hall Haven described the familiar scene in a letter to her father and mother. "The burning prairies look grand here. If you were to see such a sight [in] the East, you would think the world was on fire."[35]

Many letters to family members and friends mentioned nature; at other times the sister Saints noted these reflections in their own diaries. Eliza R. Snow celebrated this in a diary entry on 21 July 1843:

In company with Brother Allen, [I] left Nauvoo for the residence
of Sister [Leonora] Leavitt in the Morley Settlement. We rode
most of the way in the night in consequence of the annoyance of
the prairie flies. It was the season for contemplation, and while
gazing on the glittering expanse above, which splendidly contrasted with the shades that surrounded me, my mind, as if
touched by the spirit of inspiration, retraced the past and glanced
at the future, serving me a mental treat spiced with the variety of
charges subsequent to the present state of mutable existence.[36]

Zina Diantha Huntington Jacobs wrote about going into the
woods to pick fresh berries:

July 17, 1845. We started for Lima after blackberries . . . 30–31
miles. 18 July. We took a fine ramble through the woods and
bushes. . . . 23 [July]. We went to pick berries. Had a good time.
. . . While wandering in the bushes beneath the shade of large
trees, seeing the plenty of fruit that filled the woods, ah, thought
I, the care that our Bountiful Creator has even for the fowls of
heaven to prepare for them a feast.[37]

The harshness of the environment was also described in many
letters back home to friends and family, and often a comparison was
made between what these pioneers experienced in the new home
with that of their former residence. Ursulia B. Hascall's letter to a
cousin living in the East made this reference to the Mississippi Valley
weather: "It is, has been, so very warm it was as much as a Yankee
would like to do to keep from 'roasting.' I have been engaged in domestic affairs this morning, but thought I must omit some things until
I could finish this letter, as the mail goes out this afternoon."[38]

During the summer months, it was not only the heat that irri-
tated the inhabitants of Nauvoo but also a strange assortment of river
insects. The "Nauvoo flies," large, mothlike insects peculiar to the
area, plagued visitors and citizens during the day. One traveler in the
area commented, "No sooner do those [insects] who wage war during
the day retire, than their place is filled with others, labouring with
equal effect through the night, whilst the indefatigable mosquito, in
many situations, heads the attack at all times."[39]

Winter also had its challenges, as Charlotte Haven wrote to family members in New Hampshire:

This winter [1842–43] has been extremely cold; I almost despair of sunny, warm weather. . . . We had quite a fall of snow last night, and the river has been ice-bound since the middle of November. I used to think we had high winds in New England, but I look back to them now as gentle breezes compared to the violent ones we have here. Every few days we have here a perfect hurricane, lasting for forty-eight hours. Occasionally we have had a thaw, and then—oh, the mud! it seems bottomless.[40]

She described the soil at Nauvoo as being a "black, sticky loam" that, when you step in it, is virtually impossible to get out of. Nauvoo's roads and walkways were poor at best. Martha Hall Haven wrote, "The soil differs much from anything I ever saw. I have not seen a stone or any gravel in the place. The mud here sticks to my feet just like paste."[41]

There may have been as much as seventy-five miles of streets and another ninety-one miles of walkways in the city, mostly unimproved. Bathsheba W. Smith noted the problem of the roads during the wet season: "The roads have been so bad, the bridges are most all washed away, that it is almost impossible to go to or come from Macedonia [a nearby community]."[42]

Charlotte Haven related an incident of crossing one of the roads in Nauvoo when her "feet went down, down, and in all probability would have reached my antipodes had it not been for the assistance of the Judge." He helped her out, but she lost her rubber boots "far below, and there remain to be fossilized as footprints of the primeval man."[43]

Charlotte's tone changed in May, however. On 2 May 1843 she wrote that "the weather is now very fine, and we shall soon commence gardening." The frozen river opened and flowed, "majestically onward, blue and clear as crystal. Several boats pass daily." The fields around Nauvoo changed also as spring was turning into early summer. "The plain between us and the river, embracing twelve acres or more, is covered with luxuriant grass, looking bright and green."[44]

By June the gloomy feelings of winter had entirely vanished. Charlotte wrote to her sister:

The prairie flowers are to me an object of untiring interest, their beauty and variety a constant surprise; it is impossible for me to number the different species, for continually new flowers meet the eye. Pink, scarlet, and orange are now the prevailing colors.

Lavish indeed has Flora been in her decorations of these wide rolling prairies.[45]

Socially, things were changing in Nauvoo. Former attitudes colored by strict Puritan and Methodist backgrounds gave way to new expressions without the guilt. For example, Christmas was not celebrated by the Saints in New York, Ohio, Missouri, or the first years in Nauvoo with any of the festive atmosphere common to the English Saints.

So fervent were early American settlers against the "impure" practices of Europe, which gaily celebrated the day, that early colonies imposed harsh fines and even jail sentences for any idleness or feasting on Christmas. The New England and New York Saints, although accepting the message of the Restoration, struggled to determine which traditions from their past should be retained and which should be rejected. In Nauvoo, these Saints came into contact with immigrants from England with different traditions.

On 25 December 1843, Christmas was celebrated by Emma Smith and her family with all the trimmings of Christmas—caroling, visiting friends, eating a delicious dinner, and opening presents.

The Smith family members were awakened from their sleep very early in the morning by some friends. Lettice Rushton, a blind widow of Richard Rushton from England, was "accompanied by three of her sons, with their wives, and her two daughters, with their husbands, and several of her neighbors, singing, 'Mortals, awake! with angels join.'"

The music "caused a thrill of pleasure to run through my soul," Joseph noted in his diary. The rest of those in the house arose to hear the singing. Joseph thanked God and blessed Sister Rushton and the group "in the name of the Lord."[46]

A few days later, on 31 December 1843, Helen Mar Kimball joined a youth choir to serenade Emma and her family: "We met at our usual place of practice, on the hill near the temple, and although the night was unfavorable, being dark and rainy, we, nothing daunted, started out between twelve and one o'clock, we struck up and sang the New Year's hymn."[47]

Another holiday, Thanksgiving, was not celebrated in Nauvoo nor the state. Massachusetts convert Martha Hall Haven and her family had observed this holiday at home and so commenced it in Nauvoo among family members. "We have no Thanksgiving in this state," she wrote her mother and father. Her husband's sister "made a feast after the eastern style and invited all the family that is here" on the last day of November.[48]

Charlotte Haven left a description of an invitation for a party at the Rigdon home. The announcement read: "The company of Mr., Mrs., and Miss Haven is solicited to attend a party at the house of Mr. Rigdon on Thursday the 24th at three o'clock p.m. Sarah Rigdon, Eliza Rigdon. Nauvoo February 20th."

When Charlotte arrived at the Rigdon home, she was escorted through the kitchen-dining room into a room where there was a "large quilting frame, around which sat eight of the belles of Nauvoo." She was kindly introduced to everyone, and then "a seat was assigned me near the head of the frame, and, equipped with needle, thread, and thimble, I quilted with the rest." When the quilt was completed, the door separating the young women and the dining room was opened.

> The scene, how changed! Through the whole length of the room . . . a table extended, loaded with a substantial supper—turkey, chicken, beef, vegetables, pies, cake, etc. . . . All seemed more joyous; songs were sung, concluding with the two little girls singing several verses of the Battle of Michigan. . . . Then followed an original dance without music, commencing with marching and ending with *kissing!* Merry games were then introduced, The miller, Grab, etc., at nine out to a second edition of supper, and then the games were renewed with vigor. We left about ten. [The] party did not break up till twelve.[49]

Among the many activities that the women of Nauvoo engaged in, singing and playing musical instruments were always popular. On one occasion, Rachel Ivins Grant was visiting her sixteen-year-old cousin. Both young women were at the piano when Joseph Smith came to visit the family. Joseph asked Rachel to sing "In the Gloaming," a popular nonreligious song. "Why, Brother Joseph, it's Sunday!" Rachel exclaimed. To which he responded, "The better the day, the better the deed."[50]

As Nauvoo grew from a struggling community of log homes to a thriving city of brick homes and buildings, sisters took advantage of increased prosperity by offering their special talents and services to the public. Ann Pitchforth reported to her mother and father in England that she had been talking with her family in Nauvoo about teaching piano and had said, "I wonder where there is a good piano here." At this point, her daughter, little Ann, popped up her head and said, "My Grandlady [her Grandmother in England] has one piano." They all were surprised to think she still remembered her family in England.[51]

Ann Pitchforth was successful in locating a piano. Within a few months she published the following advertisement in the local Nauvoo newspaper:

> Piano-Forte Music, MRS. PITCHFORTH respectfully informs the inhabitants of Nauvoo that she has commenced teaching music on the piano-forte; and wishing to suit the circumstance of the Saints, she offers to teach at the very low rate of three dollars per quarter: so that all classes wishful to learn may be accommodated. As Mrs. P. has had the benefit of many years instruction from several of the most scientific English and German masters, and subsequently has had much experience in teaching, she flatters herself that she will be able to give satisfaction to all those who may favor her with their patronage. Reference, kindly permitted, to Elders Brigham Young and John Taylor. Enquire for Mrs. P. at Misses Bray's milliners, Main Street, or at her own residence, corner of Granger and Parley streets, one block east of the Seventies Hall.[52]

Another pastime for young women in Nauvoo was making samplers, pincushions, and dolls. In families and among friends, a "candy pull" was often suggested as entertainment. Young teenage girls enjoyed a number of outdoor activities, including horseback riding. Helen Mar Kimball went riding with her father whenever he was home.

On one occasion Heber C. Kimball had business at the Lawrence home, located several miles from Nauvoo on the prairie. The sky was somewhat cloudy during the day, but Heber told his daughter they would be back before it began to rain. Helen wrote:

> We had barely got started for home when it commenced raining. Father put his umbrella over me and told me to hold it closely over myself and not mind him. The thunder and lightning were terrific, and the wind blew and the rain poured in perfect torrents; there was no house and not even a tree to seek shelter under. . . . We soon reached Brother Winchester's house, which

Thirteen-year-old Mary Ann Broomhead's sampler embroidered in Nauvoo commemorating the Martyrdom. Making samplers was among the various activities engaged in by women and young girls of the period.

was near the outskirts of the town, but not before our clothes were drenched through.

They found warm clothing and shelter and waited out the storm. On the way home the "roads were washed smooth, and we found that a heavy freshet [a flooding of a stream because of heavy rain] had passed over the lower part of the city."[53]

Another activity that both young and older women occupied themselves with was collecting autographs and messages of advice and friendship in their autograph books.[54] Barbara Matilda Neff Moses, a daughter of a well-to-do family in the East, visited Nauvoo as a young woman newly baptized into the Church. While among the Saints, she invited well-wishers and Church leaders to leave remembrances in her autograph book.

W. W. Phelps began on a serious note and then ended by rhyming his name in a spirit of fun:

> Two things will beautify a youth,
> That is: Let *virtue* decorate the *truth*.
> And so you know; every little helps,
> Yours, W. W. Phelps

The next person to write, Joseph Smith, responded to Phelps's admonition by quoting Paul the Apostle:

> The truth and virtue both are good
> When rightly understood,
> But charity is better, Miss—
> *That* takes us home to bliss.
> And so forthwith
> Remember, Joseph Smith

Brigham Young, who was sometimes serious and at other times humorous in the messages he left in autograph books, wrote:

> To live with Saints in Heaven is bliss and glory,
> To live with Saints on Earth is another story.

Eliza R. Snow, Zion's poetess, so named by Joseph Smith, signed Barbara's autograph book on 12 May 1844:

> O God, my Father, bless her—
> Be thou her friend and guide;
> May guardian pow'rs caress her
> While watching by her side.
> An tho' the earth's foundation
> Is from its center torn;

On visions of salvation,
Let her be upward borne.
Inspire her with thy Spirit,
Go fix her hopes above;
And bring her to inherit
The fullness of thy love.

Wilford Woodruff composed an acrostic using the letters of her name:

Behold there's glories within thy reach, O virtuous maid,
Ah, maintain thy faith, for this generation will fade.
Round thy bower [abode] salvation and peace shall twine,
Blessing surround thy head through the new covenant divine.
Attend, O Barbara, to that truth and that light,
Round thy path it has shown by day and by night,
And to the brightness of its rising the Lord shall come.[55]

Another young girl, Margaret Pierce, passed her autograph book around Nauvoo and among the settlements across the river in Iowa:

This world, my dear Margaret, is full of deceit
And friendship a jewel we seldom can meet.
How strange does it seem that in searching around,
This source of delight is so rare to be found.

Friendship is like the cobbler's tie
That binds two souls in unity.
But love is like the cobbler's awl
That pierces through the soul and all.

I would write better if I could
But nature said I never should.

S. M. White—Nauvoo, August 3rd, 1843[56]

5

DAUGHTERS, WIVES, AND MOTHERS— SISTERS AT HOME

Good parents will bring up good children; and good
children will exalt themselves to good saints; and
good saints will take the kingdom, under the whole
heaven, and possess it forever and ever.
—John Taylor

he most basic dimension of society in pre-Civil War America
was the family. This was certainly true of the women of Nauvoo, whose lives revolved around their families. Like their non-Mormon neighbors, the Saints in Nauvoo reflected many of the values
and dreams of most American families.[1] Nevertheless, in some very
important ways, the sisters' values and beliefs differed from the larger
American society. The *Times and Seasons* stated, "Good parents will
bring up good children; and good children will exalt themselves to
good saints; and good saints will take the kingdom, under the whole
heaven, and possess it forever and ever."[2]

The sister Saints in Nauvoo believed that little children were
"not capable of committing sin" (Moroni 8:8) and dismissed the traditional Protestant belief in the depravity of the child. An 1843 editorial in the Nauvoo *Wasp* reported:

We hope that since we, as a people, are favored with more religious light than others that we shall not be neglected in [raising
children], but that our children may be taught the principles of
morality, industry, and virtue, and when these are attended to . . .
that we may become the praise of the whole earth.[3]

More so than during the Kirtland period, the family in Nauvoo took on added significance—eternal family organization entered the Prophet's teachings. The "celestial" family was made possible by the divine ordinances revealed in Nauvoo to Joseph Smith.

Children were a significant part of private family life but were also equally important to the community as a whole. From the moment of birth, children were considered as blessings from heaven. They were blessed as infants by the elders of the Church. Unlike other religious ceremonies of the period for infants, the blessing simply invoked divine favors for the recipient and publicly provided the young Saint with a name that would be officially entered in the records of the Church. Later at the age of eight a child was baptized into the faith and confirmed a member of the Church.

The woman's responsibility was to prepare her children for these important events. Nevertheless, these sister Saints recognized that occasionally their husbands' sometimes long absences could create a void in family life and leave family members feeling a sense of loss. Writing to her husband, Vilate Kimball noted the children's desires:

> The children are impatient to have you come home; you are losing all of the most interesting part of little David's life. A child is never so pretty and interesting as when they first begin to walk and talk. He is now well and goes prattling about the house, and you may be assured we all think him very cunning. He is called Heber altogether by the neighbors.[4]

Surprisingly, births were never mentioned in Nauvoo's local newspapers, and often journal entries and letters contained only the notice of the birth itself, with no mention of pregnancy. If it was noted, the sisters' Victorian sensibilities forced them to use some other term.

Charlotte Haven wrote to her mother on 19 February 1843 about the birth of a nephew without having mentioned the expectant mother's condition in any previous letter. "A very happy Sunday morning dawned upon us," she began her letter, "for about midnight Elizabeth [her sister-in-law] gave birth to a fine, healthy little boy." Charlotte reported that the baby weighed nine pounds and felt fine. Her letter continued:

Some children in Nauvoo had beautiful dolls like this period doll brought to Utah by a young child from the City of Joseph. The head was made of porcelain, and the hairstyle reflects the period of the 1840s.

We had two experienced Mormon women with her all day yesterday, and Dr. Weld came towards evening and tarried till after daylight. Brother H. seems to be the only one in danger; you, Mother, know already how fond he is of children—he is now carried beyond himself, so perfectly happy; in his transports of joy he laughs and cries alternately, and cannot keep quiet, but jumps up to look at the baby or its mother every few minutes.[5]

Note that while the activities of the child and father were freely discussed, nothing was said about the birth itself or the mother's condition, except that she was fine.

A few years later, Irene Hascall Pomeroy wrote to her mother in Massachusetts about the birth of a new daughter, Francis. "Dearest Mother," she started, "I have wonderful news! Last Wednesday morning at the break of day we were presented with a beautiful girl weighing eight pounds and a quarter. It is the prettiest *little* babe you ever saw." Irene sent a lock of hair to the new grandmother and another piece to the great-grandmother.

The baby was admired by friends and family. Irene noted, "It does nothing but *nurse* and sleep." On 30 September she continued her unfinished letter, "Our lovely babe is one week old this morning [and] is pretty as ever and appears to be perfectly well, excepting when I eat too much pumpkin pie." Irene was elated with the birth of her first child. "Tell Aunt Milly I am happier than I used to be, now I have such a pretty little girl to 'fix up.' "[6]

Mary Fielding Smith, like most wives of prominent community and Church leaders, sometimes had a difficult time balancing her public and private lives as a mother and a stepmother of five children. In a letter to her husband, who was touring Church branches in the Northeast, she signed it, "Your faithful companion and friend, but unhappy stepmother, Mary Smith."[7] The stress of rearing one's children was magnified by being placed in a position to replace a deceased mother.

Mary Ann Phelps, a stepdaughter of another family, recalled her own situation from a child's perspective as a woman tried to take the place of her mother: "The woman Daddy had married was so different from my mother. Well, I guess she did the best she could, but she had no management, and my mother was such a fine woman to manage and keep things going along. This made it very hard for Father."[8]

While many sister Saints arrived in Nauvoo with family members by their sides, others had left loved ones behind in order to join the Saints themselves. While physically separated from family, each of these women hoped for her family's conversion, followed by an ultimate reunion in Nauvoo. Clarissa Chase wrote to her sister about the recent April 1844 Church conference:

> There were about two hundred elders called upon at the conference to go and preach through the different towns in the United States. John Cleason is . . . going to start in about two months, and he thinks he shall call on you before he returns, and I want some of you to be ready to come home with him.[9]

A woman's experiences in Nauvoo were made up of contradictions. Nauvoo was a place alive with dinner parties, Christmas celebrations, quilting bees, cornhusking parties, circuses, Fourth of July celebrations, military parades, house-raisings, and excursions on the Mississippi River. On the other hand, it was also a city of sadness, sickness, funerals, and challenges.

Local newspapers in Nauvoo chronicled life in the city. Sometimes they made note of sorrows that beset the sister Saints and their families. One such notice appeared in the *Times and Seasons* on 2 August 1841: "Drowned—In this city July 23rd, Samuel W., aged 8 years, and James F. C., aged 6 years, both children of Stephen and Mary Luce, formerly of Maine."[10]

Emma Smith, overworked and exhausted, gave birth to a child on 6 February 1842, a son who did not survive. Only five months before, her fourteen-month-old baby boy, Don Carlos, died from the effects of malaria. In the middle of February, Joseph and Emma buried their child amidst a great deal of sorrow.

The sisters' personal letters and diaries often spoke, without self-recrimination, of their sorrows—many times without their spouses to assist and comfort them. As letters were the principal means of communication at the time, they tended to be obituary notices, reporting the deaths of friends and family.[11]

Sitting down at a small desk in a candle-lit room during a cold winter's day, Sarah Mulholland began writing her brother-in-law and sister about the events of the preceding weeks in Nauvoo:

> It is with feelings easier felt than described that I sit down to write a few lines to you. . . . We have had to *part with our dear mother;* what a heart-rending sight to stand and see such a tender and an affectionate *mother* pass through the *dark valley of death.* But it was not too trying as it might have been if she had not had such a glorious hope in the trying hour of death. The *God she served* owned *her* in the hour of *death,* and eased and softened every *pain.*

Sarah recounted how "the sweet spirit took its flight, without causing her to have a struggle or a groan." Her death "left a sweet smile on her blessed face." Sarah admitted to her sister Mary, "I miss Mother, the little dishes of butter . . . [do] not come now; no, no, Mother [is] gone."[12]

Ellen Briggs Douglas, an English convert, wrote her family in Britain, "I know not whether you will have heard or not of the great and unremedied loss that I have sustained in the death of my husband, my children of the loss of the kindest, most affectionate father, and you, my fathers and mothers, of a son and brother."[13]

The Prophet's aunt Temperance Mack wrote her daughter an "obituary letter" in September 1840:

> My dear daughter, I fear you have suffered some anxiety in consequence of not having heard from me sooner, but as sickness has been the cause I am sure you will excuse me. . . . There has been considerable sickness here of late and some deaths, among which are your cousin Don Carlos, your cousin Joseph's youngest child, and the young Elder you heard preach on the Sabbath morning after your arrival here.[14]

When Wilford Woodruff left his wife, Phebe, and his daughter, Sarah Emma, for his first mission to Great Britain in 1839, Phebe was pregnant. During his travels to England he dreamed about his wife. On 28 November 1839 he related:

> [I] had a dream while upon my bed. And in my dream I saw Mrs. Woodruff, and notwithstanding we rejoiced much having an interview with each other, yet our embraces were mixed with sorrow for after conversing a while about her domestic affairs I asked where *Sarah Emma* was, our only child. She [said] weeping and kissing me, "She is dead." We sorrowed a moment and [then] I awoke. Phebe also said she had not received my letters. Is this dream true? Time must determine.[15]

Nearly a year later on 26 November 1840, Wilford received several letters from Nauvoo, one from Sister Margaret Smoot and another from his beloved Phebe—his dream had indeed been a warning. He noted, "The letters from Phebe and Sister Smoot gave an account of the death and burial of our oldest child Sarah Emma, who died July 17, 1840, being two years and three days old."[16]

Phebe wrote to Wilford on the day following Sarah Emma's death:

> My dear Wilford, what will be your feelings, when I say that

yesterday I was called to witness the departure of our little Sarah Emma from this world? Yes, she is gone. The relentless hand of death has snatched her from my embrace. But Ah! She was too lovely, too kind, too affectionate to live in this wicked world. When looking on her I have often thought how I should feel to part with her. I thought I could not live without her, especially in the absence of my companion. But she has gone.

Phebe continued, "Yes, Wilford we have one little angel in heaven, and I think likely her spirit has visited you before this time." Her description of the last days and moments of Sarah Emma's life must have caused tears to well up in her lonely companion's eyes. "She used to call her poor papa and putty papa many times in a day. She left a kiss for her papa with me just before she died."

The walk to the cemetery was quite hard for the young mother. "She had no relative to follow her to the grave or to shed a tear for her," Phebe wrote Wilford, "only her Ma and little Wilford [a son born while Wilford was gone]."[17] Sarah Emma may have died of a respiratory infection, but many other children were attacked by a more common disease of the Mississippi Valley, the ague.

The ague—malaria, with its chills and fever—took many lives before the swampland was drained and the anopheles mosquito was somewhat controlled. Writing to her family in 1843, Sally Randall mentioned:

October 6, 1843—Dear Friends. . . . We landed in Nauvoo on the 22 [September 1843] about two o'clock in the morning. I found James [her husband] in as good health and circumstances as I expected. He has a lot with a log cabin on it. . . . It is very sickly here at present with fevers, ague, and measles. A great many children die with them.[18]

Four weeks later, Sally wrote again, but it reflected her own personal grief:

November 12 [1843]—Dear Friends. . . . George [her son] has gone to try the realities of eternity. He died the first day of this month about three o'clock in the morning. He was sick three weeks and three days with ague and fever. . . . He was taken in fits the day before he died and had them almost without cessation as long as he lived. When he breathed his last he went very easy, but, oh, the agonies he was in before—it seemed I could not endure.[19]

It did not suffice to tell others merely who had died, but the manner of their going also received a good deal of attention in the Nauvoo letters, as was common with many letters of the period.

The Saints in Nauvoo knew death by its close proximity as well as by its actuarial prevalence. While there was a powerful intimacy with death and a fascination with the spiritual aspects of it in the first half of the nineteenth century, the Saints seemed to diverge from their cultural surroundings. The letters and diaries of many non-Mormons of the period show a capacity to accept death without questioning. However, many sister Saints did not accept death with the providential resignation manifested in many other letters of the period. Zina Diantha Huntington Jacobs recorded this prayer and plea in her diary:

> Disease continues to prey upon the children. O Lord, how long shall we labor under these things, even children suffering so sore? Wilt thou hasten the time in thine own way when the Saints shall have power over the destroyer of our mortal body. Not that I would complain at thy hard dealings, O Lord. All things are right with Thee. But, oh, the weakness of human nature.[20]

The realities of the situation at Nauvoo may never be known, but historians have estimated that deaths may have averaged over two hundred sixty-three a year for the period of 1843–44.[21]

The national mortality rate was 13.5 deaths per one thousand persons. The ratio for the state of Illinois for the decade of the 1840s was identical to the national figure. Nauvoo was quite a different story, however. For the years when figures are available, the mortality estimate for the city at its lowest was 19.5 per one thousand people in 1845. At its highest, in 1844, it was nearly 26 per thousand.

Some may assume that such high mortality rates caused parents, especially mothers, to withdraw their affection from young children to buffer themselves from possible losses. However, Nauvoo letters and diaries paint a different story. In fact, the anniversary date of a child's birth was sometimes noted many years later.

Emmeline B. Harris [Wells] lost a five-week-old son named Eugene in 1844. Thirty years later, she noted in her diary:

The anniversary of Eugene's birth—he would have been thirty today. . . . It seems almost like a dream when I consider and reflect upon it; if he were here how much happiness he might bring to me. What a rock to lean upon! What a shelter and protection his strong arm might be for his nervous and delicate mother![22]

In Utah years later, joyful memories of life in Nauvoo surfaced—social activities and interaction that helped sustain the Saints during difficulties.

The Nauvoo community was concerned about relationships between men and women. Courtship and marriage were an important aspect of not only personal life but also of the community itself. In a society so dependent upon family for support and survival, especially in old age, marriage was considered the only option for young men and young women.

In one significant aspect, Nauvoo was unlike most frontier communities of the period. While men usually significantly outnumbered the women in similar towns, the numbers in Nauvoo were fairly equal.

It was not uncommon for a girl between the ages of fourteen and sixteen to be married. For example, in June 1843, Artemisia Sidnie Myers, fourteen years of age, married Warren Foote, age twenty-five.

One young couple, Martha Jane Knowlton and Howard Coray, met each other in Nauvoo at an outdoor Church service. Howard was not yet twenty-three years old and had been a Church member only a few months when Joseph Smith asked him to clerk for him. During a playful wrestling match, Joseph broke Howard's leg. Joseph tried to do everything to help the young clerk and gladly responded when asked to bless him. In the blessing he promised Howard "that [he] should find a companion." Soon thereafter, while attending a church service Howard decided to "take a square look at the congregation and see who there was; that, possibly, the fair one promised might be present." Looking intently at all the young ladies, he soon hesitated:

My eyes settled upon a young lady, sitting in a one-horse buggy. She was an entire stranger to me, and a resident of some other place. I concluded to approach near enough to her to scan her features well and thus be able to decide in my own mind, whether her looks would satisfy my taste—she had dark brown eyes, very bright and penetrating; at least they penetrated me. . . . I was decidedly struck.

Following the close of the meeting, Howard made an approach since the young woman was with an acquaintance of his. They were introduced—she was Martha Knowlton of the Bear Creek settlement. The meeting was unforgettable: "I discovered at once that she was ready, off hand, and inclined to be witty; also, that her mind took a wider range than was common of young ladies of her age. This interview, though short, was indeed very enjoyable."[23]

Martha and Howard were married shortly thereafter on 7 February 1841 in Nauvoo.

Following courtship and marriage, the community was still very interested in promoting the relationship between husbands and wives.

The men of the community were admonished to "never give [their wives] cause to repent the confidence . . . reposed in you." A faithful husband, one editorial suggested, never joked about marriage, gave up all male acquaintances of whom his wife disapproved, focused his social attentions at home, and treated his spouse with wisdom, gentleness, and love. "Never," the newspaper stated, "witness a tear from your wife with apathy or indifference."[24]

Howard and Martha Coray's home was located on the bluff of Nauvoo near the temple site. Log structures like this home were very common, especially during the early period—but they were still being built in 1845 by recent immigrants.

In Nauvoo, the power to perform marriages was apparently granted to any worthy Mormon elder, because the community's newspapers and official ledgers abounded with references to weddings conducted by scores of historically obscure men.[25]

An ordinance passed at Nauvoo in February 1842 established city-wide regulations for marriages. A minimum age of seventeen for males and fourteen for females was established. Anyone under those ages was required to obtain parental consent to marry. Officially, power to perform marriages was bestowed upon the mayor, alderman, justices of the peace, judges, and ordained ministers of the gospel.[26]

One study indicates that an average of slightly over one hundred marriages per year were performed in Nauvoo for 1843 and 1844, not including priesthood-sealed marriages that were not of public record.

The traditional marriages performed in Nauvoo were very much like any other Protestant ceremony. Charlotte Haven described one such wedding in a letter to her family in New Hampshire:

> Then the bridal party entered and seated themselves in four chairs placed in the center of the room. Mr. S. handed the license to the Prophet, who read it aloud. The four stood up, the guests keeping their seats. In a few simple words not very different from any other Protestant marriage ceremony, Mr. B—, a lawyer of Carthage, and Miss W—, a niece of Sister Emma, were united for time only. A prayer was made by Hyrum Smith, another Latter-day hymn was sung, wedding cake, apple pie, and pure cold water was passed around.[27]

The wedding party continued following the couple's departure, and dancing, eating, and playing games took place until one o'clock in the morning.

Bathsheba W. Smith recalled her 1841 wedding to George Albert Smith fondly:

> On the 25th of July, 1841, I was united in holy marriage to George Albert Smith, the youngest member of the Quorum of the Twelve Apostles, and first cousin of the Prophet (Elder Don Carlos Smith officiating at our marriage). . . . Two days after we were married, we started, carpet bag in hand, to go to his father's, who lived at Zarahemla, Iowa Territory, about a mile from the Mississippi. There we found a feast prepared for us. . . . [M]y hus-

band's father, John Smith, drank to our health, pronouncing the blessings of Abraham, Isaac and Jacob.[28]

Their marriage, in spite of numerous periods of separation while George performed his missionary duties and other severe trials caused by external persecution, was full of love and reciprocal respect. Other women were not as fortunate, however. Sabra Granger Gribble published the following in the local newspaper: "Whereas John Gribble has taken off my bed and board, [and] having had to pay his debts to this date: Notice is hereby given that I will pay no more debts of his contracting."[29]

Sabra, who signed the notice "Sabra Granger," attempted to expose her husband's false claim of abandonment and set the record straight. Her husband had filed a similar notice earlier. Cyrus Boley published a notice that his wife left him without cause; later Martha published a refutation in the *Nauvoo Neighbor*.

Another sister Saint who was abandoned by her husband was Emmeline Woodward Harris. Emmeline married the son of the local presiding elder, James Harris, on 29 July 1843 in Massachusetts. She migrated to Nauvoo with her in-laws and new husband in March 1844. In the dissension that occurred following Joseph's death, Emmeline's in-laws left Nauvoo. Before they left, however, they tried unsuccessfully to entice Emmeline and her husband to leave Nauvoo and the Church.

James and Emmeline's first son was born in September, following the elder Harris's departure. The baby died just five weeks later from "chills and fevers." The series of events shook James's faith, and he deserted Emmeline and went to New Orleans to find employment.

Emmeline was shocked by the unexpected events and became depressed as her life unraveled. She wrote, "When will sorrow leave my bosom! All my days have I experienced it, oppression has been my lot; when, O when, shall I escape the bondage?" She thought her life seemed strangely similar to the Victorian romance novels being read at the time. Emmeline continued, "Is not my life a romance? Indeed it is a novel—strange and marvelous." She had arrived in the city of the Saints as a newlywed full of expectations of what the future had in store for her:

Here am I brought to this great city by one to whom I ever expected to look for protection and left dependent on the mercy and friendship of strangers. Merciful Providence, wilt thou long suffer this news. I forever be unhappy? Will the time never come when happiness and enjoyment will be the lot of this lump of clay?

For a moment, thought Emmeline, even death "would be a comfort," but "again when I think of the gospel I feel resigned to the lot God has assigned me, but what has life ever been to me from the days of my childhood?" During this time of reflection, Emmeline reviewed the struggles she encountered from the time she was in school. She was persecuted for friendship, and when "Mormonism began to flourish, were they not harassing me on every side?" Her guardian, "who pretended so much respect for me," did not wish her to associate with her own mother and sister, "because they were Saints of the Most High God, or, as he called them, Mormons." Emmeline married, not only to escape the persecution but also, as she wrote, "He with whom I was to be connected was my lover in truth; I loved him and I believed his professions to be true."

Thinking "all danger would be past, but alas, misery presses me heavier and more heavy," she pled for comfort and consolation, "O God, my Heavenly Father, assist me; do not let it always be thus." She reminded him of the promises she received of "days of joy and gladness." She continued her prayer of supplication, "O Lord, impart thy Spirit. I grow sick at heart; in vain does the sun shine bright, my heart is faint, my soul longs."[30]

Four days later, Emmeline confided in her diary, "This day like all others is full of trouble. Sorrow and affliction are my attendants." She reminded God, "Once I could have filled this book with expressions of happiness, but, alas, sorrow is my portion. I behold those around me enjoying the society of their dearest friends while I am cut short." As all who suffer such tragedies, Emmeline wondered what was the cause of such sorrow. "Why is it? Is it because of my sin and wickedness, or is it a trial of my patience, Heavenly Parent?"

In the depths of despair Emmeline sought God in humble prayer and supplication, "In the name of the Holy Son, Jesus, do I beseech thee," she prayed. "Have mercy and forgive and grant me the desire of my heart." She had no mother or sister to advise her. Although she had friends, "dare I unbosom my heart to them? No, no, I know them not."[31]

By 27 February a new hope arose in Emmeline's heart that James would return to her. She wrote in her diary:

Last night there came a steamboat up the river. O how my youthful heart fluttered with hope. With anxiety my limbs were affected to that degree. I was obliged to lay aside my work. I rely upon the promise he has made me, and not all that has yet been said can shake my confidence in the only man I ever loved, but hope returned and was renewed in my bosom. I watched the boat and looked out at the door. I walked a few steps out of the yard. . . . I saw a person approaching. My heart beat with fond anticipation. It walked like James. It came nearer, and just as I was about to speak his name, he spoke, and I found I was deceived by the darkness.[32]

On 28 February Emmeline wrote, "Today I am alone and I have time for reflection." She could not believe that James had forgotten "all his promises, all his vows." Finally, she prayed, "O God, if he is situated so that he cannot return, allow him to write to me that I can know something about his whereabouts." A few letters arrived, but soon she lost contact with James again.

In 1888, Emmeline returned to her childhood home in New England following the death of her former mother-in-law and discovered that James had died in Bombay, India, in 1859. She also found a trunk full of letters he sent her in care of his mother, who did not forward them.[33]

Sometimes women deserted their husbands, an indication that in spite of divorce laws, some women were willing to make it alone instead of subjecting themselves to situations they felt unbearable. In a September 1842 issue of the *Wasp*, for example, Nathaniel Whiting placed the following notice: "Whereas my wife, Casander J. Whiting, eloped my bed and board about one year ago, without any just cause or provocation, and has not returned; this is, therefore, to forbid all persons trusting her on my account, as I shall pay no debts of her contracting."[34] In several cases, these notices reflected more concern about the personal property taken by the estranged spouse than the separation itself. While offering a substantial reward for returned property, several men offered one cent for their wife's return.

These few examples demonstrate the effects of combined stresses, including frontier living conditions and marriage itself. As may be expected, sometimes young women and wives chose to deviate from the society and family pressures of acceptable courtship and marriage in Nauvoo. Some eloped with visitors to the city.

During the difficult period when the Saints made the decision to abandon Nauvoo and flee west for safety in 1846, several women in the city made decisions that affected their marriage relationships. A Sister Cox wanted to leave with the Saints, but her husband decided to remain, took custody of the children, and forced her to leave the house before she could prepare for the intended journey. Another woman, Eliza Robinson Wells, a nonmember spouse of Daniel H.

A poem entitled "Love," written by Zina Diantha Huntington Jacobs in Nauvoo on 9 May 1844. She wrote, "From one short word all pleasures flow, that blessed word is Love." Many Nauvoo women spent time writing letters, writing in their journals, signing autograph books, and composing poetry, which was often published in the local newspapers.

Wells, made the choice to stay, following her husband's conversion and decision to follow the Saints west.

An obvious impact on marriage in Nauvoo was the death of a spouse. For example, on 9 August 1844, Sister Clifton's husband was run down by a riverboat while fishing. She and other family members attempted to "raise his body [from the river] by firing large guns, but without success."[35] Life without a spouse caused not only emotional trauma and pain but often severe economic deprivation as well. A widowed woman with small children was forced to totally support herself and family.

For the vast majority of Saints living in Nauvoo, their faith and commitment to the gospel was an additional reason to promote happiness within a marriage and reconciliation during times of stress.

The letters, diaries, and reminiscences reflect an unbounding sense of affection and concern between husbands and wives, especially during the most difficult periods.

While at least one contemporary religious society, the Shakers, denied the sanctity of marriage, most Christians accepted marriage as part of the eternal scheme of things. Latter-day Saint women and their spouses departed from the traditional Protestant view of marriage, however. They not only accepted marriage as ordained of God but also believed it to be necessary for one's exaltation in the eternal world to come. This cherished belief came as a result of continuing revelations given through Joseph Smith in Nauvoo.

6

NEW REVELATIONS— A TIME OF TESTING

We pondered upon them continually, and our prayers were unceasing that the Lord would grant us some special manifestation concerning these new and strange doctrines.

—Elizabeth Ann Whitney

The Church in Nauvoo was significantly different from the Church as it was in New York when it had only a few members. Even the name was changed in 1838 from the Church of Christ to The Church of Jesus Christ of Latter-day Saints. In New York, the Saints used the Bible and the Book of Mormon as their canon of scripture. By 1835, an early edition of the Doctrine and Covenants had been published as additional scripture.

During the early period of the Church's existence, Joseph Smith and Oliver Cowdery acted as the first and second elders, the only general Church organization. As the Church increased in membership, a complex leadership organization developed, including a Church First Presidency (three presiding high priests), Twelve Apostles, Seventies, and a Church Patriarch. In Nauvoo, the development continued, both doctrinally and administratively.

Church ordinances included those revealed in the New York period—baptism, confirmation, sacrament, and priesthood ordinations. In Nauvoo, additional religious rites became part of Church practice, particularly as they related to temple worship. In the temple, Joseph planned to introduce proxy baptism, washing and anointing ceremonies, endowment rituals, and sealing rites (including eternal marriage).

The Church in Nauvoo had additional publications, including newspapers, hymnals, and an enlarged edition of the Doctrine and Covenants, which included many of Joseph Smith's revelations. Joseph expanded the organization of the Church when he established the Council of Fifty and increased the role of the Council of the Twelve Apostles.

Joseph Smith was the principal reason Nauvoo grew. Thousands of Saints gathered from near and far to be near the man whom God had called to be a prophet. The Saints were eager to hear him speak and took every available opportunity to listen to his sermons. Those who arrived first were guaranteed the best seats, though women were usually accorded seats no matter when they arrived. Latecomers could expect seats only in the rear, if at all.

The Saints often met in the uncompleted temple, but "only on pleasant Sundays." Charlotte Haven described the situation: "Planks are laid loosely over the joists and some boards are placed for seats, but not half enough to accommodate the people; so men, women, and children, take with them chairs, benches, stools, etc."

Charlotte described the Sunday dress of the Saints as she watched them pass her parlor window on the way to a meeting at the temple:

Their dress you would think not very comfortable for a winter's day, many men and boys with straw hats, low shoes, and no over-coats, and women with sunbonnets, calico dresses, thin shawls, or some nondescript garment thrown over the shoulders. Their zeal must surely keep them warm.[1]

While it is certain some Saints had a large and varied wardrobe, undoubtedly many others had only a few items. Many recent converts from the British Isles or the eastern seaboard of the United States brought a few nice items with them carefully protected in heavy trunks.

In Nauvoo a few shops offered the latest styles from the East, not just accessories. Altering already-made clothing would have been the alternative for the majority, however. Some five hundred seamstresses and another one hundred tailors were found within the city of the Saints before the exodus in 1846. Most clothing in Nauvoo would have been functional, but on special occasions the women of Nauvoo would wear special dresses, along with hats and gloves and a few pieces of jewelry.

An unknown English Saint's portrait (ca. 1840) completed before her arrival in Nauvoo. Several British Saints brought valuable family heirlooms, including family paintings, with them to Illinois. They loaded their wagons with them again as they made their way to a "place prepared."

The few existing images (paintings and photographs) along with store account records suggest that Nauvoo women had a variety of fine apparel to choose from. Slippers made from magenta silk with embroidery or white and green polka dots for the teenage girl were found in stores in the city. The British Saints brought their own styles to the city of the Saints.

Participation at weddings, parties, and Church meetings naturally caused the sisters to unpack their nicest clothes to wear at these special celebrations.

Ann Pitchforth described a gathering in a letter to friends and family in England. It was not held in the temple, but rather outside in the grove: "It was a fine sight. In the center the Twelve Apostles, then the women with hundreds of parasols, then the men. On the outside were the carriages and the horses. The singing was good, the speeches witty, enlivening, and interesting."[2]

Charlotte Haven, though not a member of the Church, was a little curious to "see and hear this strange man, who has attracted so many thousands of people from every quarter of the globe":

The Judge and myself sallied forth. We had not proceeded far when a large horsesled, with a little straw on the bottom upon which were seated men and women, stopped before us; one of the men asked us to get on, and by a little crowding we placed ourselves among them and were borne along with the multitude that were thronging to hear their beloved leader. Such hurrying! One would have thought it was the last opportunity to hear him they would ever have, although we were two hours before the services were to commence. When the house was so full that not another person could stand upright, the windows were opened for the benefit of those without, who were as numerous as those within.[3]

Eliza R. Snow attended another meeting where the Prophet spoke and recorded in her diary the following:

Tuesday 13, [June 1843]. Last Sunday I had the privilege of attending meeting and in the forenoon listening to a very interesting discourse by President Joseph Smith. He took for his subject the words of the Savior to wit, "O Jerusalem, thou that killest the prophets and stonest them that are sent unto you! How oft would I have gathered you . . ." He beautifully and in a most powerful manner illustrated the necessity of the gathering and the building of the temple that those ordinances may be administered which are necessary preparations for the world to come: he exhorted the people in impressive terms to be diligent.[4]

A recent arrival to the city, Phebe Chase, wrote family members about her first few days in Nauvoo and reaffirmed her faith in Joseph's divine appointment. "I have seen him and heard him preach, and I am satisfied for myself."[5]

Rhoda Richards wrote in her diary at the conclusion of the April 1844 conference:

I have been to conference. Heard Bro. Joseph the Prophet speak upon various subjects, glorious season, blessed visions, glorious prospects the Saints have in view. It appeared to me as if the whole sectarian world must fall before him as if it was the God of heaven spake, could they but hear, but when will the ears be opened and unbelief be done—God only knows.[6]

In public and private, Joseph unfolded the "visions of eternity" to the Church. On 15 August 1840, Joseph delivered a powerful sermon at the funeral of Seymour Brunson. In this discourse, he quoted 1 Corinthians chapter 15, in particular verse 15, dealing with baptism for the dead.[7] Joseph announced to the congregation that the Lord would permit the Saints to be baptized in behalf of their deceased friends and relatives through a proxy baptism.

Joseph singled out a "widow in that congregation that had a son who had died without [being] baptized." He told her to rejoice since she could be baptized in behalf of her deceased son. "The plan of salvation," Joseph stated, "was calculated to save all who were willing to obey the requirements of the law of God."[8] He concluded, "I have laid the subject of baptism for the dead before you, you may receive or reject it as you choose."[9]

Widow Jane Neyman asked Harvey Olmstead to baptize her in the Mississippi River in behalf of her deceased son, Cyrus. Vienna Jacques rode her horse down into the river to observe and hear the ceremony better. When news reached the Prophet about the widow's action, he rejoiced and said the baptism was acceptable to the Lord. Many other faithful Saints followed suit and were baptized for their friends and relatives.

Another grieving mother, Sally Randall, had a believing heart and had her husband stand as proxy for her son who had died shortly after their arrival in Nauvoo:

> What a glorious thing it is that we believe and receive the fulness of the gospel as it is preached now and can be baptized for all our dead friends and save them as far back as we can get any knowledge of them. . . . O Mother, if we are so happy as to have a part in the first resurrection, we shall have our children just as we laid them down in their graves.[10]

Writing to her husband in England, Vilate Kimball detailed the events of the month in Nauvoo:

> Conference [October 1840] closed last Monday. It was the largest and most interesting one that has been held since the Church was organized. The people that attended were estimated at four thousand; some thought there were more. Much business was transacted and many good instructions given. Brother Joseph has

opened a new and glorious subject of late, which has caused quite a revival in the Church; that is being baptized for the dead. . . . Since this order has been preached here, the waters have been continually troubled. During the conference there were some-times from eight to ten elders in the river at a time baptizing.[11]

Vilate enthusiastically concluded, "Thus you see there is a chance for all. Is not this a glorious doctrine? Surely the Gentiles will mock, but we will rejoice to have the gospel preached to the spirits in prison and give them the privilege of coming forth in the first resurrection."

Sometime later, nonmember Charlotte Haven did mock the Saints' sincere efforts when she witnessed these baptisms in Nauvoo. She wrote her family about a stroll she took along the Mississippi River in May 1843:

Then we followed the bank toward town, and rounding a little point covered with willows and cottonwoods, we spied quite a crowd of people, and soon perceived there was a baptism. Two el-ders stood knee-deep in the icy cold water, and immersed one after another as fast as they could come down the bank. We soon observed that some of them went in and were plunged several times. We were told that they were baptized for the dead who had not had an opportunity of adopting the doctrines of the Latter-day Saints. So these poor mortals in ice-cold water were releasing their ancestors and relatives from purgatory.

Charlotte moved a little closer to get a better look and "heard several names repeated by the elders as the victims were doused, and you can imagine our surprise when the name George Washington was called. So after these fifty years he is out of purgatory and on his way to the 'celestial' heaven!"[12]

Others believed firmly the doctrine that they could become "sav-iors on Mount Zion" by assisting their friends and family members to receive baptism, and they rejoiced in the opportunity. Emma Smith was baptized in 1841 in behalf of her father (who died in January 1839) and a year later for her mother (who died in February 1842), her sister Phoebe, her Uncle Reuben Hale, her Aunt Esther Hale, and her Great-aunt Eunice Cady.[13]

Other revelations were forthcoming, including a commandment to "build a house to [the Lord's] name" (D&C 124:27), given on

21 January 1841. A temple was an essential element in Joseph's preparations in Nauvoo, "for there is not a place found on earth that he [the Most High] may come to and restore again that which was lost . . . , even the fulness of the priesthood" (D&C 124:28).

The promised temple blessings restored by God through Joseph to a group of some seventy individuals were transmitted to faithful Church members generally when the temple was completed in 1845–46. He had made it clear to those selected to receive these sacred teachings before the temple's completion that this group was a vanguard, not an elite. They would receive "what will be made known to all the Saints . . . so soon as they are prepared to receive . . . them."[14]

One important result of the private teachings revealed to Joseph's intimate associates was the recognition that we have a Heavenly Mother.[15] The knowledge about a Heavenly Mother was first publicly expressed as doctrine in a poem by Eliza R. Snow, written in 1845 while she was in Nauvoo:

Lucian Foster may have taken this daguerreotype of Eliza R. Snow in Nauvoo. The hairstyle and clothes reflect the Nauvoo period fashion.

O my Father, thou that dwellest
  In the high and glorious place;
When shall I regain thy presence,
  And again behold thy face?
In thy holy habitation
  Did my spirit once reside?
In my *first* primeval childhood
  Was I nurtur'd near thy side?

For a wise and glorious purpose
  Thou hast plac'd me here on earth,
And withheld the recollection
  Of my former friends and birth:
Yet oft times a secret something
  Whispered you're a stranger here;
And I felt that I had wandered
  From a more exalted sphere.

I had learn'd to call thee father
  Through thy spirit from on high;
But until the key of knowledge
  Was restor'd, I knew not why.
In the heav'ns are parents single?
  No, the thought makes reason stare;
Truth is reason—truth eternal
  Tells me I've a mother there.

When I leave this frail existence—
  When I lay this mortal by,
Father, mother, may I meet you
  In your royal court on high?
Then, at length, when I've completed
  All you sent me forth to do,
With your mutual approbation
  Let me come and dwell with you.[16]

Joseph may have taught this doctrine as early as 1839, while comforting Zina Diantha Huntington at his own home near the time of Zina's mother's death.[17]

So inspiring was this teaching that Bathsheba W. Smith, whom Eliza asked to read the first draft of the poem, not only recalled the moment but also could describe the very room where Eliza composed the poem.[18]

As Joseph prepared the Saints to receive all the Lord wished to restore to them at this time, he also felt an increasing anxiety about completing his work.[19] Beginning in April 1842, he started to share his premonitions about being taken from them either by death or exile before the temple could be completed.

Joseph moved ahead with the restoration of the full temple blessings, even though the temple was not completed. This decision was perhaps based on the slow progress at the temple site and the continued premonitions about his early death. Joseph's experiences in Ohio and Missouri, where several leading members of the Church had fallen away, reminded him of the problem he faced in finding stable followers who could and would continue to fulfill his vision of the kingdom following his death.

Joseph had tested his followers in the past to gauge their loyalty to himself and, more important, to the Church. In Nauvoo, however, he was planning to give the Church the keys of the kingdom, and he wanted to be certain that they were placed in the right hands.

Following the return of the Twelve from their mission to England in the summer of 1841, Joseph began to test their loyalty in preparation for sealing their civil marriages for "time and eternity," with the promise that they would "inherit thrones, kingdoms, principalities, and powers."[20]

Sometime after 1840, Joseph Smith began to teach that marriage, which was ordained of God, could continue past death if solemnized by proper priesthood authority. Like the Protestants of the day, Joseph and Emma believed during their first years of marriage that marriage was dissolved at death. Their correspondences with one another before 1840 contained statements to that effect. Beginning in 1842, however, Joseph's letters hinted of the potential eternal nature of marriage, saying, "Yours in haste, your affectionate husband until death, through all eternity forever more."[21]

Parley P. Pratt recalled an 1840 conversation with the Prophet in Philadelphia about eternal marriage: "It was from [Joseph] that I learned that the wife of my bosom might be secured to me for time and all eternity; and that the refined sympathies and affections which endeared us to each other emanated from the fountain of divine eternal love."[22]

Vilate Kimball's letters to her husband, who was serving a

Church mission in the East in 1843, reveals the hopes and convictions that these new revelations generated in the faithful. In an effort to acknowledge her love and support to her lonely husband, she wrote, "Let your heart be comforted, and if you never more behold my face in time, let this be my last covenant and testimony unto you that I am yours in time and throughout all eternity."[23] Later she penned this short verse:

> Our union then, will be increased
> With an immortal flame;
> We shall meet, our joy complete;
> We never shall part again.[24]

For Vilate and many other sister Saints in Nauvoo, the revelation of eternal marriage meant that regardless of what situation mortality placed upon her and Heber, she and her beloved husband could be together "throughout all time and eternity."

That a knowledge of such marriages was common in Nauvoo is seen in two letters, the first by lay member Jacob Scott to his daughter Mary Warnock living in Upper Canada, and another letter from non-Mormon Charlotte Haven to her family in New Hampshire. Jacob Scott wrote, "Several revelations of great utility and uncommon interest have been lately communicated to Joseph and the Church. One is that all marriage contracts or covenants are to be *Everlasting*."[25]

Writing to a sister, Charlotte Haven said, "I had heard that in some cases the marriage is not only for time but for eternity." Miss Haven urgently wished to witness such a ceremony, but this simply was not to be.[26]

Formally, Joseph taught the Saints:

Except a man and his wife enter into an everlasting covenant and be married for eternity, while in this probation they will cease to increase when they die; that is they will not have any children after the resurrection. But those who are married by the power and authority of the priesthood in this life [will] continue to increase and have children in the celestial glory.[27]

The performance of eternal marriage ceremonies was known as "sealing." A number of priesthood sealings were performed in Nauvoo before Joseph's death. For example, in November 1843, Hyrum Smith sealed the marriage of Wilford Woodruff and Phebe W. Carter "for time and eternity." A few months later, Erastus Snow observed that "according to the laws and provisions of the holy priesthood [I] was married and sealed for time and eternity to Artemsia Beman."[28]

By May 1843, the marriages of Joseph and Emma Smith, Heber and Vilate Kimball, Willard and Jennetta Richards, Hyrum and Mary Fielding, Brigham and Mary Ann Angell Young, and James and Harriet Adams were sealed. In addition, those with deceased mates were sealed to them by proxy—for example, Hyrum Smith and his first wife, Jerusha Barden.[29]

Martha Jane Knowlton married Howard Coray in 1841. Shortly thereafter she began to have dreams that were hard for her to understand:

> [Martha] had a peculiar dream. . . . She desired me to accompany her to Brother Hyrum Smith's for the purpose of getting him to interpret it. We went the next Sunday to see him, but having company, he was not at liberty to say much. . . . The next Sunday we went, but found as many at his house as the Sunday previous. He said to us, Come again the next Sunday. . . . But in a day or so he called at our house, and invited us to take a ride with him in his buggy. . . . He commenced rehearsing the revelation on [eternal] marriage. . . . This was on the 22 of July 1843. The dream was in harmony with the revelation. . . . While still in the buggy, Brother Hyrum asked my wife, if she was willing to be sealed to me; after a moment's thought, she answered, yes. He then asked me if I wished to be sealed. I replied in the affirmation. . . . He performed the ceremony, then and there.[30]

When the Nauvoo Temple was completed, thousands of Saints received the blessing of being sealed at the holy altars of the temple.

The first to be tested in preparation for receiving these ordinances were Vilate and Heber C. Kimball.[31] Heber and Vilate Kimball had already sacrificed their family, friends, homes, possessions, and, more important, a peaceful life, for the gospel. Nothing else was seemingly left to place on the altar, except their children and each other.

Then came to Heber and Vilate an Abrahamic test—something that was to them unthinkable. Joseph asked Heber to give Vilate to him as a wife. Heber, emotionally overwhelmed by the request, came home to wrestle with the request. He touched neither food nor water for three days and three nights and continually sought confirmation and comfort from God. On the evening of the third day, some kind of divine assurance came, and Heber and Vilate walked from their home to Joseph's store. Having placed her hand into the Prophet's, Heber and Vilate submitted their will to his.

Joseph wept at this act of faith, devotion, and obedience. The Prophet never intended to take Vilate from Heber—his request was only a test. Passing the test, Vilate and Heber were rewarded by being sealed for time and eternity by Joseph before they returned home.

For many disciples, another test, much more difficult, was introduced in Nauvoo by Joseph Smith—the principle of plural marriage (technically known as polygyny).[32] It is not known how extensively plural marriage was practiced in Nauvoo, but less than twenty-five individual men can be identified as participating in the Church-sanctioned practice.

This particular teaching tried the souls of the most devoted disciples. In almost every account, both of men and women, initial presentation of the principle produced "shock, horror, disbelief, or general emotional confusion." For those who accepted it, they generally went through a "period of inner turmoil lasting from several days to several months." Many prayed and fasted that God would "reveal the truth of the new beliefs to them." They often reported "a compelling personal experience revealing the truth of the new standards."[33]

Brigham Young, following his return from England, was informed of the revelation and commanded to take an additional wife. He recalled:

> Some of these my brethren know what my feelings were at the time Joseph revealed the doctrine; I was not desirous of shrinking from any duty, nor of failing in the least to do as I was commanded, but it was the first time in my life that I had desired the grave, and I could hardly get over it for a long time. And when I saw a funeral, I felt to envy the corpse its situation, and to regret that I was not in the coffin.[34]

Heber C. Kimball was warned that he would lose his apostleship and was rebuked on three separate occasions before he accepted the revelation. Another Apostle, John Taylor, said the whole Quorum of the Twelve "seemed to put off as far as we could, what might be termed the evil day" when they would take plural wives. Despite these reactions, Joseph "clapped his hands and danced like a child," so relieved he was of not carrying the burden alone anymore.[35]

The practice was both difficult and against the Saints' Puritan traditions. Following the death of their father, sixteen-year-old Emily and twenty-year-old Eliza Partridge moved into the Smith home to assist Emma with the many duties surrounding her public and private life. During this time Joseph was sealed to the two sisters.

Emily recalled, "[We] were married to Brother Joseph about the same time, but neither of us knew about the other at the time; everything was so secret."[36] Her sister remembered:

> A woman living in polygamy dare not let it be known, and nothing but a firm desire to keep the commandments of the Lord could have induced a girl to marry in that way. I thought my trials were very severe in the line, and I am often led to wonder how it was that a person of my temperament could get along with it and not rebel; but I know it was the Lord who kept me from opposing his plans, although in my heart I felt that I could not submit to them. But I did and I am thankful to my Heavenly Father for the care he had over me in those troublous times.[37]

A few sources also indicate that some of the marriages were "for eternity only."[38] Another obscure aspect of the plural marriages in Nauvoo was the practice of "sealing" a woman who was already civilly married to another man. For example, twenty-year-old Zina Diantha Huntington married Henry Jacobs 7 March 1841; later, on 27 October 1841, when Zina was sealed to Joseph Smith, Henry stood as a witness. Though married for eternity to Joseph, Zina continued to live with Henry in Nauvoo and bore him two children.[39]

In spite of the difficulties, some sister Saints became close to their sister wives. In many cases, living the principle often brought the first wife and her spouse closer together, as was demonstrated in Vilate and Heber Kimball's letters during this period.

Vilate sent her husband off on a mission in October 1842. She remained home in Nauvoo with Heber's first plural wife, Sarah Peak. Both women were pregnant at the time. In the letters between Heber and Vilate, and, in one case, Sarah added as postscript to one of Vilate's letters, an added dimension of concern and tenderness is shown.

STATE OF ILLINOIS, } ss.
Hancock County. }

Office of the Clerk of the County Commissioners' Court.

THE PEOPLE OF THE STATE OF ILLINOIS:

To any regular Minister of the Gospel, authorized to Marry by the society to which he belongs; any Justice of the Supreme Court, Judge or Justice of the Peace, **GREETING:**

These are to License and Authorize you to celebrate and certify the Marriage of Mr. *Henry B Jacobs* and Miss *Zina D Huntington* and for so doing, this shall be your sufficient warrant.

Given under my hand, and the seal of the County Commissioners' Court, at Carthage, this *6th* day of *March* A. D. *1841*

Dan'l Marshall Clk. C. C. C. H. C.

State of Illinois, } ss.
HANCOCK COUNTY. }

I Hereby certify, That I joined in the holy state of Matrimony, Mr. *Henry B. Jacobs* and Miss *Zina D. Huntington* on the *7th* day of *March* A. D. 18*41*. Given under my hand and seal, this *8th* day of *March*, A. D. 18*41*.

John C. Bennett, [SEAL.]
Mayor of Nauvoo.

Make return hereof within Thirty days

Hancock County marriage certificate for Henry Jacobs and Zina Diantha Huntington signed by Mayor John C. Bennett on 7 March 1841 when he married them. Later, Zina married Joseph Smith and following Joseph's death, Brigham Young.

To Vilate, Heber wrote, "I dream about you most every night, but always feel disappointed when I awake; behold, it is a dream, and I could cry if it would have done any good. I am quite a child some of the time." In closing the letter, Heber noted, "You [spoke] about if I had sent a kiss to you. I will send you several on the top of this page where those round marks are, no less than one dozen. I had the pleasure of receiving those that you sent. I can tell you it is a pleasure in some degree, but when I come home I will try the lump itself."[40]

Vilate noted a few days later, "Our good friend Sarah Peak, Heber's first wife, is as ever," and "we are one." Though harmony existed between the two sister-wives, Vilate admitted that the marital arrangement was stressful and difficult:

> I sometimes felt tempted and tried and feel as though my burden was greater than I could bear; it would only be a source of sorrow to you, and the Lord knows that I do not wish to add one sorrow to your heart, for, be assured, my dear Heber, that I do not love you any the less for what has transpired, neither do I believe that you do me.[41]

Not all to whom Joseph Smith confided the doctrine accepted it and passed this test of obedience. Some apostatized and became bitter enemies of Joseph and the Church as a result, including Jane Law, the wife of Joseph's counselor in the First Presidency.

For the women involved in this test, many relied on their faith and personal dedication to the gospel to sustain themselves. Some asked not to be considered but remained faithful to the Church and its other principles. When Joseph revealed the doctrine to Sarah G. Kimball, she told Joseph "to go and teach it [to] someone else."[42]

As difficult as this may have been to the sister Saints who were invited to become a second wife, the first wife also struggled tremendously. Many women in Nauvoo who began to live the law with their husbands indicated that their decisions to move forward were based on personal revelation. Vilate Kimball, having watched her husband suffer from some unknown cause, received a vision that confirmed to her the rightness in accepting this test. How unique an experience this was for the sisters involved in Nauvoo is unknown, but Vilate was not the only one to receive special divine sanction.

Vilate Kimball noted the change in Mary Ann Pratt's attitude in a letter to her husband, Heber:

I have had a visit from brother Parley [Pratt] and his wife; they are truly converted. It appears that Joseph has taught him some principles. . . . Sister [Mary Ann] Pratt has been raging against these things . . . until within a few days past. She said the Lord had shown her it was all right. She wants Parley to go ahead, says she will do all in her power to help him.[43]

Elizabeth Ann Whitney noted, "We pondered upon [these principles] continually, and our prayers were unceasing that the Lord would grant us some special manifestation concerning these new and strange doctrines."[44] Another woman, Lucy Walker, first rejected the teaching but afterwards received a manifestation and was married:

When the Prophet Joseph Smith first mentioned the principle of plural marriage to me, I became very indignant and told him emphatically that I did not wish him ever to mention it to me again, as my feelings and education revolted against anything of such a nature. He counseled me, however, to pray to the Lord for light and understanding. . . . After I had poured out my heart's contents before God, I at once became calm and composed; a feeling of happiness took possession of me, and at the same time I received a powerful and irresistible testimony of the truth of plural marriage, which testimony has abided with me ever since.[45]

There is some evidence that some of these sister Saints, once committed to the principle, not only willingly accepted it but also encouraged hesitant husbands and in some cases took the first steps in selecting sister wives themselves.

Bathsheba Smith helped her husband select five wives within a year—Lucy Meserve; Zilpha Stark; Sarah Ann Libby; Sarah's sister, Hannah Maria Libby; and Nancy Clement. Bathsheba noted:

They all had their home with us, being proud of my husband and loving him very much, knowing him to be a man of God and believing he would not love them less, because he loves me more. I had joy in having a testimony that what I had done was acceptable to my Father in Heaven.[46]

Because of the cultural difficulties, plurality was taught in a confidential way. Joseph knew that its introduction in Nauvoo would

invite severe criticism of the Church and possibly jeopardize the
safety of the leaders and the community of Nauvoo believers itself.

Based on rumors, several individuals envisioned and sometimes
practiced alternative nonmonogamous marriages quite different from
that revealed by Joseph. Of these, John C. Bennett, mayor of Nauvoo, chose to distort the teaching for his own advantage.

Capitalizing on rumors and the lack of understanding among the
Saints, Bennett presented a counter doctrine he called "spiritual
wifery." Along with several close confidants, he sought to have illicit
sexual relationships with women by telling them that they were married "spiritually," even if they had never been married legally. Bennett
and his followers claimed authority from Church leaders, including
Joseph Smith.

This scandal not only resulted in the excommunication of Bennett and others involved but also made the introduction of the plural
marriage revelation much harder. Several Saints became disillusioned
as a result, and Bennett began touring the country "exposing the evils
of Nauvoo."

The introduction of this principle caused untold hardships for the
Saints, including family problems within the homes of some of the
leading members of the Church. In reality, however, plural marriage
had little real impact on the daily lives of the vast majority of Nauvoo Saints. A few Saints did embrace the practice during the later
stages of the Nauvoo experience, but most marriages in the city were
more traditional, except that Joseph had added one additional dimension—eternal marriage.

The Nauvoo revelations and Joseph Smith's talks enhanced the
sister Saints' understanding of their eternal destiny. While the vast
majority remained faithful and loyal to his prophetic leadership, others became anxious about the startling doctrinal statements.

Sarah Hall Scott and her sister, Martha Hall Haven, arrived in
Nauvoo from New England in 1843. During April 1844, Sarah wrote
home to her mother about the affairs in the city and the important
Church conference held in Nauvoo during the beginning of the
month:

We go to meeting near the temple every Sunday. I do love to
hear the *Prophet* preach; there was over thirty baptized last Sunday in the river. Joseph baptized quite a number of them; there
was about fifteen [hundred] people at the meeting; we have the

meetings in a grove near the temple. A great many thousand people attended the conference. It closed Tuesday last.[47]

Within a short few weeks, however, Sarah Hall Scott and her husband rejected the teachings delivered during the conference, especially those eternal truths taught by Joseph in his significant funeral discourse known as the King Follett Sermon.[48]

Writing home on 16 June 1844, just eleven days before Joseph and Hyrum's assassination, Sarah's tone had significantly changed. Following a review of William Law's efforts to reform the Church and the new revelations announced during the past year, Sarah wrote to her mother:

The people of the state will not suffer such things any longer. But I am sorry that the innocent must suffer with the guilty. I believe there are hundreds of honest hearted souls in Nauvoo. . . . Any one needs a throat like an open sepulchre to *swallow down* all that is taught here.[49]

For Elizabeth H. B. Hyde, however, the teachings revealed in Nauvoo stimulated her intellect and warmed her heart, especially when taught by the Prophet himself. She recalled:

The first Sabbath which I spent in Nauvoo, I attended a meeting held in the grove. There was no one there whom I had met before. Some of the elders on the stand spoke first, then the Prophet Joseph Smith arose and commenced to speak. His words thrilled my whole being, and I knew he was a prophet of God.[50]

7

THE RELIEF SOCIETY— SISTERS UNITE

The Church was never perfectly organized until the
women were thus organized.

—Joseph Smith

The Nauvoo Relief Society had its beginnings when several female members of the Church decided to make clothing for the men working on the temple in Nauvoo. It was truly a grass roots movement that began at a meeting held in the parlor of Sarah M. Kimball in the spring of 1842.[1] Sister Kimball recalled:

A maiden lady (Miss Cook) was seamstress for me, and the subject of combining our efforts for assisting the temple hands came up in conversation. She desired to help, but had no means to furnish. I told her I would furnish material if she would make some shirts for the workmen. It was suggested that some of the neighbors might wish to combine means and efforts with ours, and we decided to invite a few to come and consult with us on the subject of forming a Ladies Society. The neighboring sisters met in my parlor and decided to organize. I was delegated to call on Sister Eliza R. Snow and asked her to write for us a constitution and by-laws and submit them to President Joseph Smith prior to our next Thursday meeting.

Eliza "cheerfully responded" and drafted a constitution similar to other female benevolent societies of the period, and then presented it

Sarah Granger Kimball's home was built before the Saints arrived in Nauvoo and was the site of a provisional meeting of sisters—a group of neighborhood friends—which later became the nucleus of the first Relief Society in 1842.

to Joseph Smith for his approval. The Prophet, while pleased about their willingness to serve, announced his intentions of organizing the women after the same pattern as the priesthood. Sarah M. Kimball recalled his words, "This is not what you want. Tell the sisters their offering is accepted of the Lord, and he has something better for them than a written constitution."[2] He did not want them to simply copy a middle-class model of contemporary women's benevolent societies and Protestant auxiliaries; he wanted them to expand their vision, which they gladly did as much from their own experience as from Joseph's prodding.[3]

The chance meeting and conversation in Sarah M. Kimball's parlor demonstrate an informal influence in Mormon society as sisters within the Church brought about their own kind of innovations through informal structures.[4]

Joseph asked them to meet with him on the following Thursday at his store. The Prophet explained that, unlike other contemporary organizations, the Society was not to have a written constitution. The voice of the Society's presidency and the decisions of the members, as recorded in the minutes, would serve as a living constitution.

This historic meeting occurred on Thursday afternoon, 17 March 1842, when twenty women met in the upper room of Joseph Smith's Red Brick Store in Nauvoo to organize, under the direction of the Prophet, the Female Relief Society of Nauvoo.[5]

The twenty women present on this historic day were Sarah M. Cleveland, Margaret A. Cook, Elvira Annie Cowles, Desdemona Fulmer, Phebe Ann Hawkes, Elizabeth Jones, Sarah M. Kimball, Martha Knight, Sophia R. Marks, Philinda Myrick, Sophia Packard, Nancy Rigdon, Athalia Robinson, Bathsheba W. Smith, Emma Smith, Eliza R. Snow, Leonora Taylor, Phebe M. Wheeler, and Elizabeth Ann Whitney.[6] One source indicates that a baby was also present on this historic day.[7]

An additional eight women—Abigail Allred, Thirza Cahoon, Cynthia A. Eldredge, Sarah S. Granger, Sarah Higbee, Marinda N. Hyde, Keziah A. Morrison, and Mary Snyder—who were not in attendance were also accepted into membership, making a total of twenty-eight official members at the founding meeting of the first Relief Society. The Society's minutes, private diaries, letters, and autobiographies of the sisters in Nauvoo reveal a great diversity among this first organized group of sister Saints.

One study suggests that in attendance on this first day were sisters of financial abundance and of the poorest circumstances in Nauvoo. Some of the women were well educated for the time, while others had had much less opportunity. Along with the older, mature sisters were several teenagers and young women. The group consisted of married women, others who were separated or widowed, and several single women. A few members were recent converts, while several had joined a decade earlier. Among those listed as founding members could be found the names of the leading women of the Church and community, while others were less well known.[8]

During this organizational meeting, Joseph instructed the Relief Society sisters that they should

> elect a presiding officer to preside over them, and let that presiding officer choose two counselors to assist in the duties of her office—that he would ordain them to preside over the Society—and let them preside just as [the] Presidency presides over the Church.[9]

It should be remembered that during this period of Church history, no attempt was made to differentiate between the terms *ordain* and *set apart*. John Taylor, who was present at the organizational meeting, later recalled:

> On the occasion of the organization of the Relief Society, by the Prophet Joseph Smith at Nauvoo, I was present [when] Sister Emma Smith was elected president and Sisters Elizabeth Ann Whitney and Sarah M. Cleveland [were chosen as] her counselors. . . . The ordination then given did not mean the conferring of the priesthood upon those sisters, yet the sisters hold a portion of the priesthood in connection with their husbands. (Sisters Eliza R. Snow and Bathsheba W. Smith stated that they so understood it in Nauvoo and have looked upon it always in that light.)[10]

During this first meeting, Joseph continued:

> Let this presidency serve as a constitution—all their decisions be considered law, and acted upon as such. If any officers are wanted to carry out the designs of the institution, let them be appointed and set apart, as deacons, teachers, etc. are among us. The minutes of your meeting will be precedent for you to act upon—your constitution—and law.

The recorder noted that Joseph "suggested the propriety of electing a presidency to continue in the office during good behavior, or so long as they shall continue to fill the office with dignity etc.—like the First Presidency of the Church."

Sister Elizabeth Ann Whitney motioned and Sister Sophia Packard seconded that Emma be chosen president, which was "passed unanimously." Elizabeth Ann Whitney and Sarah M. Cleveland were then chosen as counselors, Eliza R. Snow as secretary, and Elvira Annie Cowles as treasurer.

Joseph's reflections on this meeting and Emma's call to serve are noted in his history:

> I gave much instruction, read in the New Testament and Book of Doctrine and Covenants concerning the elect lady, and showed that the elect meant to be elected to a certain work, etc., and that the revelation [Doctrine and Covenants 25] was then fulfilled by Sister Emma's election to the presidency of the society.[11]

After John Taylor "ordained" the presidency, Joseph continued.

President Smith then resumed his remarks and gave instruction how to govern themselves in their meetings—when one wishes to speak, address the chair—and the chairman responds to the address. Should two speak at once, the chair shall decide who speaks first; if anyone is dissatisfied, she appeals to the house. When one has the floor, [she] occupies [it] as long as she pleases, etc. Proper manner of address is Mrs. Chairman or President and not Mr. Chairman, etc. A question can never be put until it has a second. When the subject for discussion has been fairly investigated, the chairman will say, are you ready for the question? etc. Whatever the majority of the house decide upon becomes a law to the society.

In his closing comments, Joseph exhorted the sisters to "not injure the character of anyone—if members of the society shall conduct [themselves] improperly, deal with them and keep all your doings within your own bosoms; and hold all characters sacred."

It is evident that those sisters assembled at this first meeting also shaped their own destiny as the discussion turned to a formal name. John Taylor suggested that the organization's name incorporate the term *Benevolent* instead of *Relief*. Emma disagreed and debated Joseph and John Taylor on the point, saying that she did "not wish to have it called after other societies in the world."

Eliza R. Snow added, "As daughters of Zion, we should set an example for all the world, rather than confine ourselves to the course which had been heretofore pursued." Joseph and John Taylor both conceded the point and the society name remained as originally suggested by the sisters.

The society's minutes indicate that Joseph's original donation of a five-dollar gold piece was supported by additional contributions at that meeting to a total of $10.62. Later, the Prophet donated a building lot for the society.[12]

The minutes of the early Relief Society are filled with historical, doctrinal, and practical gems. The sisters not only discussed their duties to the poor and needy but also spoke of spiritual gifts, such as speaking in tongues and healing the sick. On 19 April, the women met in a testimony meeting where the sisters stood one by one to share their feelings and express their spiritual experiences. Sarah

Cleveland said, "As the Prophet had given us liberty to improve the gifts of the gospel in our meetings, . . . [she] desired to speak in the gift of tongues, which she did in a powerful manner," after which a second woman interpreted. The minutes, kept by secretary Eliza R. Snow, declared the meeting "interesting."[13]

A letter written by Ellen Douglas on 2 June 1842 refers to the early meetings and types of instruction received during this initial period of organization:

> There is now in this city a female charity society of which I am a member. We are in number eight or nine hundred. Joseph Smith's wife is the head of our society, and we meet on a Thursday at ten o'clock, where we receive instructions both temporally and spiritually.[14]

Within a two-year period, 1842–44, vital links were established among the sisters and the Relief Society, the work with the poor and sick, the exercise of spiritual gifts, and temple worship.

The Relief Society was officially organized in Joseph Smith's Red Brick Store on 17 March 1842 in the upper large assembly room. The building was the focus of religious, social, military, political, and economic activity in Nauvoo between 1842 and 1844.

The importance of the Relief Society's organization is further emphasized by the Prophet's statement that "the Church was never perfectly organized until the women were thus organized."[15] The founding meeting of the Female Relief Society of Nauvoo was held in the most important building in the city during this period, Joseph Smith's store.[16]

During Joseph's lifetime, the Relief Society increased in membership from the original twenty-eight women to thirteen hundred and forty-one sisters. At the second meeting, an additional forty-four sisters applied for membership. Soon, branches of the society were organized in the adjoining Mormon communities such as Macedonia.

Seventeen-year-old Talitha C. Avery recalled, "There was no society for the young people at that time, so I, as did all the other girls, who wished to and were worthy, joined the Relief Society." She recalled the times when Joseph came to those early meetings where he "talked to us and gave us such good counsel."[17]

The dramatic increase in membership required that the society meet in diverse locations because the Red Brick Store was no longer large enough to accommodate them. The eighth meeting of the Relief Society on 26 May was the last in the Red Brick Store in 1842. General meetings were then conducted in the grove near the temple during the summer months of that year.

Between September 1842 and June 1843, no formal society meetings were held; however, their work continued. Eventually, the society began to meet in the private homes of its members in each ward, the geographical-political boundaries of the city. During its second year, 1843–44, only fourteen society meetings were reported, most of them in private homes. The sisters again adjourned for the winter, reconvening in March 1844. A "Young Ladies Relief Society of Nauvoo," an auxiliary of the women's Relief Society, was also organized during this period for young women.

The growth and ward division of the society, however, did not end the significance of the Red Brick Store. The three final meetings of the Nauvoo Female Relief Society were held in the store on 14 October 1843, 9 March 1844, and 16 March 1844.

Several factors led to the demise of the Nauvoo Female Relief Society, including Emma's personal opposition to plural marriage and her use of the Relief Society in combating the spread of this doctrine among Church sisters. Following the crisis created by Joseph Smith's death and the exodus to and settlement of the Great Basin, few society meetings were held until the organization was revived in Utah by Brigham Young in 1867.[18]

The society flourished in Nauvoo for nearly two years and saw a brief revival in Utah in the 1850s. President Brigham Young's efforts to reinstitute the society in 1867 resulted in an organized sisterhood that still exists in the LDS Church today.

The final meeting of the Nauvoo Female Relief Society occurred on 16 March 1844, just two years following its organization. Appropriately, the closing meeting of the society was held in the "room over [the] Brick Store," the place where the first Relief Society was organized.[19]

8

CHARITY—
WOMEN WITH A MISSION

The best measure or principle to bring the poor to
repentance is to administer to their wants—the
society is not only to relieve the poor, but to save
souls.

—Joseph Smith

One aspect of Joseph's charge to the sisters of the newly formed Relief Society was announced during the founding meeting. The Prophet said that the society "should provoke the brethren to good works and look to the wants of the poor, searching after objects of charity, and in administering to their wants—to assist, by correcting the morals and strengthening the virtues of the community." He remarked:

> This is a charitable society, and according to your natures; it is natural for females to have feelings of charity and benevolence. You are now placed in a situation in which you can act according to those sympathies which God has planted in your bosoms.[1]

Several weeks later, Joseph announced in the *Times and Seasons* the formation of the Relief Society:

> A society has lately been formed by the ladies of Nauvoo for the relief of the poor, the destitute, the widow, and the orphan; and for the exercise of all benevolent purposes. . . . There was a very numerous attendance at the organization of the society and also at their subsequent meetings of some of our most intelligent, hu-

mane, philanthropic, and respectable ladies; and we are well assured from a knowledge of those pure principles of benevolence that flow spontaneously from their humane and philanthropic bosoms, that with the resources they will have at command they will fly to the relief of the stranger, they will pour oil and wine to the wounded heart of the distressed; they will dry up the tears of the orphan, and make the widow's heart to rejoice.[2]

At the ninth meeting, Joseph told the sisters, "Said Jesus, 'Ye shall do the work, which you see me do.' These are the grand key words for the society to act upon."[3] On 9 June 1842, he advised the women, "If you would have God have mercy on you, have mercy on one another." He continued, "The best measure or principle to bring the poor to repentance is to administer to their wants—the society is not only to relieve the poor, but to save souls."[4]

Joseph deeded a city lot to the society, on which he hoped they would build homes for the poor. He promised to give them a house frame for the lot.

Under Emma's direction, the sisters of the Relief Society were engaged in many projects and activities beyond their traditional roles as care givers. They formed a very successful labor market in an effort to help women in the community find employment. Often goods were purchased directly for those in need instead of giving outright donations. Orphans, including motherless children, found homes; food commodities donated weekly helped feed several needy families; several children of widows received funds to pay for school tuition; elderly women's gardens were plowed and planted; destitute Saints found shoes at their doors; and others found bedding. The sisters even organized a boycott of persons who did not pay poor widows what was owed them.

Eliza R. Snow published a poem about the society's goals in the *Times and Seasons*, a few weeks following its founding:

The Female Relief Society of Nauvoo—

What Is It?

It is an Institution form'd to bless
The poor, the widow, and the fatherless—
To clothe the naked and the hungry feed,
And in the holy paths of virtue, lead.

To seek out sorrow, grief and mute despair,
And light the lamp of hope eternal there—
To try the strength of consolation's art
By breathing comfort to the mourning heart.

To chase the clouds that shade the aspect, where
Distress presides; and wake up pleasures there—
With open heart extend the friendly hand
To hail the stranger, from a distant land.

To stamp a vetoing impress on each move
That Virtue's present dictates disapprove—
To put the tattler's coinage, scandal, down,
And make corruption feel its with'ring frown.

To give instruction, where instruction's voice
Will guide the feet and make the heart rejoice—
To turn the wayward from their recklessness,
And lead them in the ways of happiness.

It is an *Order*, fitted and design'd
To meet the wants of body, and of mind—
To seek the wretched, in their long abode—
Supply their wants, and raise their hearts to God.[5]

A Nauvoo membership certificate signed by Joseph Smith for Sister Martha Goforth. Many sister Saints' names are preserved not only in private diaries, in letters, or on tombstones of Nauvoo but also in official records of the city, the county, and the Church.

By August 1843, each Relief Society group in the city wards appointed several sisters to "search out the poor, and suffering, and to call on the rich for aid and thus as far as possible relieve the wants of all."[6] Their efforts to relieve suffering among the community included providing not only physical help but spiritual sustenance as well. With Joseph Smith's approval, the sister Saints not only took care of the poor but also blessed their fellow sisters through the gifts of the Spirit.[7]

On several occasions, the society investigated reports of moral misdeeds of those in the community. The first to be considered was Clarissa Marvel, who was "accused of [telling] scandalous falsehoods on the character of President Joseph Smith without the least provocation."[8] A member of the society, Agnes Coolbrith Smith, Don Carlos's widow, responded in the young girl's defense, "Clarissa Marvel lived with me nearly a year and I saw nothing amiss of her." Unknown to Agnes at the time, her name was also in the rumor mill.

After a discussion among the sisters, they finally agreed that someone should talk with Clarissa about the accusation. No one volunteered for this unpleasant task, however. Sister Emma acknowledged that Clarissa was an orphan and needed friends, but, said she, "We intend to look into the morals of each other, and watch over each other." Eventually, the issue was resolved when Clarissa stated that she was not involved in any talk that was derogatory to the characters of Joseph Smith or Agnes Smith.[9]

Gossip and rumors were a part of even the best communities and societies. When another ingredient was added, the introduction of new teachings such as plural marriage, a powder keg was the result. The local paper ran a "recipe" for a common disease called "Scandal":

> A complete cure for a terrible disorder of the mouth commonly called, "Scandal":
>
> Take a good nature, one ounce; of an herb called by the Mormons "mind your own business," one ounce, to which add of the oil of benevolence, one drachim and of brotherly love, two ounces. You must mix the preceding ingredients with a little charity for others, and a few sprigs of "keep your tongue between your teeth." Let this compound be allowed to simmer for a short time in a vessel called circumspection, and it will be ready for use.
>
> Symptoms: The symptoms are a violent itching in the tongue and roof of the mouth when you are in company with a species of animals called "Gossips."

Applications: When you feel a fit of the disorder coming on, take a teaspoonful of the mixture, hold it in your mouth, which you must keep closely shut till you get home. [10]

Gossip continued, in spite of the society's effort to stop it. Most of the time it centered around plural marriage. One Saint noted a rumor that "an introduction of principles that would soon be, that the ancient order of God that was formerly, would again have its rounds, as it was in the days of old Solomon and David. They had wives and concubines in abundance, as many as they could support. The secret whisperings were that the same will eventually be again." [11]

In almost all the acts of the society during this period, President Emma Smith led out. She was fondly remembered years later in Utah by the sisters who recalled the great good she accomplished as president of the first Relief Society. Emmeline B. Wells, an associate of Emma at the time, recalled:

Sister Emma was benevolent and hospitable; she drew around her a large circle of friends, who were like good comrades. She was motherly in her nature to young people, always had a houseful to entertain or be entertained. She was very high-spirited, and the brethren and sisters paid her great respect. Emma was a great solace to her husband in all his persecutions and the severe ordeals through which he passed; she was always ready to encourage and comfort him, devoted to his interests, and was constantly by him whenever it was possible. She was a queen in her home, so to speak, and beloved by the people, who were many of them indebted to her for favors and kindnesses. [12]

Other duties fell upon the sisters of the society, including an effort to intercede in the Prophet's defense. The society circulated a petition that was signed by its members "for the protection from illegal suits then pending against the Prophet Joseph Smith."

Emma Smith took Amanda Barns Smith and Eliza R. Snow to see Governor Thomas Carlin in Quincy in July 1842. Eliza Snow noted in her diary on 29 July:

Just returned from Quincy, where I visited the governor [Thomas Carlin] in company with Mrs. Emma Smith who presented him a petition from the Female Relief Society. The governor received us with cordiality, and as much affability and politeness as his excellency is a master of, assuring us of his protection, by saying that the laws and constitution of our country shall be his polar star in case of any difficulty. He manifested much friendship, and it remains for time and circumstance to prove the sincerity of his profession.[13]

Joseph appreciated their help, and on 31 August he attended their meeting to thank them personally for their efforts in his behalf:

The Female Relief Society have taken a most active part in my welfare against my enemies, in petitioning to the governor in my behalf. These measures were all necessary. . . . If these measures had not been taken, more serious consequences would have resulted. I have come here to bless you. The society has done well; their principles are to practice holiness. God loves you, and your prayers in my behalf shall avail much. Let them not cease to ascend to God continually.[14]

During the first meeting of the second year of its existence, society treasurer Elvira Annie Cowles Holmes reported that about five hundred dollars was received and nearly four hundred dollars expended during the first year of the society's existence. An official report appeared in the *Times and Seasons* on 1 August 1843.

While the sister Saints reached out to those in need, not all were impressed by their acts of charity; some saw them as being less than Christian because of their beliefs.

An English clergyman, Henry Caswell, visited Nauvoo during a North American trip in 1842. He reported a visit to a Church service where he saw "many grey-headed old men . . . and many well-dressed females." The choir was made up of men and women. When the meeting ended, he "arrived at a small, but neat, tavern where I called to get dinner. An old woman, apparently the mistress of the house, was seated by the fire, devoutly reading the Book of Mormon, from which she scarcely lifted her eyes as I entered." Within a short time Caswell found his way across the river to his lodgings and reported, "I felt happy to be once more among Christians."[15]

Another gentleman living at an Indian trading post, Eben Weld, wrote family members about his brother's life in Nauvoo:

I received a letter from brother [John Fuller Weld] last July stating that he had lately been married in Nauvoo. But did not inform me whether she was one of his spiritual ones or of another kind. She was very impertinent to enquire through him how many papooses I had and wives.[16]

Charlotte Haven was not as harsh about the sister Saints, but she found many of them too zealous for her temperament. While these few observations seem judgmental, others wrote and remembered the acts of kindness and help offered to them and their families as signs of honest and sincere efforts by the sister Saints in Nauvoo to make life on the harsh frontier a little more like heaven than it otherwise would have been.

9

A Key Is Turned—
Ancient Covenants Restored

I now turn the key to you, in the name of God, and
this society shall rejoice, and knowledge and intelligence shall flow down from this time—this is the
beginning of better days to this society.

—Joseph Smith

*D*uring the weeks following the organization of the Relief Society on 17 March 1842, the Prophet Joseph met with the sisters
in the upper room of his store on eight other occasions, teaching and
giving them instruction. Years later, Bathsheba W. Smith, an original
member of the society and later its fourth general president, remembered those early sessions with Joseph in the Red Brick Store. "The
sisters flocked to our meetings every week," she reminisced, "and the
Prophet Joseph met with us as long as he could."[1]

Mercy Thompson, another member of the society in Nauvoo, remembered her feelings while attending the meetings. She said, "I
have been present at meetings of the Relief Society and heard
[Joseph] give directions and counsels to the sisters, calculated to inspire them to efforts which would lead to celestial glory and exaltation, and oh! how my heart rejoiced."[2]

The diaries, personal letters, and later reminiscences of the
women in Nauvoo reveal that, along with their American sisters, the
sisters in Nauvoo judged themselves and were judged by society by
certain notions of womanhood. While womanhood as defined by
middle-class values included four cardinal virtues—"piety, purity, sub-
missiveness, and domesticity"—working-class women understood
womanhood quite differently.[3]

In Nauvoo the vast majority of women made a financial contribution to their family economy. As the contemporary records reveal, their home production of goods such as quilts and straw hats, services provided to boarders, and outside interests such as teaching school significantly augmented a precarious family budget.

Outside the realms of family economy, however, Joseph expanded the Saints' worldview by lifting "a portion of the veil of eternity," as it were, and aroused in the Saints' hearts a desire to move beyond contemporary Protestant categories of self-definition.[4] While it is certain that many women in Nauvoo already had begun to see themselves in a new light, the catalyst for such changes was the Prophet.

This widening of views began in a historic meeting of the Relief Society on 28 April 1842 in the upper room of Joseph's Red Brick Store. The Prophet attended this, the sixth meeting of the newly organized group, and noted in his journal, "At two o'clock I met the members of the 'Female Relief Society,' and after presiding at the admission of many new members, gave a lecture on the Priesthood, showing how the sisters would come in possession of the privileges, blessings and gifts of the Priesthood."[5]

Joseph presented to the women assembled in the Red Brick Store an important sermon on the blessings that awaited them in the temple, then under construction in Nauvoo. Bathsheba W. Smith recalled that Joseph himself offered the invocation to this meeting. She said that in his prayer "his voice trembled very much." "According to my prayer," the Prophet told the society membership, "I will not be with you long to teach and instruct you, and the world will not be troubled with me much longer."[6]

Another participant, Nancy N. Tracy, recalled that during this prayer "he was full of the Spirit of God. His whole frame shook, and his face shone and looked almost transparent."[7]

Joseph Smith spoke prophetically during this sermon:

> He said as he had this opportunity, he was going to instruct the society and point out the way for them to conduct, that they might act according to the will of God—that he did not know as he should have many opportunities of teaching them—that they were going to be left to themselves—they would not long have him to instruct them—that the Church would not have his instruction long, and the world would not be troubled with him a great while, and would not have his teachings.[8]

From this time forward, Joseph indicated that his time in mortality was near an end and hastened to fulfill his vision of the kingdom.

In just over two years, the Prophet was killed, but not before he left the blueprint for the restoration of the temple covenants to those whom he had prepared, including many sisters of the Relief Society.

Eliza R. Snow's minutes demonstrate that following Joseph's statements regarding his early death, he presented a plan of action that would prepare the Saints to receive all the blessings God had promised them.

She also noted:

> He exhorted the sisters always to concentrate their faith and prayers for, and place confidence in, those whom God has appointed to honor, whom God has placed at the head to lead [Church leaders]—that we should arm them with our prayers—that the keys of the kingdom are about to be given them [Church leaders], that they may be able to detect everything false.[9]

Joseph completed his work by preparing the Saints for his departure. These preparations included organizing the Relief Society with its unique mission.

One aspect of that mission was to prepare the sisters to receive their temple blessings.[10] Elder George A. Smith indicated that Joseph may have intended to include the sisters in temple worship in Kirtland several years earlier, but "the Saints had a great many traditions which they had borrowed from their fathers" about women's role in religious ritual.[11]

Joseph indicated that the "keys of the Priesthood" (presumably referring in this case to the fulness of the priesthood) would be given both to the sisters of the society and to the members of the Church. The "keys" referred to were given in the endowment as the term took on greater meaning than before. The society minutes were amplified by Church leader and historian George A. Smith when published for the first time in Joseph Smith's history, as represented by the italicized additions in the following paragraph:

> He spoke of delivering the keys *of the Priesthood* to the Church, and *said that the faithful members* of the Relief Society *should receive them in connection with their husbands,* that *the Saints whose integrity has been tried and proved faithful, might know how to ask the*

Lord and receive an answer; for according to his prayers, God had appointed him elsewhere.[12]

Sources indicate that Joseph gave the endowment to leaders of the Church before the temple was completed, beginning on 4 May 1842.[13] Before his death, too, he sealed upon the Apostles' heads "every key, every power, and every principle" that he had received from heavenly beings.[14] His presentiments about his early death caused him to perpetuate these ordinances and keys in this way.

One of the blessings reported as a result of the endowment was the enhancement of the power of prayer. Bathsheba W. Smith recalled that Joseph "said that we did not know how to pray to have our prayers answered. But when I and my husband had our endowments in [December 1843], Joseph Smith presiding, he taught us the order of prayer."[15] On another occasion she said, "[He also] showed us . . . how to detect them when true or false angels come to us."[16]

From Joseph's comments, it is clear that he intended, even before he first gave these ordinances to the brethren, for women to receive the same rights and privileges in the endowment. He also promised the sister Saints "better days" and an increased knowledge of the Lord's plan, and he gave them the power to prepare for the great blessings that awaited them in the temple. The Prophet stated at their meeting on 28 April 1842, "I now turn the key to you, in the name of God, and this society shall rejoice, and knowledge and intelligence shall flow down from this time—this is the beginning of better days to this society."[17]

The 28 April 1842 meeting in the Red Brick Store was most memorable. The minutes for this day's meeting concluded with this reflection, "The Spirit of the Lord was poured out in a very powerful manner, never to be forgotten by those present on this interesting occasion."[18]

Six days following this meeting, nine individuals met in the same upper room of Joseph's store. Those who attended this special meeting received their temple blessings from Joseph, becoming the first in this dispensation. These leaders, including Brigham Young and Heber C. Kimball, were able to carry on this sacred work within the completed Nauvoo Temple following Joseph Smith's death. However, the work in the temple could only begin after women were also given the same blessings. It was obvious that Joseph saw the Relief Society

Sutcliffe Maudsley's portrait of Bathsheba Smith, completed in Nauvoo before she crossed the Mississippi River in 1846 to begin the long journey to the Great Basin.

organization as a means to prepare the sisters of the Church for temple worship, just as the Church's priesthood quorum prepared the brethren.

Shortly following this introduction of sacred priesthood ordinances, Bishop Newel K. Whitney spoke to the society and exuberantly addressed the sisters about the blessings that awaited them: "Rejoice while contemplating the blessings which will be poured out on the heads of the Saints. God has many precious things to bestow, ever to our astonishment, if we are faithful." The society's secretary noted that Bishop Whitney then "rejoiced at the formation of the society, that we might improve our talents and . . . prepare for those blessings which God is soon to bestow upon us."[19]

Reynolds Cahoon confirmed Joseph's intention of using the Relief Society as a means to prepare the sisters for temple ordinances when he spoke to the Relief Society in 1843: "You knew no doubt [that] this society is raised by the Lord to prepare us for the great blessings which are for us in the House of the Lord, in the Temple."[20]

In the 30 March 1842 minutes, Eliza R. Snow recorded:

Pres. Joseph Smith arose—spoke of the organization of the society. Said he was deeply interested that it might be built up to the Most High in an acceptable manner—that its rules must be observed—that none should be received into the society but those who were worthy. Proposed that the society go into a close examination of every candidate.

The minutes continue:

The society should move according to the ancient priesthood, hence they should be a select society, separate from all the evils of the world, choice, virtuous, and holy.[21]

Several of the sisters received their blessings under Joseph's direction before his death and before the temple was completed. They constituted, along with several men of the Church, the "Quorum of the Anointed"—a group of twenty-four couples and several individual men and women who received the temple endowment ordinances during Joseph Smith's lifetime.[22]

In May 1843, the way was opened for the first women to receive the blessings of the temple in the "Quorum of the Anointed." During the next weeks several sister Saints were sealed to their husbands in the "new and everlasting covenant of marriage."

During this period of spiritual and emotional outpouring, Joseph prepared Emma for her duties as the administrator of temple blessings to her sisters. As the "elect lady," she was responsible to administer the blessings of washings and anointings to her sister Saints. Sometime on or before 28 September 1843, Emma became the first woman in the new dispensation to receive the blessing of the endowment.

Soon the "Quorum of the Anointed" greatly expanded its membership and increased the frequency of meetings—some fifty-four meetings were held before Joseph's death in 1844. Still, the number of men and women participating was kept to a minimum until the temple was completed. Elizabeth Ann Whitney recalled that Joseph had been told by an angel that he was "only to reveal [the ordinances] to such persons as were pure, full of integrity to the truth, and worthy to be entrusted with divine messages."[23]

The expansion began on 1 October 1843 when Elizabeth David Durfee and Mary Fielding Smith received their blessings. Seven days later, Harriet Adams, Elizabeth Ann Whitney, Clarissa Smith, and Lucy Mack Smith were given the special blessings promised to the sister Saints in April 1842. Women were quickly brought into the "Quorum of the Anointed" during the next few weeks and months.

On Saturday morning, 23 December 1843, Phebe Woodruff walked with her husband to Emma's home at the corner of Main and Water. Along with Permelia D. Lott, Lucy Morley, Fanny Murray, Sally Phelps, Bathsheba W. Smith, Catherine Spencer, Phebe received her blessings, administered by Emma. The women then joined the brethren in a meeting of the "Quorum of the Anointed" at the Red Brick Store, which included participating in Joseph's prayer.[24]

By late December some fifty individuals met every Saturday and Sunday evening for prayer. Besides praying for the sick and those in need, time in the meetings was taken up by Joseph's lectures on various gospel themes and explanations of the sacred ordinances. In some cases, the sacrament was administered and brief testimonies were offered.

Meetings were held regularly during the winter, bringing much joy and comfort. On 27 January 1844, for example, Joseph met with the group. One participant noted:

The ["Quorum of the Anointed"] met for a meeting in the

evening at Joseph's store. [We] had a number of prayers and ex-
hortations upon the subject of holiness of heart. Brother
[Willard] and Sister [Jennetta] Richards were present. They had
both been unwell for a number of days before, but were able to attend meetings this evening and seemed to enjoy themselves well.
They had received blessings by the prayer of faith.[25]

These meetings continued during the spring and early summer
before Joseph's death in late June 1844.

The thirty sister Saints who received these ordinances were Mary
Harriet Adams, Thirza Cahoon, Lois Cutler, Elizabeth Davis Durfee,
Hannah Fielding, Marinda Nancy Hyde, Vilate Kimball, Jane Law,
Permelia Lott, Mary L. T. Lyman, Rosannah Marks, Mary Catherine
Miller, Lucy Morley, Fanny Young Murray, Sally Phelps, Jennetta
Richards, Agnes Smith, Bathsheba W. Smith, Clarissa Smith, Emma
Smith, Jane Bricknell Smith, Lucy Mack Smith, Mary Fielding
Smith, Catherine Spencer, Leonora Cannon Taylor, Mercy Fielding
Thompson, Elizabeth Ann Whitney, Phebe Woodruff, Phebe Wood-
worth, and Mary Ann Young.[26]

Following the completion of the Nauvoo Temple, a large number
of Relief Society sisters worked side by side with the brethren to help
administer the temple blessings to over five thousand Saints.

Sixteen-year-old Mary A. Phelps married Charles C. Rich in January 1845 and recalled her opportunity to participate in the ordinances of the temple:

As soon as possible, the temple was opened and dedicated to the
Lord. They opened it to all the worthy Saints, and gave their endowments, sealings, and ordinances to just as many as it was possible. . . . There were Saints working in the temple every day except Saturdays, and a greater part of the night, giving endowments until the first of February. . . . The Spirit of the Lord was
greatly manifested during that winter, and we all enjoyed the
privilege of having our endowments and sealings. I received all
these blessings in the Nauvoo Temple in common with my husband and family.[27]

10

THE CITY OF JOSEPH—
SISTERS MOURN

It pains me to write such a painful tale, but the Lord
has comforted our hearts in a measure.
—Bathsheba W. Smith

*J*ane and William Law, prominent members of the Church and
former members of the "Quorum of the Anointed" (they were
dropped from this quorum on 7 January 1844), became disenchanted
with the doctrinal developments in Nauvoo. By 28 April 1844,
William organized the Reformed Church of Jesus Christ and gathered
around him hundreds of fellow dissidents. These former brother and
sister Saints published the vitriolic *Nauvoo Expositor* on 7 June 1844.
The paper contained accusations of corruptions within the Church.
They published several affidavits, including one by Jane Law, in an
effort to incite apostasy from within and intensify persecution from
without by the non-Mormon residents of Hancock County.

The newspaper described Joseph Smith as "one of the blackest
and basest scoundrels that has appeared upon the stage of human existence since the days of Nero and Caligula," and his followers as
"hell-deserving, God-forsaken villains."[1]

The Nauvoo city council met in the wake of the paper's publication and, acting under a liberal interpretation of its charter, declared
the *Expositor* a public nuisance and ordered it destroyed.

Unaware of the real danger of this situation, Bathsheba W. Smith
wrote her husband, who was away on Church business, a long letter
and spoke briefly of the recent difficulties in Nauvoo:

There has been some excitement in town, but I do not feel [an] alarm. The Lawites had got their printing press going. Had printed one paper, and a scandalous thing it was. The City Council examined its lease and found it a [nuisance]. The [city] authorities went and burnt and destroyed the press. This made the Lawites mad. They tried to get a mob but failed. Joseph and those that were concerned in it had been tried, but were cleared. The Laws and a good many have gone and are going off.[2]

The dissidents left the community but also issued charges against the council and city mayor, Joseph Smith. This led to the issuance of a complaint on the charge of riot. Eventually, Joseph Smith surrendered to officials in Carthage, Illinois.

Non-Mormon women in Hancock County were aware of the tense situation existing in the county. Sarah Gregg, a resident of Carthage, wrote to her husband on 18 June 1844:

My dear Thomas:

My hand trembles, not from fear, though in the midst of wars alarms, but from fatigue. . . . Oh! my dear husband you have no idea what is passing here now. To see men preparing for battle to fight with blood hounds, but I hope there will be so large an army as to intimidate that "bandit horde" so there will be no blood shed. Brothers and brother-in-laws are wide awake and determined to defend their liberty or die.[3]

What Sarah Gregg was unwilling to see among her brothers was a thirst for blood, the blood of Joseph and Hyrum Smith. Another Hancock County resident understood that it was the Latter-day Saint leaders who stood in jeopardy of freedom, not the citizens of Carthage. Zina Diantha Huntington Jacobs, who was sealed to Joseph sometime earlier, wrote on 24 June 1844:

A day long to be remembered. This day Joseph, Hyrum, John P. Green, Dimick [Huntington], and others started for Carthage to be met at the Mound. [They] returned about noon accompanied by a number by the governor's orders. Took the cannons and all the U.S. arms, also the before mentioned prisoners and left this place, in the afternoon. O God, save thy servants, save them for Jesus' sake.[4]

While on the way to Carthage, a fifteen-year-old sister was called upon to help Joseph in his time of need. Mary Rich recalled:

At this time I was fifteen years old. When he found he had to go to Carthage, he wanted a man by the name of Rosecrantz, who was well acquainted with the governor, to go with him. He sent word by Mr. Rosecrantz, asking me if I would go and stay with Mr. Rosecrantz's sick wife while he went to Carthage with him. I went to stay with Mrs. Rosecrantz, and as they were going, they called at the gate with their company of about twenty men, and Joseph Smith asked me if I would bring them out a drink of water. I took a pitcher and glass and went out and gave them a drink. "Lord bless you," Joseph told me.[5]

Within a short time Joseph and Hyrum left the home and were placed in the county jail where they were later murdered. Zina Diantha characterized the day as "the ever to be remembered awful day of the 27th of June 1844":

Thus in one day about three or four o'clock [it was 5:00 P.M.] fell the Prophet and Patriarch of the Church of the Latter-day Saints, the kind husbands, the affectionate fathers, the venerable statesman, the friends of mankind, by the hand of a ruthless mob mixed with dissenters.[6]

When the bodies of Joseph and Hyrum Smith were returned to Nauvoo the day following their murders, some Saints came to the Mansion Home to view their beloved leaders' remains. Zina Diantha Huntington Jacobs recorded her experience:

This afternoon the bodies of the martyrs arrived in town. . . . I went into this house for the first time and saw the lifeless, speechless bodies of the two martyrs for the testimony which they held. Little did my heart ever think that mine eyes should witness this awful scene.[7]

A copy of an 1846 daguerreotype of Emma Hale Smith holding eighteen-month-old David Hyrum—born five months after Joseph's death.

Joseph and Hyrum's widows were devastated. Emma was five months pregnant at the time. The martyrs' mother could not be consoled; Sarah M. Kimball held her hand for a long time before the grieving woman spoke, "How could they kill my boys! O how could they kill them when they were so *precious*! I am sure they would not harm anybody in the world; . . . there was poor Hyrum, what could they kill him for—he was always mild."[8]

A few days later, Zina Diantha Huntington Jacob's diary entry stated: "It is Sunday, a lonely heart-sorrowful day. Also it rains."[9]

The feeling and the emotional state of many Saints during this fateful period has been preserved in several extant letters and diaries from the women of Nauvoo. The events of 27 June 1844 were the hardest the Saints had yet experienced.

Fifteen-year-old Mary A. Phelps's father took her to the Mansion House early in the morning before the bodies were prepared for the public viewing:

He told me that if I would get up I could go down, as he had gotten permission for me to see Joseph and Hyrum Smith as they lay at their home. I went down, saw them, and laid my hand on Joseph's forehead. The blood was oozing out of the wound in his shoulder, and the sheet that was around him was stained with blood. Still he looked very natural; Hyrum had been shot in the face and therefore did not look very natural.[10]

Vilate Kimball provided a detailed view of the confusion and intense emotional atmosphere following the martyrdom. In a letter dated 30 June 1844, Vilate wrote her husband, who was absent from Nauvoo on Church business in the month of June:

> Never before, did I take up my pen to address you under so trying circumstances as we are now placed, but as Brother Adams, the bearer of this, can tell you more than I can write I shall not attempt to describe the scene that we have passed through. God forbid that I should ever witness another like unto it. I saw the lifeless corpses of our beloved brethren when they were brought to their almost distracted families. Yea, I witnessed their tears, and groans, which was enough to rent the heart of an adamant. Every brother and sister that witnessed the scene felt deeply to sympathize with them. Yea, every heart is filled with sorrow, and the very streets of Nauvoo seem to mourn. Where it will end the Lord only knows. We are kept awake night after night by the alarm of mobs.[11]

Another letter was sent to missionary George A. Smith by his wife, Bathsheba, on 6 July 1844:

> We have had strange times since you left. You will no doubt hear, before this reaches you, of the death of our beloved brethren Joseph and Hyrum Smith. They were killed at Carthage on the 27 of June and on the 28, they were brought home, and such a day of mourning never was seen. It pains me to write such a painful tale, but the Lord has comforted our hearts in a measure. . . . Brother John Taylor was wounded but is getting better, is quite weak but quite cheerful. Brother Willard Richards was not hurt. They were both in jail at the time of the massacre. I will not write any more on that subject as I expect you will hear all the particulars before this reaches you.[12]

Writing to non-Mormon family members in the East, Hortensia Patrick Merchants lamented, "Truly, it is trying and grievous, that we cannot worship God according to the dictates of our own conscience, unmolested."[13]

While the sad news of the martyrdom spread quickly, some sister Saints had mixed emotions: their beloved prophet and patriarch were dead, but their husbands and fathers were saved. Writing to her non-member parents in England, Jennetta Richards noted her husband's presence at Carthage Jail and his miraculous escape:

> Mr. Richards [her husband] and Mr. Taylor were with Hyrum and Joseph in the room at the time. . . . Mr. Taylor and Mr. Richards were not prisoners, but were only there as company. . . . Mr. Richards was not wounded, only a ball passed under his left ear, seared his neck, and took a little off the tip of his ear. . . . I think I never can praise my Heavenly Father sufficiently for his mercies to me in preserving and restoring Mr. Richards safe and sound again. It seemed to me as though the children realized it in a great measure, they made so much work with him when he came home.[14]

Fourteen-year-old Eliza Clayton went to the jail on the day following the martyrdom. She recalled:

> I went with my sister Lucy to the jail; we found the doors and windows open and everything in confusion, as though the people had left in great haste. We went upstairs to the room in which the Prophet and his brother had been shot. Everything seemed upset. There were some Church books on the table and portraits of Joseph and Hyrum's families on the mantle piece, blood in pools on the floor and spattered on the walls, at the sight of which we were overcome with grief and burst into tears.[15]

Mary Ann Barzee Boice and her husband lived outside of Nauvoo, "a few miles from Carthage," at the time of the martyrdom. When news arrived of the death, Mary Ann and her husband went to Nauvoo "but got there too late to see their bodies." They returned home and, as they passed through Carthage, her husband wanted to go to the jail. Mary Ann remembered that her husband "wanted me to go up in the jail and see where they were slain. But I felt that I could not look upon the scene. However, he went in."[16]

In the 1 July 1844 issue of the *Times and Seasons,* an issue totally outlined in black, several articles and reports relating to Joseph and Hyrum's death were published. Among those items was a poem by Eliza R. Snow telling the awful tale in poetry. The last few lines, however, suggest the desire of many in Nauvoo at the time of trouble:

> All hearts with sorrow bleed, and ev'ry eye
> Is bath'd in tears—each bosom heaves a sigh—
> Heart broken widows' agonizing groans
> Are mingled with the helpless orphans' moans!
>
> Ye Saints! be still, and know that God is just—
> With steadfast purpose in his promise trust.
> Girded with sackcloth, own his mighty hand,
> And wait his judgments on this guilty land!
> The noble martyrs now have gone to move
> The cause of Zion in the courts above.

The death of the Prophet and Church Patriarch added to the sorrow of some sister Saints who were torn by the apostasy of family members during the period. Elvira Annie Cowles Holmes, the thirty-year-old daughter of former Nauvoo stake presidency counselor Austin Cowles, was sealed to Joseph sometime earlier. Her father withdrew from his Church position when the revelation on eternal marriage, which included provisions for plural marriage, was first read to the Nauvoo high council the year before. "He opposed this law and preached against it," she recalled.

Austin Cowles became a prominent leader in the new opposition Church in April 1844 and was one of the major supporters of the *Expositor.* Elvira Annie felt the heartache of being forced to choose between her father and the Church she so dearly loved. Her marriage to Joseph Smith only increased the gulf between her and her parents.

Now as a sorrowing widow, she faced life without support from her estranged father and mother.[17]

Eliza Dana Gibbs arrived in Nauvoo—a city of sorrow and distress—just shortly after the martyrdom, having heard the news on the way. Within a short time, she, her husband, and her sister, Mary, were

taken ill with the ague. Mary died, and "the cares of her family de-
volved on me, but the care of the babe was of short duration for it
died about a month after her mother, a sweet little angel too beautiful
for this wicked world."

She recalled, "Those were days long to be remembered, as indeed
were all the days of Nauvoo, filled up with the bitter trials and deep
sorrow and mourning, but the Lord strengthened us to struggle
through as he did many others."[18]

Following a public funeral, the two widows, Emma and Mary
Fielding Smith, held a secret burial under the cover of darkness and
began immediately to worry about their families' economic security.
Emma was the mother of three children—Joseph III, Frederick
Granger Williams, and Alexander Hale—and was pregnant with a
fourth child, David Hyrum, who was born in November 1844. Mary
was the legal guardian of five children: John, Jerusha, Sarah, Joseph
Fielding, and Martha Ann (the last two were her own children).

During the next few days and weeks, the Church attempted to
understand what had happened. Joseph's death received national attention as word spread from Nauvoo. The *New York Herald* published
an extra to announce the death of the Mormon leaders. The editor,
writing in a harsh obituary, stated, "The death of the modern ma-
homet will seal the fate of Mormonism. They cannot get another Joe
Smith. The holy city must tumble into ruins, and the 'latter day
saints' have indeed come to the latter day."[19]

Joseph's death caused great grief but helped crystallize many feelings of those in Nauvoo who were debating the doctrinal innovations
revealed by the Prophet.

During the succession crisis, many of Nauvoo's women stood
firmly to the commitment to finish one aspect of the martyred
prophet's work—the Nauvoo Temple. Later, several recalled the experience of Joseph's mantle falling on Brigham Young. Zina Diantha
Huntington Jacobs said:

> Never can it be told in words what the Saints suffered in those
> days of trial; but the sweet spirit—the Comforter—did not for-
> sake them; and when the Twelve returned, the mantle of Joseph
> fell upon Brigham. When I approached the stand (on the occa-
> sion when Sidney Rigdon was striving for the guardianship of the
> Church), President Young was speaking. It was the voice of
> Joseph Smith—not that of Brigham Young. His very person was

changed. The mantle was truly given to another. There was no
doubting in the minds of the vast assembly. All witnessed the
transfiguration, and even today thousands bear testimony thereof.
I closed my eyes. I could have exclaimed, "I know that is Joseph
Smith's voice!" Yea, I knew he had gone. But the same Spirit was
with the people; the Comforter remained.[20]

Brigham Young and the rest of the Twelve Apostles took control
of the civic and ecclesiastical departments of the community and
Church. By and large the trying experiences surrounding these events
left a committed and faithful group in the city, the dissenters having
abandoned Nauvoo. A feeling of normalcy and unity once again returned to Nauvoo as the Twelve undertook an accelerated building
pace of homes, shops, and the temple.

Contemporary accounts continue to speak of parties, marriages,
births, sickness, death, poor living conditions, and progress on the
temple.

A place of gathering in the city was the Masonic Hall (cultural
hall), where numerous activities, including plays and concerts, were held.

The hall was completed and dedicated in 1844, just before Joseph
and Hyrum's deaths. A reader of the *Nauvoo Neighbor* wrote this letter to the editor:

Mr. Editor, taking it as it is, I would ask where are we to go for
music, if we do not find it in Nauvoo? I will boldly assert,
nowhere. Witness the concert the other evening at the Masonic
Hall; got up for the most laudable and praiseworthy purpose. The
music in its selection was of the most varied character, and the
electrifying feeling that was manifest proved to demonstrate that
Nauvoo can furnish us with ladies and gentlemen whose instrumental and vocal powers are of no unpolished order. The stringed
instruments, the trumpets, flutes, and clarinets, which formed the
band, and particularly the flute and violin solos, not only gave a
magic charm but struck the numerous and admiring audience
with amaze at the consummate skill they exhibited. We could
mention several gentlemen whose talent for music was of the
highest order. The songs, too, and glees drew forth the most unbounded applause. . . . The ladies will ever be remembered for
their sweet, soothing, lively, and harmonious voices, for their
graceful appearance, and their choir selection of their pieces.[21]

Among the new activities available to the men and women in Nauvoo was the possibility of having their "images fixed" through the process of photography. For all but a select few, it was the first time to experience this most recent and amazing invention.

The daguerreotype process came to Nauvoo through Lucian Foster, a convert from New York. He established a daguerreotype studio on Parley Street. Several images were made of people who lived in the city and a few more of the city itself, especially the temple. One of these images still in existence, a family portrait, freezes in time a portion of the life in Nauvoo—the daguerreotype of Willard, Jennetta, and Heber John Richards.

A copy of the original daguerreotype of Jennetta Richards sitting on the lap of her husband, Willard (their son Heber John cuddles close to his father). The Richardses arrived at Foster's studio on 26 March 1845 to have their "likeness" preserved.

On 26 March 1845, Lucian Foster's daguerreotype studio was alive with activity. Willard Richards wrote in his journal, "10 a.m. went to Foster's daguerreotype with Jennetta and Heber John."[22] It is an unusual view, unlike many of the daguerreotypes of the day. Jennetta and Willard strike a loving pose, instead of the strict, stilled views we expect from the period.

For Willard Richards, this view became an important treasure, as his beloved companion, Jennetta, fell ill on 21 May and died on 9 July 1845, just a few months after they had their likeness made.

Jennetta Richards asked for the Twelve to come to her home and pray for her, as she felt that she could not live long. "We also prayed for my wife [Vilate Kimball], who is very sick," Heber C. Kimball noted. Heber continued, "Returned home and found Sister Whitney. She anointed my wife and sang in tongues; I also sang and the Lord blessed us."[23]

By the 20th, Vilate "was better and had a good night's rest," but Jennetta Richards grew worse during the next few days and weeks.[24] Willard Richards wrote:

> Wednesday July 9 [1845]. At day light dressed. . . . [Jennetta] very weak. [I] kneeled, prayed, and laid hands on her three times. . . . I gave her encouragement as I felt. She said, "How can I die under such progress?" About sunrise [I] sent for Levi [Richards] and about six a.m. sent for Elder Heber C. Kimball, who came and laid on hands and prayed; she revived. [I] sent for Father John Smith, John Taylor, and George A. Smith. Heber Kimball, John E. Page, Levi Richards, and myself . . . prayed and went into her room, anointed and prayed for her and felt encouraged. At fifteen minutes past ten a.m., Jennetta stopped breathing. . . . Sister Wilcox and Lucy Clayton watched, and I slept in [the] room on the floor.[25]

On the following day, 10 July, the Quorum of the Twelve Apostles met at the Richards home for their weekly meeting to console their fellow Apostle. Several sisters—including Sisters Durfee, Sessions, Clayton, and Wilcox—dressed Jennetta in her temple clothing and put her in the "coffin about sunset."

Whether Willard planned to bury his wife in the local cemetery is not known, but his young son Heber John, named after their first child, who died a few months after his birth, asked, "Pa, will you bury

Ma in the garden; if you do I can bear it. If you do not, I cannot bear it." Willard gladly complied with the young boy's desire.[26] On the following day, Willard recorded in his diary:

> Friday July 11. At dinner Rhoda Ann [nearly two years old] spoke out very pleasantly and said, "Ma is gone away. She is gone to see Uncle Joseph and Hyrum and my little brother." I wept for joy to think of the happy meeting of Jennetta and Heber John. About sunset [we] laid the coffin in a pine box in a vault in the southwest corner of the door yard. One foot east and north of the fence covering eight feet four inches long and four feet wide. Rhoda Ann called it the play house. [I threw] a dahlia on the head of the coffin in the vault and said, "I will come and fetch it with [you]."[27]

A few days following the burial, Willard went to the Seventy's Hall to see William Major's uncompleted painting of Jennetta. Later, when Rhoda Ann accompanied her father to visit the artist, she pointed out her mother's profile, "though not half done."[28]

William W. Major, an English artist, commenced painting Jennetta Richards's portrait in 1845. She died before it was completed. Ann Fox King posed in her place.

Several contemporary portraits of members of the Nauvoo community survived the exodus of the city, including the one of Jennetta Richards, completed after her death with Ann Fox King sitting in for the artist to finish the work. Besides Majors, Sutcliffe Maudsley was active in Nauvoo capturing visual images of the Saints. Maudsley's portrait paintings of Emma Smith and Mary Fielding Smith are examples of such work.

Other families were enjoying the celebrations of life with marriages and births of children. Nancy Tracy had a baby on 15 March 1845, and a few weeks later experienced a wonderful manifestation:

> I was aroused from my slumbers one night, hearing such heavenly music as I had never heard before. Everything was so still and quiet when it burst upon my ear that I could not imagine where it came from. I went up and looked out of the window. The moon shone bright as I looked over at the temple from whence the sound came. There on the roof of the building heavenly bands of music had congregated and were playing most beautifully. The music was exquisite![29]

Mary M. Kimball delivered a "daughter just at sunset by Sister Billings and Sister [Patty] Sessions, who are [the] most skillful midwives in Israel." Vilate Kimball and Sylvia Sessions Lyon assisted in the delivery. Heber C. Kimball continued his journal entry, "The God of Israel was with us, and his name shall have all the glory, and may peace rest down on thine handmaidens, that they may always be [blessed] in all such cases, from hence forth all their days and thy name shall have all the glory."[30] Other celebrations included musicals, plays, and parties.

George A. and Bathsheba W. Smith attended a gathering at Mary Ann and David Yearsley's home in 1845:

> Went to Brother David D. Yearsley's with my wife. The party consisted of about fifty. . . . Elders Orson Pratt, Willard Richards, John E. Page, John Taylor, Amasa Lyman, and their wives, besides Father and Mother, and many others composed the party. . . . Six widow Smiths were present, to wit: Aunt Lucy, widow of Joseph Smith, Sr.; Mary, the widow of Silas Smith; Mary, the widow of Hyrum; Agnes, the widow of Don Carlos; Lavira, the widow of Samuel Harrison Smith; [Emma, widow of Joseph].[31]

Zina Diantha Huntington Jacobs reflected upon the general state of affairs in Nauvoo at the time: "The Church is in prosperous circumstances, for there appears to be the most union that has ever been. The faithful are determined to keep the law of God. O Father, bind us as a people together in the bonds of love that we never shall separate. The temple prospers."[32]

While the Saints enjoyed a period of unity, a dark cloud began to descend upon the city in the summer and fall of 1845. The uneasy peace that existed between the Saints and their enemies following the murders of Joseph and Hyrum Smith was ending.

The Saints' situation became increasingly unsettled in 1845 and early 1846. The Nauvoo city charter was revoked by the Illinois state legislature on 24 January 1845 and left the Saints without a judicial system, city government, militia, or any significant legal protection from the armed mobs in the county. It was at this time that the Saints voted to rename Nauvoo "the City of Joseph" in honor of their fallen leader.

As early as 1845, state officials advised the Twelve Apostles that the Saints should leave the state if they wanted to avoid more bloodshed. Illinois governor Thomas Ford, claiming that the martyred Prophet had informed him before his death that he intended to take the Saints west, told Church leaders in the City of Joseph, "It would be good policy for your people to move to some far distant country. Your religion is new and it surprises the people as any great novelty in religion generally does. I do not foresee the time when you will be permitted to enjoy quiet."[33]

The governor simply counseled the Saints the painfully obvious: abandon Nauvoo or be destroyed by their enemies in Hancock County. This, however, was not news to the Saints, as Joseph Smith had made plans before his death to move the Church headquarters from Illinois to a "place prepared" in the West.[34]

The summer of 1845 passed fairly harmlessly, but during September a number of violent acts against the Saints and their property occurred in the outlying settlements. Church leaders signed the following statement, noting their intentions of departing Nauvoo during the next year:

> We, the undersigned members of a council of The Church of
> Jesus Christ of Latter-day Saints assembled at the house of John
> Taylor, in the city of Nauvoo on the evening of the twenty-fourth

day of September 1845, do hereby express our determination, to remove, in connection with as many of the members of the Church as will hearken to our advice on the subject from this county and state as soon as property can be disposed of, and the necessary preparations made . . . as early as next spring, in April or May. . . . As we wish for peace, at any sacrifice which is in our power to make consistent with honor and virtue.[35]

It is certain that Church leaders wanted to avoid the suffering encountered during the Missouri exodus in 1838–39.

Non-Mormon Nancy Hunter, who taught school in Hancock County briefly in the summer of 1845, wrote her fiance, John Aiton, from her home in Theoplis, Illinois, in September. She noted, "When I consented to go to Augusta I forgot, or rather it never occurred to my mind, that it was in Hancock County and that I should be fellow citizen with the Mormons." Nancy continued,

Well, when I had been there but three weeks and going on very pleasantly, a disturbance broke out between the Mormons and old settlers, and Augusta, as well as Carthage and Warsaw having rendered itself peculiarly obnoxious to the Mormons during the disturbance last season, the people being very much excited on account of threats made last year and now renewed all except two or three families, left Augusta. This of course broke up the school, and as there was nothing more for me to do at present I came home when Andrew came after me.

Nancy told John she thought he may have seen "an account of the [Hancock County] affairs in the papers." She informed him that many "false and exaggerated reports circulated, but the truth is quite bad enough." For certain, she maintained, "the Old Settlers cannot and *will not* long remain in the same county, perhaps not in the same state with the Mormons. But how [the Mormons] are to be disposed of remains yet to be decided." She continued, "Many Anties are so enraged that they would not stop at bloodshed."[36]

A few days following Nancy Hunter's letter, the anti-Mormons held a series of meetings in Carthage and Quincy, Illinois, and adopted the "Quincy Convention," demanding the removal of the Mormons by May 1846.

A young woman living in Nauvoo, Irene Hascall Pomeroy,

reported the situation in a letter to her mother in September 1845: "The Twelve had issued a proclamation that if they will let them alone . . . and do what they can to prepare us for journeying, all that follow the Twelve will go where they will not bother [the] United States with Mormon religion. . . . I think probably they will cross the Rocky Mountains to a healthier climate."[37] She was planning for her parents' arrival in Nauvoo and wanted to keep them informed of their plans, hoping they would arrive before the Saints' departure in the spring of 1846.

Bathsheba W. Smith recalled, "The fall of 1845 found Nauvoo, as it were, one vast mechanic shop, as nearly every family was engaged in making wagons. Our parlor was used as a paint shop in which to paint wagons."[38]

Church leaders were again under attack and subject to prosecution by legal means. Many went into hiding as they continued to conduct the affairs of the kingdom and prepared for the mass exodus. As a precaution, police were posted at major intersections and at the homes of Church leaders.

Even during this difficult time, the young women of Nauvoo found means to entertain themselves. Helen Mar Kimball wrote:

> The pleasure of having John Kay and Howard Egan [men who stood guard at the Young home] was always anticipated by the young people. They were very entertaining—Egan with his interesting yarns and anecdotes, and the singing by John Kay it would be useless for us to try to describe, but suffice it to say, his voice (a baritone) was most magnificent, . . . and many an evening we were thus entertained, as we circled around the "ingle side," and the hours flew by so swiftly that midnight was often there before we knew it.

Helen recalled one occasion when John Kay stood guard the "forepart of the night at the house of President Young." During the evening she and her friends gathered, and "when the moon shone brightly," she and her brother William would hitch the horses so that a dozen friends could join them on a ride to the Young family's residence.

Vilate Young, Helen's friend and the daughter of Mary Ann and Brigham Young, coaxed John Kay to join them in a drive in the moonlight:

[We] drove for an hour or more around the same block; for the sake of keeping him with us, and each time would drive closely to the President's gate, to satisfy him that all was right. The young people were incapable of feeling the weight which rested upon our fathers and mothers.[39]

The winter was cold as the sister Saints prepared for their departure. Irene Hascall Pomeroy wrote a letter to her cousin Ophelia M. Andrews a few days before Christmas 1845, and after the first paragraph she noted, "My blue ink is frozen." She continued with another ink and thanked her cousin for sending her a letter and "a catalogue for which" she was "greatly obliged."[40]

Soon scores of Saints from outlying communities arrived in Nauvoo, seeking safety from the increasing mob activity against their property and themselves. These attacks became bolder and bolder when it became evident that neither the Saints nor the state would intercede. People were encouraged to share living quarters, and others were forced to obtain shelter in the most unsuitable places in the city.

While the sister Saints prepared to move again, this time to some unknown location in the West, one anonymous sister wrote a song, "Early This Spring We Leave Nauvoo."

> Early this spring we leave Nauvoo
> And on our journey we'll pursue.
> We'll go and bid the mob farewell
> And let them go to heaven or hell.
>
> So on the way to California:
> In the spring we'll take our journey
> Far above Arkansas' fountains pass
> Between the Rocky Mountains.
>
> The mobocrats have done their best,
> Old Sharp and Williams with the rest.
> They've burnt our houses and our goods
> And left our sick folk in the woods.
>
> Below Nauvoo on the green plains,
> They burnt our houses and our grains.
> And if fought, they were hell bent
> To raise for help the government.

The old settlers that first cleared the soil,
They thought they would take a spoil.
And at first they did begin,
But not much money did bring in.

Old Governor Ford, his mind so small,
He's got no room for soul at all.
If heaven and hell should do their best,
He neither could be damned or blessed.

Backenstos, his mind so large
Upon the mob, he made a charge;
Some three or four he did shoot down
And left them dying on the ground.

The old state marshall came to town
And searched our temple up and down.
He told the Saints that he had come
And brought a writ for Brigham Young.

Old Major Warren came to town—
He rode our city up and down
And searched for hogs like a good fellow,
And at last was found in Hibbard's cellar.

So out of the way, you old state marshall,
You can't get the Twelve Apostles;
So out of the way, old Major Warren,
You can't come it over the Mormons.

Now since it's so we have to go
And leave the City of Nauvoo,
I hope you'll all be strong and stout,
And then no mob can back you out.

The Temple shining silver bright
And Christ's own glory gives the light;
High on the mountains we will rear
A standard to the nations far.[41]

Family and friends living in the East were naturally concerned about their family members in Nauvoo during this period of great agitation. Recent convert and Nauvoo resident Wealthy Richards received a letter from family member Mary E. Dewey in Massachusetts sometime in early 1846 expressing such a concern. "I want you to write me a letter and let me know how you feel about the Mormons leaving Nauvoo and going beyond the Rocky Mountains." Of course, the real question Mary was asking was, "Are you going with them?"

Mary asked Wealthy's forgiveness for being so inquisitive, but reassured her that it was because everyone at home felt "interested in your welfare whether present or absent." In particular, Wealthy's father wanted her to write back and tell him about the situation in Nauvoo since there were so many rumors about life there. Mary emphasized the situation back home: "We cannot take up a paper without seeing something about [life in Nauvoo]."42

While family members showed their concern, and the sister Saints responded to these concerns through letters, others sought a place to live in the overcrowded city.

Eliza Dana Gibbs and her husband struggled to find accommodations during this difficult period as the Saints from outlying areas sought "refuge and shelter until every house was filled to over-flowing." The Gibbs family, along with many others, sought any kind of shelter possible. "There was not a house or room" to be "rented for any price, and we had to take shelter in a place that was little more than a shelter," Eliza noted.

> It was clapboard on the outside but not plastered inside, and the clapboards were so old and warped that we could stick our hands through between the boards all around the sides of the house. Mother was quite aged and she had to sit in the big arm chair, wrapped in a bedquilt and hold Josiah close to the fire to keep from freezing.

Eliza Dana Gibbs's husband was forced to flee the city before the dawn of day without his family, being warned by an "outsider" about midnight. Eliza "had to get out of Nauvoo the best way" she could, "without any assistance." Her strong will soon prevailed, and Eliza succeeded in "getting away and joining" her husband in Montrose, across the river.43

One sister, in anticipation of her family's removal from Nauvoo, "obtained stones from the temple yard" and had "initials cut on them." A Brother Wilcox came to the home and "dug down at the end of each grave [in the yard] and placed the stones down almost to the coffins, then covered all over and dug up the rose trees we had planted there, and smoothed off the ground, and no stranger could tell where they were."[44]

The need to properly identify the grave was possibly based on the fact that many Nauvoo Saints were unable to locate family graves in the local cemetery. For example, the Stout family went "to the burying ground to seek for the grave of [their] little Lydia." In spite of their efforts, which included digging, they failed in their attempt to find the grave.[45]

In the local paper, sisters were given a suggested checklist for the upcoming journey. Among the recommended items were flour or other bread or bread stuffs in good sacks; sugar; cayenne pepper; black pepper; mustard; rice; cinnamon; cloves; nutmeg; salt; dried apples, beans, beef, bacon, peaches, pumpkin; seed grain; and soap. Women were expected to collect and prepare most items for their families for the trek West.[46]

The time came for the sister Saints who built Nauvoo to leave their homes and gardens, but not before they completed the temple and received the great blessings promised to them for their sacrifices.

11

HANDMAIDENS OF THE LORD—
SISTERS IN THE TEMPLE

A messenger was sent; . . . we were to present ourselves [at the temple] that evening. The weather
being fine we preferred to walk; and as we [walked] a
solemn covenant we entered into—to cling to each
other through time and, if permitted, throughout all
eternity, and this vow was solemnized at the holy
altar.

—Helen Mar Whitney

*I*n the midst of persecution and preparations to leave for an unknown place, the temple on the hill remained a beacon to the
Saints as they looked up and watched its progress. Its completion and
dedication dominated the Saints' personal and public lives in prayers,
sermons, donations, work, and, most important, anticipation for the
day when they could enter the holy edifice and receive the blessings
promised the faithful.

Since Joseph publicly announced the construction of the Nauvoo
Temple on 3 October 1840, work on it occupied the Saints' attention
and resources for nearly six years. Much of the city's energy during
this time went into building the temple. Two types of tithing existed
in Nauvoo: one on financial increase or earnings and one on an individual's time. Each member was expected to donate one out of every
ten days to the building of the temple.

The sister Saints sacrificed their time, talents, and possessions in
a remarkable way as they provided food, clothing, and shelter for the
construction workers. They contributed jewelry, watches, and other
family possessions to the temple committee or converted these "in-
kind" donations into cash for the temple tithing (a special donation
beyond the regular tithing on income). A Sister Stead donated a
day's work of washing clothes, which a surviving ledger reveals was

estimated to be worth almost thirty-eight cents, and Sister Marm donated two days' work washing.

Mercy Fielding Thompson, like many sisters in Nauvoo, wanted to help in any way she could. She sought the Lord in prayer for help in the matter, and the response was clear and precise, "Try to get the sisters to subscribe one cent per week for the purpose of buying glass and nails for the temple."[1]

With the support of Joseph Smith, Mercy and her sister, Mary Fielding Smith, went about drumming up support among the women of Nauvoo. Later, she enlisted the aid of the sister Saints in the British Isles by publishing a notice in the *Millennial Star*. By April 1845, about one thousand dollars was donated to the temple fund.[2]

Maybe the most novel means of raising funds for the temple was Sarah M. Kimball's effort, following the birth of her son. "My husband came to my bedside," Sarah recalled, "and as he was admiring our three-day-old darling, I said, 'What is the boy worth?'" Hiram Kimball, her successful non-Mormon merchant husband, hesitated and said, "Oh, I don't know; he is worth a great deal." Sarah suggested the sum of at least one thousand dollars, to which Hiram agreed. Sarah quickly claimed her half and told him that she wanted to donate it to the temple fund.

Later, Hiram Kimball related the incident to Joseph Smith, who promptly stated, "I accept all such donations, and from this day the boy shall stand recorded, *Church property.*" The Prophet jokingly gave Hiram Kimball two options—he could either pay five hundred dollars to the Church and retain possession of his son or receive five hundred dollars and give the boy to Joseph as Trustee and Trust.

Mr. Kimball graciously deeded the Church a piece of property well worth the amount Sarah wanted to donate to the temple fund.[3]

As funds and goods were donated to the temple fund, work proceeded quickly. One of the first official ceremonies conducted at the temple site was the cornerstone laying on 6 April 1841. A sister living nearby the temple site recalled:

> One day I looked over toward the temple and saw a large crowd gathered with some two or three women present, so I thought I would go over. I put on my bonnet and shawl and made my way over. Brother Joseph was there and seemed busily engaged over something. Finally, he looked up and saw us women. He said for

the brothers to stand back and let the sisters come up. So they gave way, and we went up. In the huge chief cornerstone was cut out a square about a foot around and about as deep lined with zinc, and in it Brother Joseph had placed a Bible, a Book of Mormon, hymn book, and other Church works along with silver money that had been coined in that year.[4]

Eventually, the Saints celebrated the laying of the final stone on the temple. Zina Diantha Huntington Jacobs recorded the events of that day on 24 May 1845: "This memorable day the sun arose clear in the east. This morning was serene and silent. The sun and moon were at about equal heights in the horizon, as if to rejoice with the Saints in praises to the Most High." She continued her lengthy diary entry:

The Saints went (all that knew it) to the Temple at 6:00 in the morning. The Twelve and the workmen, some brethren, the band with the banner of liberty floating in the gentle breeze, the last stone was laid on the temple with shouts of hosannah to God and the Lamb, Amen, and joy filled every bosom and thanks to our God that had preserved us. President Brigham Young made some remarks very appropriate. This is the seventh day even on which God rested from all his works and the Jews still keep it. O may Israel in these last days keep all thy statutes. O praise the Lord for all his goodness, yea, his mercies endureth forever. Exalt his holy name for he hath no end. He hath established his word upon the earth, no more to be thrown down. He will remember all his covenants to fulfil them in their times. O praise the Lord forever more, Amen.[5]

Helen Mar Kimball Whitney recalled this day as "one of the most interesting incidents within my recollections."[6] Helen quoted a contemporary source:

The singers sang their sweetest notes, and their voices thrilled the hearts of the assemblage; the music of the band . . . never sounded so charming; and when President Young placed the stone in position, [he] said: "The last stone is now laid upon the temple, and I pray the Almighty, in the name of Jesus, to defend us in this place, and sustain us until the temple is finished and we have all got our endowments."[7]

The sister Saints joined with the brethren and shouted, "Hosanna! Hosanna! Hosanna, to God and the Lamb, amen! amen! and amen!" This was repeated three times by those attending the service.

Work on the interior continued, and eventually the first public meeting was scheduled to be held and convened in the completed lower assembly room on 5 October 1845. Helen Mar Kimball Whitney recalled, "I was present with the choir on this occasion, also at conference the three following days [6–8 October]. The choir and orchestra occupied a gallery at the west end, opposite the stand."[8] Irene Hascall Pomeroy attended this first conference meeting in the temple and wrote to her mother and father in New England, "We went to conference every day (three days). O! such a glorious meeting. It was in the temple. There were five thousand people present."[9]

On 21 November the painters finished their work in the upper rooms in the attic, which were dedicated on 22 November 1845. It was here that the long-awaited blessings would be given to worthy Saints.

The next few days and weeks found the Saints busily preparing the temple for the commencement of administering the temple ordinances. Men and young boys went around the community in their wagons picking up potted plants and evergreens from the homes of the sisters for the "garden room" at the temple. Sisters gave up rugs and carpets, which were laid down in the attic story of the temple on 29 November by several men and Vilate Kimball, Elizabeth Ann Whitney, Sarah Whitney, and Bathsheba Smith.

Several women met at the temple and made a cotton veil for the main endowment room, which was hung on 5 December. Helen Mar Kimball Whitney recalled,

> We sat in Father's room [Heber C. Kimball's office in the attic], next to Brigham Young's [office], who, with his brother [Joseph Young] came in and sang some hymns—Sister [Mary Ann] Young assisting them. Uncle Joseph sang "The Upper California," and the rest joined in the chorus.[10]

The celestial room occupied the largest space on the attic floor. It was a "very large and spacious room, perfectly light, all nicely furnished." Two "splendid tables and four splendid sofas" were placed in the center of the room. Beneath the curtained, semicircular window on the east wall stood a third table with "the celestial and terrestrial globes" placed on it.

A number of mirrors and paintings—including portraits of Church leaders and their wives—hung on the east and north walls. On the north wall was a map of the world, and placed near it was a beautiful marble clock. Several maps of the United States, including a street map of Nauvoo, were placed on the west partition of the room.

The sister Saints made the larger area a "celestial room" through the sacrifice of their own furnishings. One observer noted that the room had a "very splendid and comfortable appearance."[11]

Following the assassination of Joseph and Hyrum, Church leaders decided that for the safety of the members of the anointed quorum, few meetings would be held and only a few new members would be admitted to the group until the temple was completed. Several priesthood leaders, however, did meet regularly for prayer. The sisters of the group waited for the opportunity to participate regularly in the special prayer meetings again and looked forward to the temple's completion.[12]

As the temple's attic area was being readied for the administration of the ordinances, Brigham Young announced that beginning Sunday morning at nine o'clock, the anointed quorum "will assemble for prayer and council. Our wives will come and partake with us. The sacrament will be administered and [we] will spend the day in those things that the Spirit shall teach." Heber C. Kimball noted in his journal that this announcement "gave great joy" to the sisters.[13]

The anticipated Sunday arrived as snow began to fall upon the men and women who walked up the bluff to the temple. The group included Mary Ann Young, Vilate Kimball, Elizabeth Ann Whitney, Marinda N. Hyde, Mary Ann Pratt, Leonora Taylor, Bathsheba Smith, Clarissa Smith, Lois Cutler, Thirza Cahoon, Permelia D. Lot, Lucy Morley, Catherine Spencer, Mary Miller, Mary Fielding Smith, Mercy R. Thompson, Agnes Smith, Sally Phelps, and Phebe Woodworth.

The meeting began after the Saints dressed in white. Following prayer and a hymn, a few spoke and then the sacrament was blessed and passed to those in attendance. "Great solemnity rested upon the brethren and sisters; great union in our meeting," one participant noted.[14] Those present were informed that they should meet at the temple every Sunday to repeat this experience.

The administering of ordinances in the new temple started on 10 December when "Sisters Mary Ann Young, Vilate Kimball, and Elizabeth Ann Whitney commenced administering [initiatory] ordinances in the Temple" at 3:00 P.M. Heber C. Kimball noted in his journal that this event reminded him of Joseph Smith's words, "The sisters are always first in all good works."[15]

By 4:25 P.M. everything was ready for the administering of the ordinances of the endowment.

Among those privileged to participate on that first day were the three sisters mentioned above and Nancy Marinda Hyde, Mary Ann Pratt, Leonora Taylor, Bathsheba W. Smith, Mariah Louisa Lyman, Mary Page, Clarissa Smith, Mary Catherine Miller, Sally Phelps, Lois Cutler, Thirza Cahoon, Phebe Woodworth, Catherine C. Spencer, Agnes M. Smith, Mercy R. Thompson, and Mary Smith.

Several couples, two men, and two single women (Mary and Agnes Smith—widows of Hyrum and Don Carlos Smith) were administered to during the afternoon and evening. The first day's work, including preparations for the following day, ended at 3:30 A.M. on the 11th.

Several more sisters received their blessings on the second day, including Mother Lucy Mack Smith. The martyred Prophet's sister Sophronia and her husband also received their temple blessings at the time. The anxiety of the Saints wishing to receive these special blessings was so great that the temple was thronged with those wishing to enter. On 18 December, Brigham noted, "In consequence of the great pressure of business during the past week, it was decided to devote Saturday to the purpose of washing" the temple clothing utilized. However, when "all those officiating in the ordinances [felt] that the work should not cease, it was determined that the clothes should be washed during the night."[16]

The sister Saints were busily preparing to attend the temple. Irene Hascall Pomeroy sent a letter to her cousin on the day before Christmas. She reflected on the activities of the Saints during the week, "The Temple still progresses. Hundreds have received their endowments."[17]

In preparation for administering one of the most important ordinances, the "sealing" of a husband and wife (eternal marriage), Mary Ann Young, Vilate Kimball, Elizabeth Ann Whitney, Eliza R. Snow, Mary and Agnes Smith, Mercy R. Thompson, and Sarah Ann Whit-

Sutcliffe Maudsley's painting (ca. 1842) of Lucy Mack Smith sitting in her rocking chair underneath one of the book of Abraham facsimiles. Mother Smith lost her husband and four sons in death while she resided in the City of the Saints on the banks of the Mississippi River. When family members, including grandchildren, departed west she remained behind with her daughter-in-law Emma.

ney completed working on the cushions and upholstery of the new altar.[18] On the following day, Brigham Young noted in his journal:

> [7 January 1846] This afternoon, the new altar was used for the first time, and four individuals and their wives were sealed. The altar is about two and one-half feet high and two and one-half feet long and about one foot wide, rising from a platform about eight or nine inches high and extending out on all sides about a foot, forming a convenient place to kneel upon. The top of the altar and the platform for kneeling upon are covered with

cushions of scarlet damask cloth; the sides of the upright part or body of the altar are covered with white linen.[19]

On the same day, 7 January 1846, young Samuel Richards, who was laboring on the temple construction to finish the building for completed dedication, received the invitation to come to the temple to receive his own blessings. On 20 January he began serving as an endowment worker, helping the other Saints to receive their blessings. Three days later, he noted in his journal, "Father John Parker's family received their endowments, his daughter Mary being my intended wife. After which I obtained permission of President Joseph [Young] for her to have the privilege of spending her time in the temple also."

Mary received the call and accepted the assignment to work with her fiance in the temple. On 29 January Mary stayed late following the conclusion of her labors in the temple to be "sealed upon the altar, husband and wife for time and all eternity by Amasa Lyman at twenty-five minutes to nine, witnessed by Phinehas Richards and C. W. Wandell and recorded by F. D. Richards (No. 541)."

The newlywed couple continued their labors in the temple for the next two days, and finally on 31 January they left the temple and went to Mary's home and "spent the night" together for the first time.[20]

Mary's delayed honeymoon was occasioned by the pressure to give everyone who was worthy an opportunity to receive these ordinances. By early January, Church leaders decided to "continue the administration of the ordinances of endowment night and day."[21] Many of the temple workers stayed all day and all night in the temple, obtaining only a few hours of sleep before continuing their labors. The Saints were determined to receive their blessings before they left the city. Irene Hascall Pomeroy wrote her mother that old "Mrs. Pond's mother is well, [but] does not wish to leave this place until she gets her endowments in the temple."[22]

The intense physical and emotional stress caused by mob action, preparations for the exodus west, the completion of the temple, and the everyday concerns of living on the frontier were released in various ways. During the spiritually charged period of December 1845 and January 1846, the Saints took time to refresh their minds and bodies through social recreation in the temple. William Clayton , as scribe, recorded such experiences in Brigham Young's manuscript history on 30 December 1845 and 2 January 1846. The work in the temple began at 8:10 A.M.; some twelve hours later, the endowment services ended for the day.

> The labors of the day having been brought to a close at so early an hour, viz.: eight-thirty, it was thought proper to have a little season of recreation, accordingly Brother Hanson was invited to produce his violin, which he did, and played several lively airs accompanied by Elisha Averett on his flute, among other some very good lively dancing tunes. This was too much for the gravity of Brother Joseph Young who indulged in dancing a hornpipe, and was soon joined by several others, and before the dance was over several French fours were indulged in. The first was opened by myself with Sister Whitney and Elder Heber C. Kimball and [Vilate]. The spirit of dancing increased until the whole floor was covered with dancers [as we] danced before the Lord.

The dancing continued for several hours, followed by more singing. Sister Elizabeth Ann Whitney was invited to sing and invoked "the gift of tongues, sang a beautiful song of Zion in tongues. The interpretation was given by her husband, Bishop Whitney and me," Brigham had recorded.[23] Another participant noted, "Altogether it was one of the most touching and beautiful exhibitions of the power of the spirit in the gift of tongues, which was ever witnessed."[24] Brother Brigham and Heber followed Elizabeth and spoke in tongues themselves.

On Friday, 2 January 1846, the labor of administering the endowment continued all day. Following the close of the services, Brigham Young invited those present to stay and enjoy a concert of instrumental and vocal music and dancing. Brigham Young, William Clayton noted, "alluded to the privilege which we now have of meeting in this house, and said that we would worship God in the dance, as well as in other ways."[25]

At another meeting, Brigham defended the Saints' right to dance in the temple:

> Now as to dancing in this house—there are thousands of brethren and sisters that have labored hard to build these walls and put on this roof, and they are shut out from any opportunity

of enjoying any amusement among the wicked—or in the world—
and shall they have any recreations? Yes! Where? Why, in the
Temple of the Lord. That is the very place where they can have
liberty—and we will enjoy it this winter and then leave it.[26]

Helen Mar Kimball, just a few days before her marriage, "with
quite a number of young friends, had the privilege of receiving the
holy ordinances" on New Year's evening.[27] The day was rainy, one diarist noted:

The ground [is] soft, and the mud very deep. A heavy mist rests
on the low ground under the bluffs, the sunlight is very dim being
nearly shut out the day, heavy clouds, which overspread the
whole face of the sky, and everything around wears a gloomy and
dismal aspect—but notwithstanding the unfavorable appearance
of things the brethren and sisters [assembled] together in the
house of the Lord to receive their endowments.[28]

Helen, along with her young friends, knelt down in the celestial
room following the services "in thanksgiving to God for His great
mercy and goodness to us in granting us this opportunity of meeting
together in the House of the Lord." They prayed to God that

He would continue to bless us . . . and that we might be enabled
to continue in Nauvoo in peace until all the faithful Saints had
received their endowments, and that when the time to leave here
should arrive that we might have those things that we need to
enable us to go away in comfort.

Following the prayer, Helen witnessed the marriage of two
friends. Many of those in attendance remained in the temple and participated in a marriage supper in the young couple's honor.

The wedding celebration continued until 2:30 A.M., when the sisters "retired to the side rooms, [with] the brethren stretching themselves upon the floor or on the sofas." Those in attendance were soon
in the embrace of "tired nature's sweet restorer, balmy sleep," with the
exception of the newlyweds, who with "a few of their friends, who,
being unable to close their eyes in sleep from the abundance of their
joy, passed the short hours of the morning in agreeable
conversation."[29]

A month later, Helen Mar was summoned to the temple again: "At twilight on the 3rd of February 1846, a messenger was sent by my father." The messenger informed "Horace K. Whitney and myself . . . we were to present ourselves [at the temple] that evening." She continued:

> The weather being fine we preferred to walk; and as we passed through the little graveyard at the foot of the hill a solemn covenant we entered into—to cling to each other through time and, if permitted, throughout all eternity, and this vow was solemnized at the holy altar. Though gay and high minded in many other things we reverenced the principles taught us by our parents and held them sacred, also the covenants which we had . . . made at [the temple].

On the following day, Helen Mar's parents hosted a "wedding party" for their new son-in-law and daughter:

> President Brigham Young and Bishop Newell K. Whitney were invited with members of their families and a few of our most intimate friends to attend . . . given at my father's house in honor of our marriage. . . . We had no glittering surroundings, nor had we any use for rich and costly gifts, but we had what is better, warm and loving hearts, that were knitted together by past scenes of sorrow and suffering. It was the pure and genuine friendship that could neither be bought or sold.

The party, which included music and dancing, lasted until midnight, "when the music ceased and the blessings of God were invoked upon us all and all of His people, of whatever nation they might be."[30] The newlyweds made their final preparations, and then with Church leaders left Nauvoo for the wilds of Iowa.

Before they left, however, the Saints wanted to complete the temple and dedicate the entire building to the Lord. As a result, Brigham announced to the Saints on 24 January 1846, "We shall drop all political operations and church government, and by so doing I propose that all the Saints lay down their property to be used in building the Temple, the Nauvoo House and helping the poor away [from Nauvoo]."[31]

Finally, Church leaders announced that Nauvoo must be evacuated before their enemies "hedged up the way" before their escape into the wilderness. Those unable to receive their temple blessings were promised that other temples, even bigger than this one in Nauvoo, would be built. On 3 February, Brigham went to the temple to inform those Saints waiting at the door that he "was going to get [his] wagons started and be off." He noted:

> I walked some distance from the Temple supposing the crowd would disperse, but on returning I found the house filled to overflowing. Looking upon the multitude and knowing their anxiety, as they were thirsting and hungering for the word, we continued at work diligently in the house of the Lord. Two hundred and ninety-five persons received ordinances.[32]

Brigham went home and helped Mary Ann prepare for their departure. On Friday, two days later, Brigham went back to the temple and helped administer the ordinances to many more brothers and sisters. Finally, Brigham met in the temple for the last time on Sunday, 8 February 1846:

> I met with the Council of the Twelve in the southeast corner room of the attic of the Temple. We knelt around the altar, and dedicated the building to the Most High. We asked his blessing upon our intended move to the west; also pled him to enable us some day to finish the Temple, and dedicate it to him, and we would leave it in his hands to do as he pleased. . . . We asked the Lord to accept the labors of his servants in this land. We then left the Temple.[33]

When the brethren and sisters stopped administering the ordinances of the endowment and headed west across the Mississippi River in February 1846, approximately 6,000 persons had received their temple blessings, as many as 295 in a single day.

Construction work, including plastering and painting the interior, continued until the temple was completely done. It was dedicated in a private service on 30 April and in several public services beginning on 1 May 1846.

Even before the dedication services began, the Church offered to sell the temple to the Catholic Church, hoping to receive much-needed funding to "help the poor Saints to move west."[34] Negotiations between the Catholic and Latter-day Saint representatives stalled, however. Nevertheless, rumors of the sale were widespread. Nancy Hunter, a non-Mormon Illinois resident, wrote this to her fiance in Minnesota:

> Now methinks were I an inhabitant of Hancock County, I would much rather the Mormons would have possession than the Catholics. Doubtless they have deep designing well laid plans and when once they get a foothold, there is no telling what they may do connected as they are with a foreign power.[35]

Eventually gutted by an arsonist fire in 1848, the temple was sold to the French-Icarians for one thousand dollars, but before they could restore the building, the walls were toppled by a tornado in 1850. By order of the city council, the remaining west facade was razed.

Not all of the women in Nauvoo rejoiced in the blessings given in the temple. One woman's derogatory statements were published in a local newspaper,[36] and another woman wrote with her husband an anti-Mormon tract about the temple.[37] For the vast majority of women in Nauvoo, however, the temple was worthy of every sacrifice, the endowment proved to be an uplifting experience, and participation in the sacred ordinances helped sustain them during their flight to freedom across the Mississippi River and ultimately to the Great Basin. Martha Jones Thomas summed up her feelings about the temple when she wrote:

> We esteemed it a privilege to work on the House of God . . . until it was finished. We were then called to the house to receive the blessings the Lord has in store for the faithful, which amply paid them for all their labors. Those days were grand and glorious. . . . The Saints were in the depths of poverty, but we rejoiced in building the House of the Lord.[38]

Mercy Thompson recalled years later what Joseph Smith had said following Emma's administration of initiatory ordinances: "They will bring you out of darkness into marvelous light." For Mercy and many other sister Saints, the instruction and blessing received in the Nauvoo Temple did indeed bring them "out of darkness into marvelous light."[39]

12

Into the Wilderness—
Women Pioneers

We started west in the spring with an old wagon, one
yoke of oxen, one cow and all the things we could
load in the wagon. We felt to rejoice that we escaped
with our lives.

—Mariah Pulsipher

The family of Julia Ann Hooker Shumway arrived at the Nauvoo
ferry crossing on 4 February 1846.[1] As they waited in nearly
zero-degree weather at the foot of Parley Street with an ox-drawn
wagon, they must have considered the beautiful city they were leaving behind and the uncertain destination of their journey ahead.
Soon they began their famous trip across the Mississippi River, the
first of many who would follow in the next days, weeks, and months.

The crossing occurred with the help of flat-bottomed ferry boats,
designed to carry one wagon and propelled by paddle wheels. Later,
during a brief period the river froze, which allowed the wagons to
cross the river on the ice.

Many sister Saints in Nauvoo picked out only those items from
their homes that they thought would be necessary for the long march
west, leaving many personal treasures and furnishings behind. One
item that many sisters fortuitously took was paper or journals and ink.
For some it may have been the last few cents they owned which purchased these items. For others, it was a gift from a friend.

Patty Bartlett Sessions began a "day book" in February 1846, just
two days before leaving her home to cross the river for Iowa. She
wrote on that day, "A Day Book given to me Patty Sessions by Sylvia
Lyon this 10th day of Feb. 1846. Patty Sessions her book. I am now

fifty one years six days old. February 10, 1846, City of Joseph, Hancock County, Illinois."

She continued her first entry, "My things are now packed ready for the west, have been and put Richard's wife to bed [as a midwife she had delivered a baby] with a daughter. In the afternoon put Sister Harriet Young to bed with a son." On the following day, she made herself a "cap, and in the evening went to the [Seventies] Hall to see the scenery of the massacre of Joseph and Hyrum Smith."

On 12 February, Patty and husband bade her older married children and "friends good-bye and started for the west," seeking refuge from the rising storm of anti-Mormon activity in Hancock County.

The first night on the trail was pleasant, providing a time to relax from the busy rush of leaving the city. She noted on 13 February, "attended prayers in our wagon and have eaten our own breakfast." On Valentine's Day, Patty wrote:

This morning it snows. Sister Oakly has set up all night because her wagon did not get across the river. I gave her and Mariann and Carlos Murray some breakfast. We are now ready to leave the bank of the river [and] go to the other camp. Three o'clock—we have arrived to the other camp on Sugar Creek. It has just [stopped] storming. The ground covered with snow and water and is very bad underfoot. Attended prayer in Father John Smith's tent.

The following day was Sunday, and time was taken to write letters to family members still in Nauvoo and to visit other sisters in the camp. The Sessions did not yet have a tent. On 19 February she noted, "It snows hard, the wind blows and no tent yet." Soon cloth arrived for the flaps, but "no twine to sew it with." On 23 February canvas arrived, and Patty began to sew it for the tent. Two days later, she trudged through the snow to "put Jackson Redding wife [Jane Whiting Redding] to bed."

A few days later, John Scott's wife had a miscarriage, and Patty helped all she could to care for and comfort her. When one of the companies moved from Sugar Creek on 28 February, Patty and her husband went along. Within a few days they lost their cow, and Patty was forced to take over driving the wagon as her husband went to look for it. On 6 March Patty backtracked ten miles to help her daughter. She wrote, "I go back ten miles" to see Sarah Ann, who was "sick." Two days later, Sarah Ann delivered a son. Patty's children's families were now catching up with them. By 9 March, Patty and her family were sixty miles from Nauvoo: "Everyone together . . . but our cow." [2]

Escaping Nauvoo did not, however, end the persecution. Many Saints found shelter and employment in several communities in an effort to prepare for the journey west.

In Farmington, Iowa, several Latter-day Saint families sought refuge. Eliza Dana Gibbs recalled,

> They would take [a] man if they knew he was a Mormon and hang him up to a tree or anything that would answer their purpose in the street in open daylight. They would hang him until nearly dead before taking him down. One old gentleman by the name of McBride, an old revolutionary soldier, died in consequence of the hanging. They would also cut holes in the ice in the river and hold them in the water until nearly dead. [3]

A young teenager, Mary Ann Stearns, reported that she left the city on 14 February 1846. She wrote:

> Our teams crossed the Mississippi and started westward, six emigrant wagons . . . [including] a one-horse wagon . . . with little Parley driving old Dick. Mother had arranged for her wagon quite comfortably. Grandfather Frost had made some chests to fit the wagon in which were packed all that was in wisdom to take with us and on which our bed was made. . . . Most of our provisions were in the big wagon, but mother had a goodly supply cooked and along with us ready for immediate use.

Though time does change some things, not so for all—the children "commenced calling for [the goodies] as soon as we had gotten fairly started." Soon the family crossed the river on a ferry boat, when "it commenced snowing." As they "traveled along we passed camp after camp of the Saints just by the roadside, sitting around the campfire with the snow coming down in great flakes." Mary noted the conditions of those huddled around the fires:

> Women and children with damp and drabbled clothing, men wading around caring for the cattle that were to be their pro-

pellers to a place of safety, mothers trying to prepare food for their families over the blazing log heaps, a sight fit to daunt the stoutest heart, but no, every one of our acquaintances that we greeted in passing had a cheering word and a smiling countenance.

One sister, a sixty-year-old woman, Mother McArthur, was never forgotten by young Mary. She was "seated by her campfire with an umbrella over her head and the bread pan in her lap, making some of her good biscuits," Mary vividly recalled. Her husband, standing close by, asked the family, "Won't you stay to dinner?" The family, however, continued its journey through the snowfall. Sister McArthur, "with smiling face said, 'We'll overtake you before long.' "[4]

Widowed Mary Fielding Smith, the legal guardian of John, Jerusha, and Sarah Smith (children of Hyrum and Jerusha Barden) and the parent of two children herself, Joseph F. and Martha Ann, left the city alone to face the difficult march west. Martha Ann recalled the difficult experience when they left later in the year:

> We left our home just as it was, our furniture, and the fruit trees hanging full of rosy cheeked peaches. We bid goodbye to the loved home that reminded us of our beloved father everywhere we turned.
>
> I was five years old when we started from Nauvoo. We crossed over the Mississippi in the skiff in the dusk of the evening. We bid goodbye to our dear old feeble grandmother [Lucy Mack Smith]. I can never forget the bitter tears she shed when she bid us goodbye for the last time in this life. She knew it would be the last time she would see her son's family. We did not realize this so much at that time as we have since.[5]

Eliza Marie Partridge Lyman did not dare brave the cold the first few nights after her departure: "We went to John Tanner's [who lived on the Iowa side of the river] and stayed several days as the weather was very cold and we were not in a hurry to camp out till we were obliged to. After a few days we left Father Tanner and joined the camp of Saints on Sugar Creek."[6]

Before moving on to the Sugar Creek encampment, Eliza Marie and her sister-wives, Diantha and Caroline, waited for their husband to return. Amasa Lyman went back across the river to visit another

Sutcliffe Maudsley's painting of Eliza Partridge, completed in Nauvoo. Eliza married Joseph Smith, and later, following the Martyrdom, married Amasa Lyman.

wife who remained. While at the Tanners', Eliza Marie wrote, "I cut and made a dress for Sister Tanner." In the evening Brother Lyman returned to his family, "bringing his wife Maria with him, I was heartily glad to see her," Eliza Marie wrote. A special bonding between them began already and would only increase on the journey west.[7]

While many Saints made their preparations to leave Nauvoo, Louisa Barnes Pratt wondered what to do, as her husband, Addison, was on a Church mission in the Pacific Islands. Without his support and without any other relatives in town, she felt overwhelmed by the call to leave Nauvoo and asked Church leaders for advice. Brother Brigham responded cheerfully, but clearly, "Ox team salvation is the safest way."

Louisa questioned why "those who had sent my husband to the ends of the earth did not call to inquire whether I could prepare myself for such a perilous journey." She was told:

"Sister Pratt, they expect you to be smart enough to go yourself without help, and even to assist others." The reply awakened in me a spirit of self-reliance. I replied, "Well, I will show them what I can do."

Determined to go it alone, Louisa outfitted a wagon and drove out of Nauvoo feeling "comparatively happy."[8]

Eliza R. Snow left Nauvoo with Hannah Hogaboon and Stephen Markham in February 1846. Eliza wrote in her diary,

We left our home and went as far as Brother Hiram Kimball's where we spent the night and through the generosity of Sister [Sarah] Kimball and mother [Lydia] Granger, made some additional preparations for our journey.[9]

On 13 February, the following day, Eliza crossed the Mississippi River, where she found her brother Lorenzo encamped in a tent next to Mary Ann Yearsley's family. "We lodged in Brother Yearsley's tent which before morning was covered with snow."

14th After breakfast I went into the buggy and did not leave till the next day. Sister [Hannah Hogaboon] Markham and I did some needlework though the melting snow dripped through our cover.[10]

During the next few days in camp, Eliza spent time writing in her diary and composing poems. "My dormitory, sitting room, writing office, and frequently dining room," she wrote, "was the buggy in which Mrs. [Hannah] Markham, her little son, David, and I rode." On 19 February, a "snowstorm commenced in the night and continued through the day." She "amused" herself by writing the following:

The Camp of Israel
A Song for the Pioneers, No. 1

Altho' in woods and tents we dwell
Shout, shout, O Camp of Israel
No *christian mobs* on earth can bind
Our thoughts, or steal our peace of mind.

Chorus

Tho' we fly from vile aggression
We'll maintain our pure profession—
Seek a peaceable possession
Far from Gentiles and oppression.

We better live in tents and smoke
Than wear the cursed gentile yoke—
We better from our country fly
Than by mobocracy to die.

We've left The City of Nauvoo
And our beloved Temple too,
And to the wilder we'll go
Amid the winter frosts and snow.

Our homes were dear—we lov'd them well
Beneath our roofs we hop'd to dwell,
And honor the great God's commands
By mutual rights of christian lands.

Our persecutors will not cease
Their murd'rous spoiling of our peace
And have decreed that we must go
To wilds where reeds and rushes grow.

The Camp—the Camp—its numbers swell
Shout, shout O Camp of Israel!

> The King the Lord of hosts is near
> His armies guard our front and rear.

During one particularly cold evening, Eliza's feet were frostbitten, "which occasioned me considerable inconvenience for several weeks." On 28 February, the first company of some six to seven hundred Saints moved out from the temporary camp. They were able to travel only four miles because of the condition of the road. Eliza wrote:

> We traveled four miles and put up for the night when the prospect, at first sight, was dreary enough. It was nearly sunset—very cold, with four or five inches of snow on the ground, but with brave hearts, strong hands, and plenty of spades and shovels, the men removed the snow, and suddenly transformed the bleak desert into a joyous town of cloth houses with log-heap fires, and a multitude of cheerful inhabitants. The next day the Nauvoo Band came up, and its stirring strains were wafted abroad and re-echoed on the responsive breeze.

Eliza wrote another poem, "Let Us Go."

> Let us go—let us go to the wilds for a home
> Where the wolf and the roe and the buffalo roam—
> Where beneath our own vines, we in peace, may enjoy
> The fruits of our labors, with none to annoy.
>
> Let us go—let us go where our Rights are secure—
> Where the waters are clear and the atmosphere pure—
> Where the hand of oppression has never been felt—
> Where the blood of prophets have never been spilt.
>
> Let us go—let us go where the Kingdom of God
> Will be seen in its Order extending abroad—
> Where the Priesthood of heaven, unopposed will go forth
> In the regeneration of man and of earth.

Eliza knew that her situation was better than that of many of the sisters who came out of Nauvoo. They "walked all day, rain or shine, and at night prepared supper for their families, with no sheltering tents," she wrote. These sisters made "their beds in, and under, wagons that contained their earthly all." She continued her narrative:

> Frequently with intense sympathy and admiration I watched the mother when, forgetful of her own fatigue and destitution, she took unwearied pains to fix up in the most palatable form . . . food, and as she dealt it out, was cheering the hearts of her children, while, as I truly believe, her own was listed to God in fervent prayer that their lives might be preserved, and, above all, that they might honor him in the religion of which she was an exile from the home once sacred to her, for the sake of those precious ones which God had committed to her care.[11]

The prayers were always answered, but not in the way these mothers hoped for. One sister lost her four-year-old daughter, little Mary. The mother cried out, "Oh, I can never leave her here in this lonely place." The grief-torn sister was consoled when someone suggested that the body be taken back to Nauvoo to be laid by "loved ones and then it would not seem so terrible." When they returned to the city, it was "as still as death, and few persons seen on the streets. . . . The little grave was soon ready, and the little pilgrim was laid to rest until the resurrection's morn."[12]

Eliza Snow's diary continued as her company arrived at the small community of Farmington on 3 March 1846, "Camp moved in a body eight miles which was on the bank of the Des Moine [River]." The journey became somewhat easier, as they were slowed down for several days by "mud and water" on the trail during the first few days. "We passed through the town of Farmington where the inhabitants manifested great curiosity and more levity than sympathy for our houseless situation."

During the evening while in camp, Eliza was "agreeably surprised by Sister [Elizabeth Ann] Whitney's appearance in front of the buggy where I was seated eating my supper." She rejoiced at the opportunity of visiting with a friend from Nauvoo, "having been before this time separated from all old associates."[13]

It was about six weeks since the first sister Saints left Nauvoo, and now on the trail they met together on 5 April 1846 to refresh themselves physically and spiritually. Eliza noted:

At four o'clock, according to the instruction that each tent should meet together in their several divisions and partake of the sacrament, we attended to the ordinance for the first time since we left the City. My heart was made to rejoice in the privilege of once more commemorating the death of him whom I desire to behold. Roll on ye wheels of time! Hasten thou long anticipated period when he shall again stand upon the earth.[14]

A few days later Heber C. Kimball walked past Eliza's "study" and, after the usual greetings, she told him that she wanted to be considered as one of his children. He consented, and immediately "I told him that I should claim a father's blessing." He responded positively to the request. Eliza demanded it then and there at her buggy. He replied, "Now?" She informed him that she was ready, and he then said, "A father's blessing shall rest upon you from this time forth." Eliza finished her daily entry, "From this time I call him father."[15]

Zina Diantha Huntington Jacobs was pregnant when she left Nauvoo in February 1846. A few weeks later on 22 March, Zina delivered a baby boy, whom she named Henry Chariton, after the name of his father and the river beside which he was born. Her personal history recounts the events:

We reached the Chariton River between three and four weeks after leaving Nauvoo. I had been told in the Temple that I should acknowledge God even in a miracle in my deliverance in woman's hour of trouble, which hour had now come. We traveled one [morning] about five miles, when I called for a halt in our march. There was but one person with me—Mother Lyman. There on the bank of the Chariton River, I was delivered of a fine son. Occasionally the wagon had to be stopped that I might take breath. Thus I journeyed on. But I did not mind the hardship of my situation, for my life had been preserved, and my babe was so beautiful.[16]

Ten days later, Eliza Marie Partridge Lyman arrived at the Chariton River:

Started early in the morning, traveled twelve miles, came to the Chariton river, too, in the rest of our loading and crossed over. We went on to the bluff on the opposite side and camped for the night. Two brethren from Brother Pratt's came, met us before we crossed the river with seven yoke of oxen to help us on the rest of the way to their camp, a distance of seven miles on the west side of the east fork of Shoal Creek. At the river we came across Henry Jacob's wagon in the mud. His wife Zina, sick in bed on top of the load, so near the wet cover she could hardly raise her head, a babe in her arms, but a few days old, and no other wagon near or friend to do any thing for her except her husband.[17]

It was in trials that the Nauvoo sisterhood blossomed as they reached out to touch each other's lives.

Many sister Saints did not leave in February for several reasons. Diantha Farr was married to William Clayton on 9 January 1845, and now as her husband crossed the river with three wives, five children, and his mother, young seventeen-year-old Diantha was left in the city in the last stages of pregnancy.

On 16 March 1846, nearly a month following her husband's departure into the wilderness, Diantha wrote:

My beloved, but absent William:

It rejoiced my heart to hear a word from you, but it would have given me more joy to have had a line from you, but I am thankful for a little. You know that is the way to get more. To tell you I want to see you is useless, yet true you are constantly in my mind by day and I dream about you almost every night. As to my health it is about the same as when you left, only a little more so. I often wish you had taken your house along, for it looks so lonesome. It seems a long time since I saw you, but how much longer it will be before I can have the privilege of conversing with you face to face it is yet unknown to me. Father is going as fast as he can. He wants to get away soon after conference if possible. Mother sends her best respects to you. Often says how lonesome it seems. Don't you think William will come tonight. I expect it would cheer her heart as well as mind to hear your voice once more. Dear William, write as often as you can send, for one line from you would do my heart good. I must draw to a close for I am in haste. I will try to compose myself as well as I can. I never shall consent to have you leave again. Farewell, Farewell.[18]

Just shy of one month later, William Clayton camped at Locust

Creek on 15 April. He was tired, having been on watch the previous evening, but news arrived from Nauvoo—good news about his young wife. In a letter delivered to a nearby pioneer camp, William learned that Diantha delivered a "fine fat boy" fifteen days earlier on 30 March.

Clayton wrote in his diary:

Wednesday, [April] 15th. . . . This morning Ellen Kimball came to me and wished me much joy. She said Diantha has a son. I told her I was afraid it was not so, but she said Brother Pond had received a letter. I went over to Pond's and he read that she had a fine fat boy on the 30th [March], but she was very sick with ague and mumps. Truly I feel to rejoice at this intelligence, but feel sorry to hear of her sickness.

During the evening William Pitt's band played, and at the conclusion Clayton invited some of his fellow band members to come to his tent to celebrate the birth of his son. "We had a very pleasant time," Clayton noted, "playing and singing until about twelve o'clock and drank health to my son. . . . This [early] morning I composed a new song 'All Is Well.' " He concluded his diary entry:

I feel to thank my Heavenly Father for my boy and pray that he will spare and preserve his life and that of his mother and so order it so that we may soon meet again. O Lord bless thine handmaid and fill her with thy Spirit, make her healthy that her life may be prolonged and that we may live upon the earth and honor the cause of truth. In the evening I asked the President if he would not suffer me to send for Diantha. He consented.[19]

Another sister Saint still in Nauvoo was Irene Hascall Pomeroy. Irene asked her family, including her father, mother, and brother—all living in the East—to bring supplies to Nauvoo as they began their preparations to go west. She moved from her home and in January was living at Lorin Farr's home, next to the Woodruff home. Among the unusual items requested were her "paint brushes and that piece of green paint" she gave her brother. She also asked them to visit a neighbor, and if his "fig tree is alive I want you [to] press a leaf for me."[20]

During the late spring and early summer, converts still arrived in the city for a short rest before beginning their trek across Iowa. Ursulia B. Hascall left Boston on a ship bound for New Orleans with her son, Thales. She and her son were seasick most of the time, and then Thales "caught the measles on board ship." She arrived at the mouth of the Mississippi exhausted and hungry. Ursulia wanted to travel "steerage passage" to conserve the little funds she had, but found the boat "crowded with all kinds of human beings, horses, and dogs. No place for us there." They spent four dollars for a cabin and began their last leg of the journey to Nauvoo.

After several delays, Ursulia and Thales arrived at one of the docks along the river at Nauvoo. "I saw Irene [her sister] come bounding across lots, you may guess the rest, I found her babe much handsomer than I expected." She argued that the baby girl did not have "one homely feature." In Nauvoo the tired and hungry travelers found lots of food, including pork, dried mackerel, veal, sugar, and "a box of raisins." She told her sister and brother-in-law that they all expected to begin their journey west in about two weeks.[21]

The Hascall-Pomeroy families left Nauvoo on 30 May with a "good wagon" at four o'clock in the afternoon. "[We] went down to the Mississippi River [and] found a boat to convey us across."

Ursulia wrote her sister's family on 19 September 1846 and described their departure with three yoke of oxen, and "with flour enough to last us one year, ham, sausages, dry fish, lard, . . . hundred pounds of sugar, sixteen of coffee, ten of raisins, rice with all the other items we wish to use in cooking."

Ursulia described the wagon as "long enough for both our beds made on the flour barrels, chest, and other things." She and her son slept at the back, and her sister, son-in-law, and granddaughter slept at the front, "if we camped too late to pitch our tent." The wagon was painted red. They attached a "hen coop on the end with four hens" in it. The canvas was painted also so that "the heaviest showers and storms do not beat through only a few drops now and then."

They camped the first night some three miles from the river. Before retiring they had a dinner which consisted of bread, milk, and a piece of pie. Within a few days they commenced their "journey in earnest." She continued, "It was not many days before we bid adieu to the last house we expected to see." They traveled for "hours and saw nothing but the wide expanse of heaven and the waving prairie grass, not a tree or a bush."[22]

In Nauvoo, Jane Snyder Richards prepared to leave her home on 10 June 1846. At the time of her departure she was nearly eight months pregnant. While on the road west, Jane was left with her sister-wife, Elizabeth McFae Richards, when their husband began his missionary journey to England.

Jane gave birth to a son, who died shortly after birth, a few days following her husband's departure. A midwife came to her assistance, and upon completion of her duties asked rather gruffly, "Are you prepared to pay me?" Jane responded, "If it were to save my life, I could not give you any money, for I have none; but if you see anything you want, take it." At this point the woman rummaged through the wagon and took a beautiful woolen bedspread, saying, "I may as well take it, for you'll never live to see it." The woman hurriedly left Jane with a dead baby at her side and went back to her position in the wagon company.

Jane's only child, a two-year-old daughter named Wealthy, was also ill and died shortly after their arrival at the Mormon staging ground. Elizabeth also was sick during the entire period and relied upon Jane to assist her. During all these afflictions Jane stated that she only lived because she could not die.[23]

Another sister Saint who remained in Nauvoo during the spring, Martha Haven, wrote to her mother in Sutton, Massachusetts, in July 1846, just as she was preparing to go west with her husband, Jesse. Abigail Hall, her mother, visited her briefly in Nauvoo. Martha's letter begins, "The joy of meeting and the pain of separating have passed, and I am again alone." She wrote from Nauvoo:

> I have been anxious to hear from you, to know how you got home. I should have written long before this had I known where to have told you to direct your letters. We think soon of going to Farmington, Iowa. We shall probably stay there till fall; so direct your letters there till you hear to the contrary. My health has been growing poorer since you left. Have been to meeting but once since I went with you.

Her husband "talks of boxing our things ready for the wilderness." She reported to her mother, "We have sold our place for a trifle to a *Baptist minister*. All we got was a cow and two pairs of steers, worth about sixty dollars in trade." She continued, "I feel thankful that I have had the privilege of having a visit from my *dear* Mother. I can

A very large canvas portrait of Louisa Maria Tanner Lyman, Amasa Lyman, and son Francis Marion Lyman, completed in Nauvoo. The family carefully loaded this family portrait and transported it across the plains to their new home in the West.

tell you I felt lonesome enough after I got home from the river the day you started."[24]

Sarah Leavitt and her family left Nauvoo, but soon her husband became ill. As Sarah and her daughters tried to comfort him, he began to sing, "Come, let us anew, our journey pursue, Roll around with the year, And never stand still till the Master appears." Sarah recalled that he "sang that hymn as long as he had strength to sing it and then wanted Elisa [one of his daughters] to sing it. He died without a struggle or a groan." A grave was prepared, and the family said good-bye as they turned their faces west. Sarah, taking command of the situation, noted, "A few days later we all started for the bluffs."[25]

Finally by the end of summer in 1846, several vigilante groups stepped up pressure on the remaining Saints in Nauvoo to force their exodus. The majority of Saints evacuated the city by fall 1846. Many were camped along the trail leading to Winter Quarters, where Brigham Young established a temporary Church headquarters. While many Saints made their way to the Indian lands of Nebraska, a few hundred Mormons remained in Nauvoo.

Several sister Saints remained in the city, including Joseph and Hyrum's sisters, Lucy Millikin, Sophronia McCleary, Catherine Salisbury, and their mother, Lucy Mack Smith. Emma also stayed behind. When mob violence increased, she left Nauvoo and traveled 120 miles to the north to Fulton City, where she stayed for five months before returning to the city. "I [have] no friend left but God and no place to go but home," she noted.[26] Sarah Kimball remained behind with her husband, but several years later finally made the trek west to Salt Lake City.

Among those who still found themselves in the city were recent converts who had just arrived in Nauvoo and were now without funds to continue their trip west. Eventually, the anti-Mormons attacked them in what has become known as the Battle of Nauvoo, a week of skirmishes in which several Mormons were killed, including Captain William Anderson, his son Augustus, and David Norris.

After four days of fighting in the streets, the defenders surrendered. These Saints were then forced to cross the river to Montrose, where they were critically short of supplies and shelter. As many as seven hundred refugees were camped along the banks of the Mississippi River. Many had neither wagon nor tent to protect themselves from the elements. Food was scarce, and many starved or died from exposure during the next few days.

Jane Johnston recalled that as she approached the river to cross to Iowa during the speedy retreat, a mob surrounded her wagon and demanded that she give them any weapons she had in her possession. "I then had a pistol in my bosom," she said, "which I drew out and told them it was there, and that I would use it before I gave it up." The mob retreated, but threatened to return at night and throw her into the river.

Jane crossed the river with her family; her husband was in Canada at the time. Lacking provisions and shelter, Jane received a half bushel of corn meal and a half dozen cucumbers, borrowed a tent, and "had women that were being delivered of child put in it." She continued her story:

> I was the mid-wife, and delivered nine babies that night. We had nothing to sweeten anything until the Lord sent honey dew, which we gathered from the bushes until we got all the sweets we wanted. I also boiled maple juice and got cakes of maple sugar.[27]

Widow Mary Field hurriedly packed her wagon and took her six children down to the main ferry. Her daughter recalled:

> We hurried to pack some food, cooking utensils, clothing and bedding, which was afterward unpacked and strewn over the ground by the mob as they searched for fire-arms. A sympathetic member of the mob offered to carry mother's baby down to the ferry. Mother had some bread already in the kettles to bake. Of course she did not have time to bake, so she hung it on the reach of our wagon and cooked it after we crossed the Mississippi River.

Mary continued her story about the hasty exodus from Nauvoo following the Battle of Nauvoo:

> The suffering and sadness of that camp I shall never forget. It is impossible to describe the cries of the hungry children, the sadness of others for the loss of their loved ones. What a terrible night of misery. We didn't even have a light, except a candle which flickered out in the wind and rain as it was carried from one place to another.[28]

When news of this situation reached Brigham Young, he sent

supplies to relieve their suffering and to bring them to the main staging grounds at Winter Quarters. Twenty wagons, seventeen oxen, forty-one cows, and several volunteers arrived on 6 October.

On 9 October, before starting their movement westward, these Saints witnessed what to them was a miracle sent from God. Even as the Lord had fed the children of Israel in the wilderness with manna, a flock of quail landed in the Saints' camp. The birds were exhausted and easy to kill. These birds provided much needed nourishment for the camp.

A second rescue mission was sent from Winter Quarters, arriving in late October to assist those still remaining. The majority of those who wanted to go west were evacuated to Winter Quarters by November 1846.

Many sisters were unable to keep a daily record of their escape from Nauvoo, but later in Utah, they recalled their experiences and had them recorded in autobiographies or reminiscences. Mariah Pulsipher remembered,

> We started west in the spring with an old wagon, one yoke of oxen, one cow, and all the things we could load in the wagon. We felt to rejoice that we escaped with our lives. We traveled on with a small company through mud and storm, stopping along the way as the men could find work.[29]

These sister Saints, along with their families, made their way across the river and into the wilderness of Iowa with at least one hope. "The universal desire [of the Mormons] seems to be to get away to a land of peace," reported an adept editor of the *Illinois State Register* to the people of the state that was unable to protect these citizens from their enemies.[30]

13

A Time to Remember—
The Nauvoo Legacy

The society has done well—their principles are to
practice holiness. . . . By seeing the blessings of the
endowment rolling on and the kingdom increasing
and spreading from sea to sea, we will rejoice.
—Joseph Smith

A crucial and unsung legacy of sister Saints in Nauvoo was the
support system they supplied to their fathers, brothers, husbands, and sons; they helped make Nauvoo and its men successful.
Men and women worked together on the necessities for immediate survival, but the women did almost all the domestic chores, freeing men
to go hunting and fishing, plan political campaigns and run for office,
or go on Church missions and attend priesthood quorum meetings.

The universal trials of frontier life—neverending work, sickness,
poverty, and death—exacted a heavy price from the sister Saints
gathered together on the banks of the Mississippi River. Nevertheless,
their efforts, trials, and stories had a tremendous impact beyond Nauvoo. The social organizations in Utah, both formal and informal,
took their forms from those developed in Nauvoo during the seven
years of sojourn (1839–46).

Following the Saints' departure from their city in 1846 and during the next several decades, sister Saints participated in many causes
in their new wilderness home in Utah. They brought with them a
tradition of participation in the Church. The sister Saints in New
York, Ohio, Missouri, Illinois, and Winter Quarters received personal
revelations, prophesied, spoke in tongues, and performed various
Spirit-directed activities in formal and informal settings.

An unknown English Saint's portrait (ca. 1840). Many of the early Saints did not leave a personal record of their experience in the City of Joseph; but they, like this unknown Church member, left spiritual roots for Latter-day Saint women. They created a legacy—practical and spiritual—that will always be remembered

These same sister Saints prayed and voted, along with their male family members, in Church meetings and elsewhere; in Nauvoo they participated in sacred temple ceremonies and ritual. The involvement of women in diverse enterprises in Nauvoo was quite remarkable for the time. The Relief Society, unlike many of the women's benevolent societies of the day, went beyond the responsibilities of taking care of the poor in Nauvoo and contributed in various practical ways to the community, including the building of the temple.

The Utah pioneer woman's activity in many spheres increased following the Civil War period as women found opportunities to channel their energy in improving the quality of life in the state and the nation. Zina Diantha Huntington Jacobs Young, for example, studied obstetrics and was a midwife in Utah.

Before 1850, most women in America continued to "adhere to an interpretation of evangelical womanhood which stressed invisible influence."[1] The sisters in Nauvoo, on the other hand, were involved in administrative and spiritual service and leadership among the women of their communities as they administered their society and programs in Nauvoo and later in Utah.

The Nauvoo generation of sisters had a long-lasting effect upon the Church's women's organizations in Utah. The first five Relief Society presidents—Emma Smith, Eliza R. Snow, Zina Diantha Huntington Young, Bathsheba W. Smith, and Emmeline B. Wells—all participated or associated with the sisters who were members of the Nauvoo Female Relief Society.[2] While each had their own distinctive administrative style, unique talents, and vision of the sisterhood, all were profoundly influenced by the Nauvoo experience, an experience that helped shape the sister Saints' experience during the next one hundred and fifty years.

There were other legacies of Latter-day Saint women who lived in the frontier of the Mississippi Valley from 1839–46. Joseph empowered the sisters in Nauvoo when he said, "I now turn the key to you in the name of God." They paved the way for social, political, economic, religious, and personal advancement, not just for the few Anglo-Saxon Mormon women gathered together in Nauvoo but for all women throughout the world from that time forward. A moral order was established that would call into question previously conceived ideas about the role and status of women, especially those clothed in religious language.[3]

The shackles of false traditions that disenfranchised women since the earliest time, except in those rare moments when people of God experienced Zion in all its characteristics, were now to be removed in dramatic ways.

The organization of the first Relief Society in Nauvoo preceded the convention of 1848 in Seneca Falls, New York, which has been generally identified as the beginning of the women's movement in America.

Women Church leaders noted this correlation on several occasions. Sarah G. Kimball wrote, "The sure foundations of the suffrage cause were deeply and permanently laid on the 17th of March 1842."[4] Emmeline B. Wells noted that women's formal and informal participation in religious activities in Nauvoo initiated

> one of the most important eras in the history of woman. It presented the great woman-question to the Latter-day Saints, previous to the woman's rights organizations, . . . not in any aggressive form as woman opposed to man, but as a co-worker and helpmeet

in all that relates to the well-being and advancement of both, and mutual promoting of the best interests of the community at large.[5]

Initially a large area of responsibility for the sisters in Nauvoo was simply a formalization of labors commonly performed by women in the community and family circles. Mormon women provided for the poor, comforted the bereaved, and cared for the sick, all of which figure largely in their writings. Nevertheless, a seed was planted in Nauvoo and nurtured by the sisters following their exodus west that had profound theological and social ramifications.

The teachings and vision of the sisters in Nauvoo sparked strong feelings of the possibility of a new and brighter day for women. This was especially true in the "blessing meetings" at Winter Quarters and in Salt Lake City, which was a feature of the sisters' religious life in Kirtland, but expanded in Nauvoo. "Altho' thrust out from the land of our forefathers and from the endearments of civiliz'd life," wrote Eliza R. Snow in late spring 1847, "this is truly a glorious time with the mothers and daughters in Zion."[6]

The sisters were empowered in Nauvoo through the blessing received in their call to serve in the community.

Eventually, during the 1867 reinstitution of the Relief Society in the various units of the Church in Utah, additional activities beyond the traditional roles assigned to women were rapidly introduced. The sisters increased their roles in economic, political, and commercial activities. They built and owned Relief Society halls; ran cooperatives; raised silk; bought, stored, and sold grain; and collectively supported the medical education of women as doctors and nurses, eventually establishing their own Deseret Hospital in Salt Lake City.

One scholar of the women's movement noted recently:

One of the interesting anomalies of nineteenth-century women's history is the fact that one of its most vocal feminist groups comprised the Mormon women of Utah defending their territorial right to vote and their religious practice of polygyny, called "plural," or "patriarchal" marriage. Utah was the second territory in the United States to grant female suffrage. . . . Utah women were the first to vote in the country.[7]

Mormon women understood their positions, and when the

women's rights controversy stormed during the late 1860s and early 1870s, Eliza R. Snow proclaimed that Mormon women in Utah enjoyed more "rights than any women in the world."[8]

Within two years of obtaining the franchise, the sisters in Utah established the *Woman's Exponent*, a newspaper owned, managed, supported, and produced by women for women. The *Woman's Exponent*, the second women's periodical in the trans-Mississippi West, provided jobs for the sisters in Utah as editors, business agents, and compositors, and served as an outlet for dozens of women who wanted to write poetry and prose. It carried the news of the day and discussed women's rights issues throughout the nation. Its masthead declared for "The Rights of Women of Zion, and the Rights of Women of All Nations."

The 1870s saw doors open wider for women in Utah.[9] In 1872 Georgie Snow and Phoebe W. Couzins were admitted to the Utah bar, and within two years Elizabeth Stowe Higgs and Anna King were seated on the jury at a coroner's inquest, the first female jurors in the territory and the nation.[10] By this time it was reported that Utah developed a "respectable class of professional and highly literate women," and another visitor marveled that "they close no career on a woman in Utah."[11]

Romania B. Pratt Penrose, the first Utah woman to earn her M.D., and Ellis Shipp, who in 1878 also became a medical doctor, helped prepare the way for the establishment of the Deseret Hospital in Salt Lake City. Susa Young Gates published another women's periodical, *Young Woman's Journal*, beginning in 1889.

Ironically, it was the violation of the traditional stereotype as housekeeper that apparently aroused a great deal of the antipolygamy criticism. It is certain that Mormon women were in "double jeopardy" as they attempted to hold fast to their beliefs on one hand while attempting to fulfill their vision of self-definition, often misunderstood and certainly misrepresented by many non-Mormons.[12] When the sisters in Utah defended their religious practices, such as plural marriage, they challenged the contemporary view of dependent womanhood, urging a vision of more competent womanhood. An editorial in the *Woman's Exponent* stated: "We have left the petted slave in the Greek household, to go onward and forward. We have left the idle toy and the painted doll. . . . God lead us to find the true Woman in the free American home.[13]

In 1891, the women of the Church joined the National Council of Women, and within the year the Relief Society changed its name to the "National Women's Relief Society." When Utah was admitted as a state into the Union, women voted, and Dr. Martha Hughes Cannon was elected a state senator.

In 1898 the first full-time independently authorized single women missionaries were called, Amanda Inez Knight and Lucy Jane Brimhall. During the same year the Relief Society Nurse School was organized in Salt Lake City. On Susan B. Anthony's birthday, the sisters from Utah presented her a black dress made of Utah silk.

Another legacy from Nauvoo, manifested in Utah during the nineteenth century, was the establishment of a community of women, the presence of sisterhood, cooperation, and female bonding.

It is true that as in all aspects of Church organization, times have changed the nineteenth-century women's groups as they attempt to fulfill a mission in an ever-expanding Church with new challenges and focuses.[14] One of the significant benefits of any study of history is the amazing realization that people and societies change, that life a short time ago was very different.

The diaries, letters, and other primary documents from Nauvoo deepen this realization. Nevertheless, while the form and function of the early Church women's organizations have been modified over time, the spiritual heritage of Nauvoo and early Utah still remain a vitalizing link among the Saints, especially those who seek their spiritual roots among the teachings of Joseph Smith and the lives and thoughts of the early sister Saints on the Illinois frontier along the banks of the Mississippi River.

In 1881, Sarah M. Kimball, an original member of the Relief Society and at the time its general secretary, prepared a time capsule to be opened in 1930, the one hundredth anniversary of the establishment of the Church. When opened, a message from her was found which stated:

Hon. Secretary: This is dedicated to you with the fond hope and firm belief that you are enjoying many advantages and blessings that were not enjoyed by your predecessors. May God abundantly bless you and your labors. (Signed) Sarah M. Kimball, Sec. Relief Society, Salt Lake City, April 1st, 1881.

This was the hope of sister Saints ever since Joseph had said that they would see "better days." Sarah M. Kimball hoped for the same thing when she prayed that the next generation of women would be "enjoying many advantages and blessings that were not enjoyed by [our] predecessors."[15]

Another participant in the Nauvoo experience, Elizabeth Ann Whitney, wrote in 1878:

> The [1842] Relief Society was small in numbers, but the Prophet foretold great things concerning the future of this organization, many of which I have lived to see fulfilled; but there are many things which yet remain to be fulfilled in the future.[16]

Zina Diantha Huntington Young, Jane S. Richards, and Bathsheba W. Smith wrote to the sisters "throughout the world" a letter of greetings in preparation for celebrating the fiftieth anniversary of the founding of the Relief Society. They said on that occasion:

> It will be fifty years on Thursday, March 17, 1892, since Joseph Smith the Prophet organized the Relief Society in Nauvoo, Illinois, by divine inspiration. . . . This most momentous event for women, causes us to view with wonder the past, with gratitude the present, and with faith the future.[17]

While the legacy of the sister Saints in Nauvoo is to be remembered and celebrated, it was the future to which these sisters looked, a future in which "many things yet remain to be fulfilled" for the women of the Church and the world. As the Prophet Joseph Smith said, "The society has done well—their principles are to practice holiness. . . . By seeing the blessings of the endowment rolling on and the kingdom increasing and spreading from sea to sea, we will rejoice."[18]

During an early meeting of the sisters in Nauvoo, Lucy Mack Smith shared her vision of the sisterhood she expected to enjoy with them then and in the future, a vision that remains with the sister Saints today: "We must cherish one another, watch over one another, comfort one another, and gain instruction . . . that we may all sit down in heaven together."[19]

ABBREVIATIONS USED IN NOTES

The abbreviations listed below have been used to simplify references in the notes that follow:

BLUCB   Bancroft Library, University of California, Berkeley, Berkeley, California

HBLLBYU   Harold B. Lee Library, Brigham Young University, Provo, Utah

History of the Church   *History of The Church of Jesus Christ of Latter-day Saints*, ed. B. H. Roberts, 7 vols., Salt Lake City: The Church of Jesus Christ of Latter-day Saints, 1932–51

HLSMC   Huntington Library, San Marino, California; all material from HLSMC is reproduced with permission

JD   *Journal of Discourses*, 26 vols. (London: Latter-day Saints' Book Depot, 1854–1886)

JH   Journal History of The Church of Jesus Christ of Latter-day Saints, LDS Church Archives

LDS Church Archives   Archives Division, Church Historical Department, The Church of Jesus Christ of Latter-day Saints, Salt Lake City, Utah; all material from LDS Church Archives is used with permission

MHS   Minnesota Historical Society, St. Paul, Minnesota

Millennial Star   *The Latter-day Saints' Millennial Star*

MLUU   J. Willard Marriott Library, University of Utah, Salt Lake City, Utah

RLDLA   Library and Archives, the Reorganized Church of
               Jesus Christ of Latter Day Saints, Independence, Mis-
               souri

USHS   Library Archives, Utah State Historical Society, Salt
               Lake City, Utah

NOTES

Preface

1. A series of Nauvoo letters written by Martha and Sarah are found in George F. Partridge, ed., "The Death of a Mormon Dictator: Letters of Massachusetts Mormons, 1843–1848," *The New England Quarterly* 9 (December 1936): 583–617.

2. For a beginning bibliography, see Carol Cornwall Madsen and David Whittaker, "History's Sequel: A Source Essay on Women in Mormon History," *Journal of Mormon History* 7 (1980): 123–45, and Patricia Lyn Scott and Maureen Ursenbach Beecher, "Mormon Women: A Bibliography in Process, 1977–1985," *Journal of Mormon History* 12 (1985): 113–28. Carol Cornwall Madsen is preparing an important manuscript for publication dealing with the lives of the women of Nauvoo, tentatively titled *Faith and Community: Women of Nauvoo, Their Personal Writings*.

3. A historiographical essay is Glen M. Leonard, "Recent Writing on Mormon Nauvoo," *Western Illinois Regional Studies* 11 (1988): 69–93. See also "Selected Bibliography of Published Material," in Richard Neitzel Holzapfel and T. Jeffery Cottle, *Old Mormon Nauvoo and Southeastern Iowa* (Santa Ana: Fieldbrook Productions, Inc., 1991), 237–53, and the entire issue of the *Journal of Mormon History* 16 (1990), which contains several important essays, including two about the meaning of Nauvoo from an RLDS and a non-Mormon perspective.

4. Louise A. Tilly, "Gender, Women's History, and Social History," unpublished manuscript in author's possession; for a discussion relating to other issues raised currently about women's history, see Ellen Carol DuBois and Vicki L. Ruiz, *Unequal Sisters: A Multicultural Reader in U.S. History* (New York: Routledge, 1990).

5. See Spencer J. Palmer, "Eliza R. Snow's 'Sketch of My Life: Reminiscences of One of Joseph Smith's Plural Wives,'" *BYU Studies* 12 (Autumn 1971): 128.

Chapter 1.
An Unknown Story

1. Mary Ann Weston Maughan, "Autobiography of Mary Ann Weston Maughan," typescript, USHS; published extracts are found in Kenneth W. Godfrey, Audrey M. Godfrey, and Jill Mulvay Derr, *Women's Voices: An Untold History of the Latter-day Saints, 1830–1900* (Salt Lake City: Deseret Book Co., 1982), 34–42.

2. Mary Ann Weston Maughan, "Autobiography."

3. A distinction should be made between contemporary sources and later reminiscences. The reminiscences and autobiographical recollections of the "Old Nauvooers" seem to follow certain themes, including those relating to Joseph Smith, the martyrdom, and the exodus; see Glen M. Leonard, "Remembering Nauvoo: Historiographical Considerations," *Journal of Mormon History* 16 (1990): 25–26.

4. Cited in Julie Roy Jeffrey, "Ladies Have the Hardest Time, That Emigrate by Land," in *The Private Side of American History: Readings in Everyday Life*, ed. Gary B. Nash and Cynthia J. Shelton, 2 vols. (New York: Harcourt Brace Jovanovich, 1987), 1:439.

5. A published source of several early Latter-day Saint women's letters, diaries, and autobiographical sketches is Godfrey et al., *Women's Voices*.

6. See Donald Q. Cannon, "Spokes of the Wheel: Early Latter-day Saint Settlements in Hancock County, Illinois," *Ensign* 16 (February 1986): 62–68, and Stanley B. Kimball, "Nauvoo West: The Mormons of the Iowa Shore," *BYU Studies* 18 (Winter 1978): 132–42.

7. See "A Record of the Organization, and Proceedings of the Female Relief Society of Nauvoo," 17 March 1842, LDS Church Archives. For a comprehensive account of the history of the Relief Society, see Jill Mulvay Derr, Janath Cannon, and Maureen Ursenbach Beecher, *Women of Covenant: The Story of the Relief Society* (Salt Lake City: Deseret Book Co., forthcoming).

8. Relief Society Minutes, 30 March 1842, LDS Church Archives.

9. This body of Saints used various titles to identify itself, including Ancient Order, Council of the Priesthood, First Quorum, Holy Order, Holy Quorum, Quorum of the Anointing, Quorum of the Priesthood; however, the most frequently used designation was "Quorum." In this study the term "Quorum of the Anointed" is used to distinguish it from all other organizations.

10. Orson F. Whitney, "Women's Work and 'Mormonism,'" *Young Woman's Journal* 27 (July 1906): 293.

11. Clara L. Clawson, "Pioneer Stake," *Woman's Exponent* 34 (July–August 1905): 14.

12. See *History of the Church*; Joseph Smith, *Teachings of the Prophet Joseph Smith*, sel. Joseph Fielding Smith (Salt Lake City: Deseret Book Co., 1938); Andrew F. Ehat and Lyndon W. Cook, eds., *The Words of Joseph Smith* (Provo: Religious Studies Center, Brigham Young University, 1980).

Chapter 2.
Coming to Nauvoo—Sisters Gather

1. For a broader discussion on women on the trail, see Paula Petrik, "The Gentle Tamers in Transition: Women in the Trans-Mississippi West," *Feminist Studies* 11 (Fall 1985): 677–94.

2. See Lavina Fielding Anderson, "They Came to Nauvoo," *Ensign* 9 (September 1979): 21–25.

3. Woman pioneer scholar Julie Roy Jeffrey suggested, "The major impulse behind emigrating appears to have been economic." See Julie Roy Jeffrey, *Frontier Women: The Trans-Mississippi West, 1840–1880* (New York: Hill and Wang, 1979), 29.

4. Drusilla Dorris Hendricks, "Reminscences of Drusilla Hendricks," LDS Church Archives.

5. Sarah D. Rich, Autobiography, LDS Church Archives.

6. Emma Smith to Joseph Smith, 9 March 1839, Joseph Smith Papers, LDS Church Archives.

7. Mary Fielding Smith to Joseph Fielding, June 1839; quoted in Edward W. Tullidge, *The Women of Mormondom* (New York, 1877), 255.

8. Martha Pane Jones Thomas, Autobiography, HBLLBYU.

9. Nancy N. Tracy, "Narrative by Mrs. N. N. Tracy," BLUCB.

10. Elizabeth Haven Barlow to Elizabeth Howel Bullard, 24 February 1839, in private possession; originally published in Ora H. Barlow, *The Israel Barlow Story and Mormon Mores* (Salt Lake City: Ora H. Barlow, 1968).

11. Cited in Maureen Ursenbach Beecher, *Eliza and Her Sisters* (Salt Lake City: Aspen Books, 1991), 47–48.

12. Quoted in "Julia," in *Our Pioneer Heritage*, comp. Kate B. Carter (Salt Lake City: Daughters of Utah Pioneers, 1966), 9:450.

13. Richard P. Howard, ed., *The Memoirs of President Joseph Smith III, 1832–1914* (Independence: Herald Publishing House, 1979), 5.

14. A discussion on the early Saints in England is found in Lavina Fielding Anderson, "In the Crucible: Early British Saints," *Ensign* 9 (December 1979): 51–55.

15. Jane Carter Robinson Hindly, "Jane C. Robinson Hindly Reminiscences and Diary," LDS Church Archives.

16. Quoted in Conway B. Sonne, *Saints on the Seas: A Maritime History of Mormon Migration, 1830–1890* (Salt Lake City: University of Utah Press, 1983), 53.

17. William Clayton, Diaries 1840–1842, 9–10 September 1840, HBLLBYU; a published version is James B. Allen and Thomas G. Alexander, eds., *Manchester Mormons, The Journal of William Clayton* (Salt Lake City: Peregrine Smith, 1974).

18. Ann H. Pitchforth to Saints in the Isle of Man, n.d.; originally published in *Millennial Star* 8 (15 July 1846): 12.

19. "Mary Field Garner Papers," HBLLBYU.

20. Quoted in Vida E. Smith, "Two Widows of the Brick Row," *Journal of History* 3 (April 1910): 202.

21. *Quincy Whig*, 14 April 1841.

22. *Fort Madison Courier*, 13 November 1841.

23. G. Lewis, *Impressions of America and the American Churches* (Edinburgh: W. P. Kennedy, 1845), 265.

24. Eliza Dana Gibbs, Autobiography, HBLLBYU.

25. Aurelia S. Rogers, *Life Sketches of Orson Spencer and Others, and History of Primary Work* (Salt Lake City: Geo. Q. Cannon and Sons Co., 1898), 16.

26. Ibid., 36–37.

27. Jane Manning James, "Biography of Jane Elizabeth Manning James," LDS Church Archives; a treatment of Jane James's life is Linda King Newell and Valeen Tippetts Avery, "Jane Manning James: Black Saint, 1847 Pioneer," *Ensign* 9 (August 1979): 26–29.

28. Quoted in "Joseph Smith, the Prophet," *Young Woman's Journal* 16 (December 1905): 553.

29. Jane Manning James, "Biography."

30. Helen Mar Whitney, "Scenes and Incidents in Nauvoo," *Woman's Exponent* 11 (15 October 1882): 74.

31. Isaac C. Haight, Journals 1813–1862, 13 September–18 November 1843, HLSMC.

32. Mary Ann Stearns Winters, "An Autobiographical Sketch of the Life of the Late Mary Ann Stearns Winters," LDS Church Archives.

33. J. D. Cummings, comp., "A Brief Sketch of the Life of Mary Ann Yearsley," LDS Church Archives.

34. Charlotte Haven to family, 3 January 1843; originally published in "A Girl's Letters from Nauvoo," *Overland Monthly* (December 1890): 616–38; several extracts from these letters have been published in William Mulder and A. Russell Mortensen, eds., *Among the Mormons: Historic Accounts by Contemporary Observers* (New York: Alfred A. Knopf, 1958), 116–27.

35. *Times and Seasons*, 15 May 1843.

Chapter 3.
Daily Life—Women on the Illinois Frontier

1. Emerson Hough, *Passing of the Frontier: A Chronicle of the Old West* (New Haven: Yale University Press, 1918), 134.

2. Adade Mitchell Wheeler and Marlene Stein Wortman, *The Roads They Made: Women in Illinois History* (Chicago: Charles H. Kerr Publishing Company, 1977), 21.

3. See William W. Fowler, *Women on the American Frontier* (Hartford: S. S. Scranton and Co., 1978), 192.

4. Much of the information in this chapter is based on Wheeler and Wortman, *The Roads They Made*, 21–34; Ida Blum, *Nauvoo, Gateway to the West* (Carthage: Journal Printing Company, 1978), 70–71; Jerry Mack Johnson, *Down Home Ways* (New York: Greenwich House, 1984); and Richard Neitzel Holzapfel and T. Jeffery Cottle, *Old Mormon Nauvoo and Southeastern Iowa* (Santa Ana: Fieldbrook Productions, Inc., 1991), 3–6.

5. Theodore Turley, "Reminiscences and Journal, 1839–1840 July," LDS Church Archives.

6. Talitha C. Avery, "A Sketch of Talitha C. Avery's Life," HBLLBYU.

7. See *Millennial Star* 2 (August 1841): 49–53.

8. See Lee C. LaFayette, "Recollections of Joseph Smith," LDS

Church Archives; a published version is Hyrum L. Andrus and Helen Mae Andrus, comps., *They Knew the Prophet* (Salt Lake City: Bookcraft, 1974), 145.

9. Abigail Pitkin to Rebecca Raymond, LDS Church Archives; quoted in E. Cecil McGavin, *Nauvoo, the Beautiful* (Salt Lake City: Bookcraft, 1972), 41–42.

10. Charlotte Haven to family, 3 January 1843; see note 22 for chapter 1.

11. Charlotte Haven to sister Isa, 22 January 1843.

12. Bathsheba W. Smith to George A. Smith, 15 June 1844, George A. Smith Collection, LDS Church Archives; extracts of several Bathsheba W. Smith letters are included in Kenneth W. Godfrey, Audrey M. Godfrey, and Jill Mulvay Derr, *Women's Voices: An Untold History of the Latter-day Saints, 1830–1900* (Salt Lake City: Deseret Book Co., 1982), 122–33.

13. Ann H. Pitchforth to mother and father, 23 April 1845, HBLLBYU.

14. *Nauvoo Neighbor*, as cited in Mary K. Stout, "From a Nauvoo Pantry," *New Era* 3 (December 1973): 43.

15. Bathsheba W. Smith to George A. Smith, 15 June 1844.

16. Bathsheba W. Smith to George A. Smith, 2 September 1843.

17. Quoted in Edward F. Parry, comp., *Stories About Joseph Smith the Prophet* (Salt Lake City: Deseret News Press, 1934), 34–35.

18. Mary Field Garner, Papers, LDS Church Archives.

19. Stout, "From a Nauvoo Pantry," 43–44.

20. Drusilla Dorris Hendricks, "Reminiscences of Drusilla Hendricks" LDS Church Archives.

21. Irene Hascall Pomeroy to Ursulia B. Hascall, 26 July 1845, Hascall Family Letters, 1845–54, LDS Church Archives.

22. Thomas Gregg, *The History of Hancock County, Illinois* (Chicago: Charles E. Chapman, 1880), 296.

23. Reviews of the development of the home building in Nauvoo can be found in Robert M. Lillibridge, "Architectural Currents on the Mississippi River Frontier: Nauvoo, Illinois," *Journal of the Society of Architectural Historians* 19 (October 1960): 109–14, and Betty I. Madden, *Art, Crafts, and Architecture in Early Illinois* (Urbana: University of Illinois Press, 1974), 195–208.

24. Charlotte Haven to family, 3 January 1843.

25. Charlotte Haven to mother, 19 February 1843.

26. Sally Randall to family, 6 October 1843, LDS Church Archives.

27. Ann H. Pitchforth to mother and father, 28 April 1845.

28. Hortensia Patrick to Delana Patrick, 15 January 1844, RLDLA.

29. See Dennis Rowley, "Nauvoo: A River Town," *BYU Studies* 18 (Winter 1978): 255–72.

30. *History of the Church* 5:8.

31. Vesta Crawford, "Vesta Crawford Notes," MLUU; as quoted in Linda King Newell and Valeen Tippetts Avery, *Mormon Enigma: Emma Hale Smith, Prophet's Wife, "Elect Lady," Polygamy's Foe, 1804–1879* (Garden City, New York: Doubleday, 1984), 112.

32. Elizabeth Ann Whitney, "A Leaf from an Autobiography," *Woman's Exponent* 7 (15 November 1878): 91.

33. In Edward William Tullidge, *Women of Mormondom* (New York, 1877), 213.

34. "Mother," *Young Woman's Journal* 22 (January 1911): 45.

35. *History of the Church* 4:16.

36. Joseph Smith to Emma Smith, 9 November 1839, Joseph Smith Collection, LDS Church Archives; a published version of Joseph Smith correspondences can be found in Dean C. Jessee, comp. and ed., *The Personal Writings of Joseph Smith* (Salt Lake City: Deseret Book Co., 1984).

37. Emma Smith to Joseph Smith, 6 December 1839.

38. Quoted in Joseph B. Noble, "Early Scenes in Church History," *Juvenile Instructor* 15 (15 March 1880): 112.

39. Zina Diantha Huntington Jacobs, Diary 1844–1845, 10, 12, 14–21 April 1845, LDS Church Archives; a published version can be found in Maureen Ursenbach Beecher, ed., " 'All Things Move in Order in the City': The Nauvoo Diary of Zina Diantha Huntington Jacobs," *BYU Studies* 19 (Spring 1979): 291–320.

40. Ida Blum, *Nauvoo, Gateway to the West* (Nauvoo, Illinois: Ida Blum, 1974), 58–60.

41. *History of the Church* 6:166.

Chapter 4.
Nauvoo—A City of Women

1. See Jill Mulvay Derr's important study, " 'Strength in Our Union': The Making of Mormon Sisterhood," in *Sisters in Spirit*, ed. Maureen Ursenbach Beecher and Lavina Fielding Anderson (Urbana: University of Illinois Press, 1987), 153–207.

2. Annie Wells Cannon, "Achievement," *Relief Society Magazine* 23 (March 1936): 159.

3. Carroll Smith-Rosenberg, "The Female World of Love and Ritual: Relations Between Women in Nineteenth-Century America," in *Women's Experience in America: An Historical Anthology*, Ester Katz and Anita Ropen, eds. (New Brunswick: Transaction Books, 1980), 259, 265. A recent critique is Nancy Grey Osternd, *Bonds of Community: The Lives of Farm Women in Nineteenth-Century New York* (Ithaca: Cornell University Press, 1991), 1–15.

4. See, for example, Don Harrison Doyle, *The Social Order of a Frontier Community, Jacksonville, Illinois, 1825–70* (Urbana: University of Illinois Press, 1983).

5. Sarah Hall Scott to Abigail Hall, 13 April 1844, RLDLA.

6. Vilate Kimball to Heber C. Kimball, 7 June 1843, Kimball Papers, LDS Church Archives.

7. Glen M. Leonard, director of the Museum of Church History and Art, The Church of Jesus Christ of Latter-day Saints, Salt Lake City, Utah, is preparing for publication some ninety letters written from Nauvoo. In conversation with the authors on this subject, he reviewed the correspondences' history.

8. Vilate Kimball to Heber C. Kimball, 9 June 1844.

9. Bathsheba W. Smith, Autobiography, HBLLBYU.

10. Maureen Ursenbach Beecher warns against "lumping all similar experiences into the same sort of bag, romanticizing them into generalizations which eventually become little more than sentimentality. Robbed of her own individual character, the one becomes representative of the many, and the face under the sunbonnet becomes blurred." See Maureen Ursenbach Beecher, "Under the Sunbonnets: Mormon Women with Faces," *BYU Studies* 16 (Summer 1976): 473.

11. Bathsheba W. Smith to George A. Smith, 2 September 1843, George A. Smith Collection, LDS Church Archives.

12. Bathsheba W. Smith to George A. Smith, 2 October 1842.

13. This story is found in Orson F. Whitney, *Life of Heber C. Kimball* (1888: reprint, Salt Lake City: Bookcraft, 1967), 265–66.

14. Brigham Young to Mary Ann Young, 15 September 1839, Philip Blair Collection, MLUU.

15. Louisa Barnes Pratt, Louisa Barnes Pratt Collection 1831–1924, LDS Church Archives; quoted in Beecher, "Under the Sunbonnets," 473; see also S. George Ellsworth, ed., *The Journals of Addison Pratt* (Salt Lake City: University of Utah Press, 1990),

116–17. Later in the April 1850 general conference she was called to go with Thomas Tomkins to Tahiti, where her husband was serving another mission for the Church.

16. Bathsheba W. Smith to George A. Smith, 16 July 1843.

17. Eliza R. Snow, Diaries 1842–1844, 12 April 1843, Eliza R. Snow Collection, LDS Church Archives; a published version is Maureen Ursenbach, "Eliza R. Snow's Nauvoo Journal," *BYU Studies* 15 (Summer 1975): 391–416.

18. Mary Ann Phelps Rich, "The Life of Mary A. Rich: 1820–1912," HBLLBYU. Within a short time, Mary's mother died, leaving five children, including an eighteen-month-old baby to take care of. Mary wrote, "It was now that the knowledge which I had gained at Brother Murdock's was of such a benefit to me."

19. See Calvin S. Kunz, "A History of Female Missionary Activity in The Church of Jesus Christ of Latter-day Saints, 1830–1898," Masters thesis, Brigham Young University, Provo, Utah, 1976.

20. Nancy N. Tracy, "Narrative of Mrs. N. N. Tracy," BLUCB.

21. Wilford Woodruff, Journals 1833–1898, 28 August 1844, Wilford Woodruff Collection, LDS Church Archives; a published version is Scott G. Kenney, ed., *Wilford Woodruff's Journals: 1833–1898 Typescript*, 9 vols. (Midvale: Signature Books, 1983).

22. *Millennial Star*, January 1845.

23. Louisa Tanner Follett, 1844–1845 Diary, 5 September 1845, LDS Church Archives.

24. Ibid., 7 September 1845.

25. Margaret Gay Judd Clawson, Autobiography, LDS Church Archives.

26. *Nauvoo Neighbor*, 21 May 1845.

27. Joseph Holbrook, "The Life of Joseph Holbrook," LDS Church Archives; see also Jill Mulvay Derr, "Zion's Schoolmarms," in *Mormon Sisters: Women in Early Utah* (Salt Lake City: Olympus Publishing Co., 1976), 68.

28. This metaphor can be found in several sources, including Mercy Thompson, "Recollections of the Prophet," *Juvenile Instructor* 27 (1 July 1892): 440.

29. Eliza R. Snow, Diaries, 19 December 1843.

30. Charlotte Haven to brother and sister, 5 March 1843; see note 22 for chapter 1.

31. Charlotte Haven to friends at home, 26 March 1843.

32. Jennetta Richards to Wealthy Richards, 4 July 1843, HBLLBYU.

33. Mary Ann Stearns Winters, "An Autobiographical Sketch of the Life of the Late Mary Ann Stearns Winters," LDS Church Archives.

34. Charlotte Haven to brother and sister, 5 March 1843.

35. Martha Hall Haven to Calvin and Abigail Hall, 27 December 1843; reproduced in George F. Partridge, ed., "The Death of a Mormon Dictator," *New England Quarterly* 9 (December 1936): 568–91.

36. Eliza R. Snow, Diaries, 21 July 1843.

37. Zina Diantha Huntington Jacobs, Diary 1844–1845, 17 July 1845, LDS Church Archives.

38. Ursulia B. Hascall to Ophelia M. Andres, 4 July 1845, Hascall Family Letters, 1845–54, LDS Church Archives; a published version of Ursulia and Irene Hascall Pomeroy Nauvoo correspondences is A. R. Mortensen, ed., "Letters of a Proselyte: The Hascall-Pomeroy Correspondence," *Utah Historical Quarterly* 15 (January 1857): 53–70 and (April 1957): 133–51.

39. William Oliver, *Eight Months in Illinois: With Information to Immigrants* (Newcastle-upon-Tyne: William Andrew Mitchell, 1843), 148.

40. Charlotte Haven to brother and sister, 5 March 1843.

41. Martha Hall Haven to father and mother, 23 December 1843.

42. Bathsheba W. Smith to George A. Smith, 15 June 1844.

43. Charlotte Haven to brother and sister, 5 March 1843.

44. Charlotte Haven to home friends, 2 May 1843.

45. Charlotte Haven to sister, 4 June 1843.

46. *History of the Church* 6:134.

47. Helen Mar Whitney, "Scenes and Incidents in Nauvoo," *Woman's Exponent* 11 (15 November 1882): 90.

48. Martha Hall Haven to Calvin and Abigail Hall, 27 December 1843.

49. Charlotte Haven to brother and sister, 5 March 1843.

50. Quoted in Leonard J. Arrington and Susan Arrington Madsen, *Mothers of the Prophets* (Salt Lake City: Deseret Book Co., 1987), 113.

51. Ann H. Pitchforth to mother and father, 23 April 1845, HBLLBYU.

52. *Nauvoo Neighbor*, 29 October 1845.

53. Helen Mar Whitney, "Scenes and Incidents in Nauvoo," *Woman's Exponent* 11 (15 September 1882): 57.

54. See Leonard J. Arrington, "Voices From the Past: Surprising

Lines in an Autograph Book," *This People* (Spring 1988): 15–16.

55. Barbara Matilda Neff Moses, Autograph Book, LDS Church Archives.

56. Margaret Pierce, Autograph book, LDS Church Archives.

Chapter 5.
Daughters, Wives, and Mothers—Sisters at Home

1. See M. Guy Bishop, "Preparing to 'Take the Kingdom': Childbearing Directives in Early Mormonism," *Journal of the Early Republic* 7 (Fall 1987): 275–90.

2. *Times and Seasons*, 1 March 1845.

3. *Wasp*, 1 February 1843.

4. Vilate Kimball to Heber C. Kimball, 11 October 1840, Kimball Papers, LDS Church Archives.

5. Charlotte Haven to mother, 19 February 1843; see note 22 for chapter 1.

6. Irene Hascall Pomeroy to Ursulia B. Hascall, 26 September 1845, Hascall Family Letters, 1845–54, LDS Church Archives.

7. Quoted in Leonard S. Arrington and Susan Arrington Madsen, *Mothers of the Prophets* (Salt Lake City: Deseret Book Co., 1987), 100.

8. Mary Ann Phelps Rich, "The Life of Mary A. Rich: 1820–1912," HBLLBYU.

9. Clarissa Chase to Catherine Chase Marsh, 21 April 1844, LDS Church Archives.

10. *Times and Seasons*, 2 August 1841.

11. See Ronald K. Esplin, "Sickness and Faith, Nauvoo Letters," *BYU Studies* 15 (Summer 1975): 425–34.

12. Sarah Mulholland to William and [Mary] Warnock, 2 February 1842, RLDLA.

13. Ellen Douglas to family, 1 February 1843, LDS Church Archives.

14. Temperance Mack to Harriett Whittmore, 16 September 1840, RLDLA.

15. Wilford Woodruff, Journals 1833–1898, 28 November 1839, Wilford Woodruff Collection, LDS Church Archives.

16. Ibid., 26 November 1840.

17. Phebe Woodruff to Wilford Woodruff, 18 July 1840, Wilford Woodruff Collection, LDS Church Archives.

18. Sally Carlisle Randall to George and Betsy Carlisle, 6 October 1843, HBLLBYU; extracts from Sally Carlisle Randall letters are found in Kenneth W. Godfrey, Audrey M. Godfrey, and Jill Mulvay Derr, *Women's Voices: An Untold History of the Latter-day Saints, 1830–1900* (Salt Lake City: Deseret Book Co., 1982), 134–46.

19. Sally Carlisle Randall to family, 12 November 1843.

20. Zina Diantha Huntington Jacobs, Diary, 7 August 1845, LDS Church Archives.

21. Information and statistics for this section are found in Guy Bishop, Vincent Lacey, and Richard Wixom, "Death at Mormon Nauvoo, 1843–1845," *Western Illinois Regional Studies* 19 (Fall 1986): 71–77.

22. Emmeline B. Wells, Diary 1874, 23 September 1874, HBLLBYU.

23. Howard Coray, Autobiography, LDS Church Archives.

24. *Nauvoo Neighbor*, 6 September 1843.

25. See "Marriage Records, Nauvoo, Illinois, 1842–45," LDS Church Archives, and Lyndon Cook, *Civil Marriages in Nauvoo and Some Outlying Areas, 1839–1845* (Provo: Liberty Publishing Co., 1980); a discussion on the nature of nineteenth-century marriages is Mary E. Stovall, "Did Grandmother Have a Happy Marriage? Myths and Realities of American Families," in Dawn Hall Anderson and Marie Cornwall, eds., *Women and the Power Within* (Salt Lake City: Deseret Book Co., 1991), 69–92.

26. See *Nauvoo Neighbor*, 20 September 1843.

27. Charlotte Haven to sister, 15 October 1843; see note 22 for chapter 1.

28. In Edward William Tullidge, *Women of Mormondom* (New York, 1877), 154–55.

29. *Nauvoo Neighbor*, 21 May 1845.

30. Emmeline B. Harris [Wells], Diaries 1844–1847, 20 February 1845, HBLLBYU.

31. Ibid., 24 February 1845.

32. Ibid., 28 February 1845.

33. It is reported that this tiny but determined Mormon matriarch went immediately to the cemetery and stood on the grave of her mother-in-law and, with her arm raised over the grave, called down a curse on the old woman; see Janet Peterson and LaRene Guant, *Elect Ladies* (Salt Lake City: Deseret Book Co., 1990), 82.

34. *Wasp*, 3 September 1842.

35. *Nauvoo Neighbor*, 9 August 1844.

Chapter 6.
New Revelations—A Time of Testing

1. Charlotte Haven to mother, 19 February 1843; see note 22 for chapter 1. A detailed discussion on period clothing is Carma de Jong Anderson, "A Historical Overview of the Mormons and Their Clothing, 1840–1850, Ph.D. diss., Brigham Young University, 1992.

2. Ann H. Pitchforth to saints, no date, HBLLBYU; later published in *Millennial Star* 8 (15 July 1846): 12–15.

3. Charlotte Haven to sister Isa, 22 June 1843.

4. Eliza R. Snow, Diaries 1812–1844, 13 June 1843, Eliza R. Snow Collection, LDS Church Archives.

5. Phebe Chase to Charles Marsh, 14 September 1843, LDS Church Archives.

6. Rhoda Richards, Diaries 1784–1879, 7 April 1844, LDS Church Archives.

7. See M. Guy Bishop, "What Has Become of Our Fathers?" *Dialogue: A Journal of Mormon Thought* 23 (Summer 1990): 85–97.

8. JH, 15 August 1840.

9. Ibid., 21 August 1840.

10. Sally Carlisle Randall to Betsy Carlisle, 21 April 1844, HBLLBYU.

11. Vilate Kimball to Heber C. Kimball, 11 October 1840, Kimball Papers, LDS Church Archives.

12. Charlotte Haven to family, 2 May 1843.

13. See Linda King Newell and Valeen Tippetts Avery, *Mormon Enigma: Emma Hale Smith, Prophet's Wife, "Elect Lady," Polygamy's Foe, 1804–1879* (Garden City, New York: Doubleday, 1984), 105. The first baptisms for the dead were performed without keeping records and without concern for gender. Later, these procedures were changed, beginning with the instructions received on 6 September 1842 (D&C 128).

14. *History of the Church* 5:2.

15. See Linda P. Wilcox, "The Mormon Concept of a Mother in Heaven," in *Sisters in Spirit*, eds. Maureen Ursenbach Beecher and

Lavina Fielding Anderson (Urbana: University of Illinois Press, 1987), 64–77.

16. *Times and Seasons*, 15 November 1845.

17. According to Susa Young Gates, Joseph Smith told Zina that she would meet her mother again, and "more than that, you will meet and become acquainted with your eternal Mother, the wife of your Father in Heaven." Susa Young Gates, *History of the Young Ladies' Mutual Improvement Association* (Salt Lake City: General Board of the YLMIA, 1911), 15–16.

18. See Julia P. M. Farnsworth, "A Tribute to Bathsheba W. Smith," *Young Woman's Journal* 21 (November 1910): 608.

19. See Ronald K. Esplin, "God Will Protect Me until My Work Is Done," *Ensign* 19 (August 1989): 16–21.

20. See M. Guy Bishop, "Eternal Marriage in Early Mormon Marital Beliefs," *The Historian* 52 (Autumn 1990); 77–88.

21. Joseph Smith to Emma Smith, 16 August 1842, Joseph Smith Collection, LDS Church Archives.

22. *Autobiography of Parley Parker Pratt*, ed. Parley P. Pratt [,Jr.] (Salt Lake City: Deseret Book Co., 1938), 297–98.

23. Vilate Kimball to Heber C. Kimball, 8 June 1843.

24. Vilate Kimball to Heber C. Kimball, 11 November 1843.

25. Jacob Scott to Mary Warnock, 5 January 1844, RLDLA.

26. Charlotte Haven to sister, 15 October 1843.

27. *History of the Church* 5:391–92; see also D&C 131:1–4.

28. Erastus R. Snow, Sketchbook 1818–1847, 22 June 1841–6 April 1847, HLSMC.

29. See Andrew F. Ehat, "Joseph Smith's Introduction of Temple Ordinances," Masters thesis, Brigham Young University, Provo, Utah, 1981, 63–64.

30. Howard Coray, "Reminiscences," LDS Church Archives.

31. For a more detailed discussion of these events, see Stanley B. Kimball, *Heber C. Kimball: Mormon Patriarch and Pioneer* (Urbana: University of Illinois Press, 1981), 93–112.

32. Several important studies discuss the nature and growth of polygamy in Nauvoo. A brief overview is found in Daniel Bachman and Ronald K. Esplin, "Plural Marriage," in *Encyclopedia of Mormonism*, ed. Daniel H. Ludlow, 4 vols. (New York: Macmillan Publishing Company, 1991) 3:1091–95.

33. See Lawrence Foster, *Religion and Sexuality: Three American Communal Experiments of the Nineteenth Century* (New York: Oxford University Press, 1981), 153.

34. Sermon of Brigham Young, delivered in the Bowery in Provo, Utah, 14 July 1855, *JD* 3:266.

35. Helen Mar Whitney, "Life Incidents," *Woman's Exponent* 11 (1 August 1882): 39.

36. Emily Dow Partridge Young, "Incidents in the Life of a Mormon Girl," *Woman's Exponent* 13 (1 December 1884): 102.

37. Eliza Partridge Lyman, "Autobiography and Diary to 1844," LDS Church Archives.

38. Helen Mar Whitney to [her children], 30 March 1881, Helen Mar Whitney Papers, LDS Church Archives.

39. Later, when the temple was completed, this sealing was reconfirmed and Zina was then sealed to Brigham Young "for time" as Henry stood as witness again.

40. Heber C. Kimball to Vilate Kimball, 16 October 1843.

41. Vilate Kimball to Heber C. Kimball, 16 October 1842; see Helen Mar Whitney, "Scenes and Incidents in Nauvoo," *Woman's Exponent* 11 (1 June 1882): 1–2.

42. Sarah G. Kimball, as quoted in Andrew Jenson, *The Historical Record*, 6 vols. (Salt Lake City: Andrew Jenson, 1887), 6:232.

43. Vilate Kimball to Heber C. Kimball, 27 June 1843; see Whitney, "Scenes," 15 September 1882, 57.

44. Elizabeth Ann Whitney, "A Leaf from an Autobiography," *Woman's Exponent* 7 (15 December 1878): 105.

45. Lucy W. Kimball, as quoted in Jenson, *The Historical Record* 6:229.

46. Bathsheba W. Smith, Autobiography, HBLLBYU.

47. Sarah Hall Scott to Abigail Hall, 13 April 1843, RLDLA.

48. In this address, Joseph Smith articulated the Mormon doctrine of deity and eternal progression. See Donald Q. Cannon, "The King Follett Discourse: Joseph Smith's Greatest Sermon in Historical Perspective," *BYU Studies* 18 (Winter 1978): 179–92, and Stan Larson, "The King Follett Discourse: A Newly Amalgamated Text," *BYU Studies* 18 (Winter 1978): 209–25.

49. Sarah Hall Scott to Abigail Hall, 16 June 1844.

50. "Elizabeth H. B. Hyde," *Utah Genealogical and Historical Magazine* 3 (October 1912): 207.

Chapter 7.
The Relief Society—Sisters Unite

1. For a fuller treatment of Sarah M. Kimball's life, see Jill C. Mulvay, "The Liberal Shall Be Blessed: Sarah M. Kimball," *Utah Historical Quarterly* 44 (Summer 1976): 205; for a personal view on the Relief Society, see Maureen Ursenbach Beecher, "From Nauvoo: Sisterhood and the Spirit," in Dawn Hall Anderson and Marie Cornwall, eds., *Women Steadfast in Christ* (Salt Lake City: Deseret Book Co., 1992), 53–68.

2. Augusta Joyce Crocheron, *Representative Women of Deseret* (Salt Lake City: J. C. Graham and Co., 1884), 26–27.

3. Maureen Ursenbach Beecher suggests some of the ways Mormon women marked, "their own trails, diverging from the paths of their predecessors," in "Eddies in the Mainstream: Mormon Women and American Society," *Sidney B. Sperry Symposium: A Sesquicentennial Look at Church History* (Provo: Religious Instruction, 1980), 45–56.

4. See Maureen Ursenbach Beecher, "The 'Leading Sisters': A Female Hierarchy in Nineteenth Century Mormon Society," *Journal of Mormon History* 9 (1990): 26.

5. Unless otherwise stated, quotations in this chapter are from the Relief Society Minutes, 17 March 1842, LDS Church Archives.

6. In some Church history articles and books, the number of women present at the meeting is given as eighteen (see, for example, *History of Relief Society, 1842–1966* [Salt Lake City: The General Board of Relief Society, 1966], 18). The original minutes have the names of Athalia Robinson and Nancy Rigdon, both daughters of Sidney Rigdon, crossed out, probably done by the secretary following their apostasy in 1844. A common practice in the nineteenth-century Church was to literally "blot out" the names of those who had left the faith (see Alma 1:24 for possible justification).

7. Elvira Annie Cowles Holmes, "The Story of the Life of Elvira Annie Cowles," HBLLBYU.

8. See Maureen Ursenbach Beecher and James L. Kimball, Jr., "The First Relief Society: A Diversity of Women," *Ensign* 9 (March 1979): 25–29.

9. Relief Society Minutes, 17 March 1842.

10. "Relief Society Reports," *Woman's Exponent* 9 (1 September 1880): 53–54.

11. *History of the Church* 4:552.

12. Relief Society Minutes, 17 March and 9 June 1842.

13. Ibid., 19 April 1842.

14. Ellen Briggs Douglas to mother and father, 2 June 1844, LDS Church Archives.

15. Recollection of Sarah M. Kimball; see Sarah M. Kimball, "Auto-Biography," *Woman's Exponent* 12 (1 September 1883): 51.

16. Joseph Smith's General Store, often called the Red Brick Store because of the color of paint on the interior walls of its main room, was located on the south side of Water Street near Granger. The two-story brick structure was completed in late 1841 and was the scene of a wide variety of functions and activities involving the leading members of the Church and citizens of Nauvoo; see Richard Neitzel Holzapfel and T. Jeffery Cottle, *Old Mormon Nauvoo and Southeastern Iowa* (Santa Ana: Fieldbrook Productions, Inc., 1991), 144–47.

17. Talitha C. Avery, "A Sketch of Talitha C. Avery's Life," HBLLBYU.

18. Richard L. Jensen indicates that the "gap is more apparent than real" as he chronicles several types of meetings, both informal and formal, that existed over several years until the first formal women's organization in Utah, the Female Council of Health, began in 1851. See Richard L. Jensen, "Forgotten Relief Societies, 1844–67," *Dialogue: A Journal of Mormon Thought* 16 (Spring 1983): 105–25.

19. Relief Society Minutes, 16 March 1844.

Chapter 8.
Charity—Women with a Mission

1. Relief Society Minutes, 17 March 1842, LDS Church Archives.

2. *Times and Seasons*, 1 April 1842.

3. Ibid., 26 May 1842.

4. Ibid., 9 June 1842.

5. Ibid., 1 July 1842.

6. Relief Society Minutes, August 1843.

7. See Claudia Lauper Bushman, "Mystics and Healers," in *Mormon Sisters: Women in Early Utah* (Salt Lake City: Olympus Publishing

Co., 1976), 1–23, and Linda King Newell, "Gifts of the Spirit: Women's Share," in *Sisters in Spirit,* eds. Maureen Ursenbach Beecher and Lavina Fielding Anderson (Urbana: University of Illinois Press, 1987), 111–50.

8. Relief Society Minutes, 24 March 1842.

9. For a discussion of the context of this investigation, see Linda King Newell and Valeen Tippetts Avery, *Mormon Enigma: Emma Hale Smith, Prophet's Wife, "Elect Lady," Polygamy's Foe, 1804–1879* (Garden City, New York: Doubleday, 1984), 108–10.

10. *Nauvoo Neighbor,* as quoted in Mary K. Stout, "From a Nauvoo Pantry," *New Era* 3 (December 1973): 44.

11. Oliver H. Olney, Journals, Beinecke Library, Yale University Library, New Haven, Conn., as cited in Richard S. Van Wagnor, *Mormon Polygamy: A History* (Salt Lake City: Signature Books, 1986), 17.

12. Emmeline B. Wells, "LDS Women of the Past: Personal Impressions," *Woman's Exponent* 36 (February 1908): 1.

13. Eliza R. Snow, Diaries 1842–1844, 29 July 1842, Eliza R. Snow Collection, LDS Church Archives.

14. Relief Society Minutes, 31 August 1842.

15. Henry Caswell, *The City of the Mormons; or three days at Nauvoo in 1842 by the Rev. Henry Caswall, M.A.* (London: Printed for J.G. F. & J. Rivington, 1842), 8–19.

16. Eben Weld to Martin Weld, 10 February 1846, Weld Papers, MHS; a published version is found in "A New Englander in the West: Letters of Eben Weld, 1845–50," *Minnesota History* 15 (September 1934): 306.

Chapter 9.
A Key Is Turned—Ancient Covenants Restored

1. Bathsheba W. Smith, quoted in Clara L. Clawson, "Pioneer Stake," *Woman's Exponent* 34 (July, August 1906): 14.

2. Mercy Fielding Thompson, "Recollections of the Prophet Joseph Smith," *Juvenile Instructor* 27 (1 July 1892): 398.

3. See Barbara Welter, "The Cult of True Womanhood, 1800–1860," *American Quarterly* 18 (Summer 1966): 151–74, and Carol Lasser, "Gender, Ideology, and Class in the Early Republic," *Journal of the Early Republic* 10 (Fall 1990): 331–37.

4. The 1830 revelation to Emma (D&C 25) granted her personal

religious authority unusual for the era, with some exceptions in the Protestant world; see Louis Billington, " 'Female Laborers in the Church': Women Preachers in the Northeastern United States, 1790–1840," *Journal of American Studies* 19 (December 1985): 369–94. An Irish female preacher, Jane Johnston, was converted to the Church in England and eventually arrived in Nauvoo; see Jerry D. Spangler, "Jane Johnston: Methodist Minister to Mormon Pioneer," *Ensign* 11 (April 1981): 66–68.

5. *History of the Church* 4:602.

6. Bathsheba W. Smith, "Recollections of Joseph Smith," *Juvenile Instructor* 27 (1 June 1892): 345.

7. Nancy N. Tracy, "Autobiography: Life and Travels of Nancy N. Tracy," *Woman's Exponent* 38 (November 1909): 39–40.

8. Relief Society Minutes, 28 April 1842, LDS Church Archives; see also *History of the Church* 4:604.

9. Ibid; see also *History of the Church* 4:604–5.

10. An important interpretation of these events is found in Carol Cornwall Madsen, "Mormon Women and the Temple: Toward a New Understanding," in *Sisters in Spirit*, eds. Maureen Ursenbach Beecher and Lavina Fielding Anderson (Urbana: University of Illinois Press, 1987), 80–110.

11. Sermon of George A. Smith, delivered in the Old Tabernacle in Salt Lake City, Utah, 18 March 1855, *JD* 2:214.

12. *History of the Church* 4:604, or *Teachings of the Prophet Joseph Smith*, sel. Joseph Fielding Smith (Salt Lake City: Deseret Book Co., 1938), 226.

13. *History of the Church* 5:1–2.

14. Quoted in Wilford Woodruff, *Deseret News Weekly*, 15 March 1892.

15. Smith, "Recollections," 345.

16. "A Notable Event—The Weber Stake Reunion," *Deseret Evening News*, 23 June 1903.

17. Relief Society Minutes, 28 April 1842. When published in *History of the Church* and *Teachings of the Prophet Joseph Smith*, the phrase was changed to read "I now turn the key in your behalf" (see *History of the Church* 4:607; *Teachings*, 228–29).

18. *History of the Church* 4:607.

19. Relief Society Minutes, 27 May 1842.

20. Ibid., 13 August 1843.

21. Relief Society Minutes, 30 March 1842.

22. See D. Michael Quinn, "Latter-day Saint Prayer Circles," *BYU Studies* 19 (Fall 1978): 82–96, and Andrew F. Ehat, "Joseph Smith's Introduction of Temple Ordinances and the 1844 Mormon Succession Question," Master's thesis, Brigham Young University, Provo, Utah, 1981.

23. Elizabeth A. Whitney, "A Leaf from an Autobiography," *Woman's Exponent* 7 (15 December 1878): 105.

24. See Wilford Woodruff, Journals, 1833–1898, 23 December 1843, Wilford Woodruff Collection, LDS Church Archives.

25. Ibid., 27 January 1844.

26. See Quinn, "Prayer Circle," 86–87; and Ehat, "Introduction of Temple Ordinances," 107.

27. Mary Ann Phelps Rich, "The Life of Mary A. Rich: 1820–1912," HBLLBYU.

Chapter 10.
The City of Joseph—Sisters Mourn

1. *Nauvoo Expositor*, 7 June 1844.

2. Bathsheba W. Smith to George A. Smith, 15 June 1844, George A. Smith Collection, LDS Church Archives.

3. Sarah D. Gregg to Thomas Gregg, 18 June 1844, HBLLBYU.

4. Zina Diantha Huntington Jacobs, Diary 1844–1845, 24 June 1844, LDS Church Archives.

5. Mary Ann Phelps Rich, "The Life of Mary A. Rich: 1820–1912," HBLLBYU.

6. Zina Diantha Huntington Jacobs, Diary, 27 June 1844.

7. Ibid., 28 June 1844.

8. Sarah M. Kimball to Sister Heywood, n.d., Kimball Papers, LDS Church Archives.

9. Zina Diantha Huntington Jacobs, Diary, 30 June 1844.

10. Mary Ann Phelps Rich, "Life."

11. Vilate Kimball to Heber C. Kimball, 30 June 1844, Kimball Papers, LDS Church Archives; complete published version of the letter is Ronald K. Esplin, "Life in Nauvoo, June 1844: Vilate Kimball's Martyrdom Letters," *BYU Studies* 19 (Winter 1979): 231–40.

12. Bathsheba W. Smith to George A. Smith, 6 July 1844.

13. Hortensia Merchants to William Patrick, 10 July 1844, RLDLA.

14. Jennetta Richards to Rev. John Richards, 8 July 1844, LDS Church Archives.

15. Eliza Clayton, "Reminiscences of Nauvoo," in Leonard J. Arrington, ed., *Voices from the Past: Diaries, Journals, and Autobiographies* (Provo: Brigham Young University Press, 1980), 15.

16. Mary Ann Barzee Boice Journal, in private possession of Dana Roper, Laguna Hills, California.

17. Elvira Annie Cowles, "Story of the Life of Elvira Annie Cowles," HBLLBYU.

18. Eliza Dana Gibbs, Autobiography, HBLLBYU.

19. *New York Herald*, 8 July 1844.

20. In Edward William Tullidge, *Women of Mormondom* (New York, 1877), 326–27.

21. *Nauvoo Neighbor*, 30 October 1844.

22. Willard Richards, Journals 1836–1853, 26 March 1845, Richards Collection LDS Church Archives.

23. Heber C. Kimball, Journals 1801–1848, 19 June 1845, Kimball Collection, LDS Church Archives; a published version is Stanley B. Kimball, ed., *On the Potter's Wheel: The Diaries of Heber C. Kimball* (Salt Lake City: Signature Books, 1987).

24. Ibid., 20 June 1845.

25. Willard Richards, Journals, 9 July 1845.

26. Ibid., 10 July 1845.

27. Ibid., 11 July 1845.

28. Ibid., 21 July 1845.

29. Nancy Naomi Alexander Tracy, Autobiography, HBLLBYU.

30. Heber C. Kimball, Journals, 13 March 1845.

31. George A. Smith, George A. Smith Collection 1844–1925, LDS Church Archives; published extracts are found in Zora Smith Jarvis, *Ancestry Biography and Family of George A. Smith* (Provo: Brigham Young University Press, 1962), 102–10.

32. Zina Diantha Huntington Jacobs, Diary, 10 March 1845.

33. *History of the Church* 7:398.

34. See Ronald K. Esplin, "A 'Place Prepared' in the Rockies," *Ensign* 18 (July 1988): 7–13.

35. "Agreement to leave Nauvoo," 25 September 1845, Nauvoo City Collection, LDS Church Archives.

36. Nancy Hunter to John Felix Aiton, 30 September 1845, John F. Aiton and Family Papers, MHS.

37. Irene Hascall Pomeroy to Ursulia B. Hascall, 26 September

1845, Hascall Family Letters, 1845–54, LDS Church Archives.

38. In Tullidge, *Women of Mormondom*, 321.

39. Helen Mar Whitney, "Scenes in Nauvoo, and Incidents from H. C. Kimball's Journal," *Woman's Exponent* 12 (15 June 1883): 9–10.

40. Irene Hascall Pomeroy to Ophelia M. Andrews, 20 December 1845.

41. "Early This Spring We Leave Nauvoo," Mormon File, HLSMC.

42. Mary E. Dewey to Wealthy D. Richards, 24 January 1846, Richards Correspondences Collection, HLSMC.

43. Eliza Dana Gibbs, Autobiography.

44. Mary Ann Stearns Winters, "An Autobiographical Sketch of the Life of the Late Mary Ann Stearns Winters," LDS Church Archives.

45. Juanita Brooks, ed., *On the Mormon Frontier: The Diary of Hosea Stout, 1844–1861*, 2 vols. (Salt Lake City: University of Utah Press, 1964), 1:51.

46. *Nauvoo Neighbor*, 29 October 1845.

Chapter 11.
Handmaidens of the Lord—Sisters in the Temple

1. Mercy Fielding Thompson, "Reminiscences of Mercy Fielding Thompson," LDS Church Archives.

2. *Times and Seasons*, 15 March 1845.

3. Augusta Joyce Crocheron, *Representative Women of Deseret* (Salt Lake City: J. C. Graham and Co., 1884), 25–26.

4. Nancy Naomi Alexander Tracy, Autobiography, HBLLBYU.

5. Zina Diantha Huntington Jacobs, Diary 1844–1845, 24 May 1845, LDS Church Archives.

6. Helen Mar Whitney, "Scenes in Nauvoo, and Incidents from H. C. Kimball's Journal," *Woman's Exponent* 11 (1 April 1883): 162.

7. Ibid., 169–70.

8. Ibid., 15 April 1883, 169.

9. Irene Hascall Pomeroy to Ashbel G. Hascall, October 1845, Hascall Family Letters, 1845–54, LDS Church Archives.

10. Whitney, "Scenes," 1 June 1883, 6.

11. Heber C. Kimball, Journals 1801–1848, 11 December 1845, Kimball Collection, LDS Church Archives.

12. William Clayton wrote during this post-martyrdom period,

"We have to use the greatest care and caution and dare not let it be known that we meet" (see William Clayton, Journals 1840–1853, 22 December 1844, LDS Church Archives.

13. Heber C. Kimball Journals, 5 December 1845.

14. Ibid., 7 December 1845.

15. Ibid., 10 December 1845.

16. *History of the Church* 7:547; see also 20 December 1845 entry in *History of the Church* 7:548.

17. Irene Hascall Pomeroy to Ophelia M. Andrews, 20 December 1845.

18. See Whitney, "Scenes," 1 October 1883, 71.

19. *History of the Church* 7:566.

20. S. W. Richards, Diaries 1839–1909, 7–31 January 1846, LDS Church Archives.

21. *History of the Church* 7:570.

22. Irene Hascall Pomeroy to Ursulia B. Hascall, fall 1845.

23. *History of the Church* 7:557.

24. William Clayton, quoted in Heber C. Kimball, Journals, 30 December 1845.

25. Ibid., 2 January 1846.

26. Ibid., 26 January 1846.

27. Whitney, "Scenes," 15 August 1883, 42.

28. William Clayton, quoted in Heber C. Kimball, Journals, 1 January 1845.

29. Ibid., 1 January 1846.

30. Helen Mar Whitney, "The Last Chapter of Scenes in Nauvoo," *Woman's Exponent* 12 (1 November 1883): 81.

31. *History of the Church* 7:576.

32. Ibid., 579.

33. Ibid., 580.

34. See Richard E. Bennett, *Mormons at the Missouri, 1846–1852—"And Should We Die . . ."* (Norman, Oklahoma: University of Oklahoma Press, 1987), 40, 250 n. 68; see also E. Cecil McGavin, *The Nauvoo Temple* (Salt Lake City: Deseret Book Co., 1962), 109–10.

35. Nancy Aiton to John Felix Aiton, n.d., John Felix Aiton Papers, 1835–1888, MHS.

36. *Warsaw Signal,* 13 April 1846.

37. See I. McGee Van Dessen and Maria Van Dessen, *A Dialogue between Adam and Eve, the Lord and the Devil, Called the Endowment* (Albany: C. Killmer, 1847).

38. Martha Jones Thomas, Autobiography, HBLLBYU.

39. Mercy Thompson, "Recollections of the Prophet," *Juvenile Instructor* 27 (1 July 1892): 440.

Chapter 12.
Into the Wilderness—Women Pioneers

1. An overview of the Saints' departure from Nauvoo and trek across Iowa to Winter Quarters can be found in Richard E. Bennett, *Mormons at the Missouri, 1846–1852: "And Should We Die . . ."* (Norman: University of Oklahoma Press, 1987), 12–45, and Stanley B. Kimball, "The Iowa Trek of 1846: The Brigham Young Route from Nauvoo to Winter Quarters," *Ensign* 2 (June 1972): 36–45.

2. Patty Bartlett Sessions, Diaries 1846–1880, 10 February–5 March 1846, LDS Church Archives.

3. Eliza Dana Gibbs, Autobiography, HBLLBYU.

4. Mary Ann Stearns Winters, "An Autobiographical Sketch of the Life of the Late Mary Ann Stearns Winters," LDS Church Archives.

5. Quoted in Don Cecil Corbett, *Mary Fielding Smith, Daughter of Britain* (Salt Lake City: Deseret Book Co., 1970), 195.

6. Eliza Marie Partridge Lyman, Diaries 1820–1885, 9 February 1846, HLSMC.

7. Ibid., 10 February 1846.

8. Quoted in Lavina Fielding Anderson, "They Came to Nauvoo," *Ensign* 9 (September 1979): 22–23.

9. Eliza R. Snow, Diaries 1846–1849, 12 February 1845, HLSMC; a typescript of these diaries was kindly provided by Maureen Ursenbach Beecher.

10. Ibid., 13 February 1845.

11. Eliza R. Snow, "Sketch of My Life," HBLLBYU.

12. Mary Ann Stearns Winters, "Autobiographical Sketch."

13. Eliza R. Snow, Diaries, 3 March 1846.

14. Ibid., 5 April 1846.

15. Ibid., 8 April 1846.

16. Quoted in Janet Peterson and LaRene Gaunt, *Elect Ladies* (Salt Lake City: Deseret Book Co., 1990), 50–51.

17. Eliza Marie Partridge Lyman Diaries, 2 April 1846.

18. Diantha Farr Clayton to William Clayton, 16 March 1846, LDS Church Archives.

19. William Clayton, Journals 1840–1853, 15 April 1846, LDS Church Archives; a published version is *William Clayton's Journal; A Daily Record of the Journey of the Original Company of "Mormon" Pioneers from Nauvoo, Illinois, to the Valley of the Great Salt Lake* (Salt Lake City: Clayton Family Association, 1921).

20. Irene Hascall Pomeroy to Ursulia B. Hascall, 23 January 1846, Hascall Family Letters, 1845–54, LDS Church Archives.

21. Ursulia B. Hascall to Wilson Andrews, 2 May 1846.

22. Ursulia Hascall to Wilson Andrews, 19 September 1846.

23. E. B. Wells, "Life Sketch of Mrs. Jane Snyder Richards," LDS Church Archives.

24. Martha Hall Haven to Abigail Hall, 4 July 1846; reproduced in George F. Partridge, ed., "The Death of a Mormon Dictator," *New England Quarterly* 9 (December 1936): 609–12.

25. Sarah Studevant Leavitt, *History of Sarah Studevant Leavitt,* ed. Juanita L. Pulsipher (n.p., n.d.) 34.

26. Emma Smith, quoted in Vesta Crawford, "Vesta Crawford Notes," as cited in Linda King Newell and Valeen Tippetts Avery, *Mormon Enigma: Emma Hale Smith, Prophet's Wife, "Elect Lady," Polygamy's Foe, 1804–1879* (Garden City, New York: Doubleday, 1984), 243.

27. "Jane Johnston Statement," Joseph Smith Black Diary, HBLLBYU.

28. Mary Field Garner, Papers, HBLLBYU.

29. Mariah Pulsipher, Autobiography, HBLLBYU; a published version is Kenneth Glyn Hales, comp., *Windows: A Mormon Family* (Tucson: Skyline Printing, 1985).

30. *Illinois State Register,* 13 March 1846.

Chapter 13.
A Time to Remember—The Nauvoo Legacy

1. See Anne M. Boylan's case study, "Evangelical Womanhood in the Nineteenth Century: The Role of Women in Sunday Schools," *Feminist Studies* 4 (October 1978): 62–80.

2. This insight is described by Jill Mulvay Derr and Susan Oman,

"The Nauvoo Generation: Our First Five Relief Society Presidents," *Ensign* 7 (December 1977): 36–43.

3. A fuller treatment of this issue may be found in Leonard J. Arrington, "The Legacy of Early Latter-day Saint Women," *John Whitmer Historical Association Journal* 10 (1990): 3–17; a critique of Arrington's essay was published in the same issue. An insightful discussion of modern lessons based on the history of the Relief Society is Janath R. Cannon and Jill Mulvay Derr, "Resolving Differences/Achieving Unity: Lessons from the History of Relief Society," in Mary E. Stovall and Carol Cornwall Madsen, eds., *As Women of Faith* (Salt Lake City: Deseret Book Co., 1989), 122–47.

4. Sarah G. Kimball, *Woman Suffrage Leaflet*, (1892); quoted in Arrington, "Legacy," 14.

5. Emmeline B. Wells, "Women's Organizations," *Woman's Exponent* 8 (15 January 1880): 122.

6. Eliza R. Snow, Diaries 1846–1849, 1 June 1847, HLSMC.

7. Joan Iversen, "Feminist Implications of Mormon Polygyny," *Feminist Studies* 10 (Fall 1984): 505.

8. "Great Indignation Meeting," *Deseret News Weekly* 19 January 1879; for a brief overview of Latter-day Saint women's participation in the suffrage movement, see Carol Cornwall Madsen, "Woman Suffrage," in *Encyclopedia of Mormonism*, ed. Daniel H. Ludlow, 4 vols. (New York: Macmillan Publishing Company, 1991), 4:1572–73.

9. In writing an introductory history of the women of Nauvoo, the authors wanted to remind today's community of Saints once again of women's firsts in Utah, though we recognize, as Mary Stovall Richards points out in a review essay, the need for Mormon women's histories to get beyond this stage; see Mary Stovall Richards's review of Janet Peterson and LaRene Gaunt's *Elect Ladies*, in *BYU Studies* 31 (Winter 1991): 103–6.

10. *Woman's Exponent* 3 (15 September 1874): 61.

11. Quoted in Iversen, "Feminist Implications," 510.

12. See Davis Bitton and Gary L. Bunker, "Double Jeopardy: Visual Images of Mormon Women to 1914," *Utah Historical Quarterly* 46 (Spring 1978): 184–202.

13. "Education of Women," *Woman's Exponent* 1 (April 1, 1873): 163.

14. This transition is described in Carol Cornwall Madsen, "A Legacy Challenged: The Relief Society in Transition, 1830–1920,"

unpublished manuscript in authors' possession, being prepared for publication.

15. Quoted in *A Centenary of Relief Society, 1842–1942* (Salt Lake City: General Board of Relief Society, 1942), 31.

16. Elizabeth Ann Whitney, "A Leaf from an Autobiography," *Woman's Exponent* 7 (15 November 1878): 91.

17. Relief Society Presidency, "Letter of Greeting," March 1892, LDS Church Archives.

18. Relief Society Minutes, 31 August 1842, LDS Church Archives.

19. Relief Society Minutes, 24 March 1842.

PHOTOGRAPHIC SOURCES

The abbreviations listed below have been used to simplify references in the photographic sources that follow:

DUP   The National Society Daughters of the Utah Pioneers Memorial Museum, Salt Lake City, Utah

HBLLBYU   Photoarchives, Harold B. Lee Library, Brigham Young University, Provo, Utah

LDS Church   Archives Division, Church Historical Department,
Archives   The Church of Jesus Christ of Latter-day Saints, Salt Lake City, Utah; all photographs from LDS Church Archives are used with permission

MCHA   Museum of Church History and Art, The Church of Jesus Christ of Latter-day Saints, Salt Lake City, Utah; all photographs from MCHA are used with permission

RLDSLA   Library-Archives, Reorganized Church of Jesus Christ of Latter Day Saints, Independence, Missouri; all photographs from RLDSLA are used with permission

---

In the photographic sources below, the number of the page on which a photograph appears is followed by date and photographer (where known), collection name (where applicable), and repository. Professional photographer Ronald Read provided most of the visual reproductions of artifacts and paintings for this publication.

Frontispiece
   Page ii.   Ca. 1845, probably Lucian Foster, LDS Church Archives.

Chapter 1.
An Unknown Story

Chapter 2.
Coming to Nauvoo—Sisters Gather

Chapter 3.
Daily Life—Women on the Illinois Frontier

Chapter 4.
Nauvoo—A City of Women

Chapter 5.
Daughters, Wives, and Mothers—Sisters at Home

Chapter 6.
New Revelations—A Time of Testing

INDEX